WOMEN IN GERMAN YEARBOOK

12

EDITORIAL BOARD

Leslie A. Adelson, Cornell University, 1992–2000
Angelika Bammer, Emory University, 1992–2000
Barbara Becker-Cantarino, Ohio State University, 1992–2000
Jeannine Blackwell, University of Kentucky, 1992–97
Gisela Brinker-Gabler, State University of New York, Binghamton, 1992–97
Helen L. Cafferty, Bowdoin College, 1992–97
Jeanette Clausen, Indiana University–Purdue University Fort Wayne, 1995–2000
Susan L. Cocalis, University of Massachusetts, Amherst, 1992–97
Gisela Ecker, Universität-Gesamthochschule-Paderborn, 1992–97
Ruth-Ellen B. Joeres, University of Minnesota, Minneapolis, 1992–97
Anna K. Kuhn, University of California, Davis, 1992–97
Sara Lennox, University of Massachusetts, Amherst, 1992–2000
Ricarda Schmidt, University of Sheffield, England, 1992–2000
Inge Stephan, Humboldt-Universität zu Berlin, 1995–2000
Arlene Teraoka, University of Minnesota, Minneapolis, 1995–2000
Susanne Zantop, Dartmouth College, 1995–2000

PAST EDITORS

Marianne Burkhard, 1984–88
Edith Waldstein, 1984–87
Jeanette Clausen, 1987–94
Helen Cafferty, 1988–90

WOMEN IN

Feminist Studies in German Literature & Culture

GERMAN

Edited by Sara Friedrichsmeyer & Patricia Herminghouse

YEARBOOK

12

University of Nebraska Press, Lincoln and London

© 1996 by the University of
Nebraska Press. All rights
reserved. Manufactured in
the United States of America.
Published by arrangement
with the Coalition of
Women in German.
♾ The paper in this book
meets the minimum require-
ments of American National
Standard for Information
Sciences – Permanence of
Paper for Printed Library
Materials, ANSI Z39.48-1984.
ISBN 0-8032-4783-4 (cloth)
ISBN 0-8032-9791-2 (paper)
ISSN 1058-7446

CONTENTS

Acknowledgments vii
Preface ix

Sara Lennox 1
Feminist German Studies across the Disciplines:
Introduction to Grossmann, Ferree, and Cocks

Atina Grossmann 11
Remarks on Current Trends and Directions in German Women's History

Myra Marx Ferree 27
Sociological Perspectives on Gender in Germany

Joan Cocks 39
On Commonality, Nationalism, and Violence:
Hannah Arendt, Rosa Luxemburg, and Frantz Fanon

Todd Kontje 53
Gender-Bending in the Biedermeier

Irmela Marei Krüger-Fürhoff 71
Epistemological Asymmetries and Erotic Stagings:
Father-Daughter Incest in Heinrich von Kleist's *The Marquise of O...*

Helen G. Morris-Keitel 87
Not "until Earth Is Paradise":
Louise Otto's Refracted Feminine Ideal

Barbara Hales 101
Woman as Sexual Criminal: Weimar Constructions of the Criminal *Femme Fatale*

Kathrin Bower 123
Searching for the (M)Other: The Rhetoric of Longing in Post-Holocaust Poems
by Nelly Sachs and Rose Ausländer

Charlotte Melin 149
Renderings of *Alice in Wonderland* in Postwar German Literature

Helgard Mahrdt 167
"Society Is the Biggest Murder Scene of All": On the Private and Public Spheres in Ingeborg Bachmann's Prose

Frederick A. Lubich 189
Interview with Elisabeth Alexander: The Mother Courage of German Postwar Literature

Karen Hermine Jankowsky 203
Remembering Eastern Europe: Libuše Moníková

Leslie A. Adelson 217
Now You See It, Now You Don't: Afro-German Particulars and the Making of a Nation in Eva Demski's *Afra: Roman in fünf Bildern*

Sara Friedrichsmeyer and Patricia Herminghouse 233
Towards an "American Germanics"?: Editorial Postscript

About the Authors 241
Notice to Contributors 245
Contents of Previous Volumes 247

ACKNOWLEDGMENTS

In addition to members of the Editorial Board, the following individuals reviewed manuscripts received during the preparation of volume 12. We gratefully acknowledge their assistance.

Karen Achberger, St. Olaf College
Nora Alter, University of Florida
Katharina von Ankum, University of Cincinnati
Friederike Eigler, Georgetown University
Silke von der Emde, Vassar College
Tamara Evans, City University of New York, Graduate Center
Elke Frederiksen, University of Maryland, College Park
Marjanne Goozé, University of Georgia
Marjorie Gelus, California State University, Sacramento
Katharina Gerstenberger, University of Cincinnati
Gail Hart, University of California, Irvine
Barbara Mabee, Oakland University
Claudia Mayer-Iswandy, Université de Montréal
Magda Mueller, California State University, Chico
Ann Marie Rasmussen, Duke University
Karen Remmler, Mt. Holyoke College
Azade Seyhan, Bryn Mawr College–Haverford College
Katrin Sieg, Indiana University
Patricia Simpson, University of Michigan
Margaret Ward, Wellesley College
Sabine Wilke, University of Washington
Linda Worley, University of Kentucky

Special thanks to Victoria Hoelzer-Maddox for manuscript preparation. We would also like to acknowledge the assistance of Franziska Mosthaf and Teresa Dueppmann.

PREFACE

One of the highlights of the annual Women in German Conferences has always been the opportunity to interact both personally and professionally with our invited guests. It has long been a tradition to include contributions from these guests in our yearbook, either revisions of their conference presentations or, in the case of authors and filmmakers, original work. Proudly we look back on recent volumes that include pieces by women writers, performers, and scholars from both Germanies and from Austria, contributions by both American and German filmmakers, articles by German feminist publishers, and a speech by a prize-winning author, herself a member of WIG.

The 1995 conference was organized around the issue of cross-disciplinary work and brought noted scholars from three cognate disciplines to meet with Women in German members in St. Augustine, Florida. We asked Sara Lennox, one of the conference planners, to introduce their yearbook contributions with a theoretical overview of the issues involved in cross-disciplinary work and to draw some conclusions from their articles for feminist work in German Studies. Her introduction is followed by expanded versions of the conference papers presented by the three invited scholars: historian Atina Grossmann, sociologist Myra Marx Ferree, and political theorist Joan Cocks.

The three subsequent articles offer new perspectives on nineteenth-century literature and culture. Todd Kontje argues that, despite the return to conservative values in many areas of cultural and political life following the German Wars of Liberation, writers did not necessarily revert to normative sex-roles in their writing. Through an examination of Theodor Körner's patriotic poetry and selected novels by Caroline de la Motte Fouqué and Henriette Frölich, he demonstrates that the questioning of conventional gender roles that began with the French Revolution continued well into the Biedermeier period. Rereading the father-daughter relationship in Kleist's *The Marquise of O...*, Irmela Marei Krüger-Fürhoff draws on comparisons with the *tableax vivants* and theater of Kleist's day to underscore the erotic component of the work. The scandalous hints of incest in the father-daughter relationship are read as a Kleistian parody of bourgeois expectations. Helen G. Morris-Keitel analyzes heterosexual relations in Louise Otto's *Castle and Factory*. She argues that by granting success only to the one relationship that moves toward genuine partnership, Otto hints at the cultural changes upon which realization of her ideals will depend.

This questioning of society is continued by Barbara Hales, who identifies in various cultural products of the Weimar era a connection between female sexuality and criminality. This preoccupation with the criminal *femme fatale,* she argues, exposes a widespread uneasiness with modernity in general. In her comparison of the poetry of Nelly Sachs and Rose Ausländer, Kathrin Bower finds that despite many differences, both poets confronted the trauma of exile and the Holocaust through language. Both, she contends, used the poetic word to express the tensions between mourning and a form of hope represented by the (M)other. Ausländer is one of the women writers—along with Sarah Kirsch, Elisabeth Plessen, and Angelika Mechtel—whose works Charlotte Melin deals with in her analysis of the reworkings of the Alice in Wonderland motif. Comparing the versions of Alice in the works of these four women writers to those of male writers H.C. Artmann and Jürg Federspiel, she concludes that the protean character basic to all Alice variations is viewed by the female writers as essential to psychological well-being and by the male writers as indicative of a loss of identity.

Feminists have often questioned the applicability of the Frankfurt School's cultural criticism for their work. Helgard Mahrdt addresses this still open question with an analysis of the private and public spheres that connects Ingeborg Bachmann's work to the Frankfurt School's critique and at the same time provides avenues for understanding the importance of gender throughout her *ouevre*. Following this contribution on one of the icons of feminist readers and scholars, the next article takes up the life and work of a living, and far more controversial writer: Frederick A. Lubich offers an interview with Elisabeth Alexander, whose approach to feminism has provoked debate within the literary establishment and especially among feminists.

For the last several decades, members of Women in German have been questioning and expanding the definition of German literature. The final two articles contribute new insights to this discussion. Karen Jankowsky offers a reading of *The Façade* by our guest at the 1996 conference, Libuše Moníková, a Czech writer who lives in Germany and writes in German. This work, according to Jankowsky, provokes readers to an understanding of the fluid boundaries between nations, cultures, and genders. Eva Demski's *Afra: Roman in fünf Bildern* is the focus of Leslie A. Adelson's inquiry, a novel she understands as a blending of the history of Germany with that of Afra, a child of mixed race living in a small Bavarian village. Reading the text for the discursive functions of blackness and whiteness, she challenges our profession to embrace an expanded understanding of German culture. The volume ends with the editors' reflections on the role of WIG in the evolution of an "American Germanics" that differs in substantial ways from what has been typically understood as *Germanistik*.

The editors gratefully acknowledge the ongoing support of the University of Cincinnati and the University of Rochester.

Sara Friedrichsmeyer
Patricia Herminghouse
July 1996

Feminist German Studies across the Disciplines: Introduction to Grossmann, Ferree, and Cocks

Sara Lennox

The following three essays, written by historian Atina Grossmann, sociologist Myra Marx Ferree, and political theorist Joan Cocks, are a feminist contribution to the ongoing debate about the role of multi- and interdisciplinary work in the emerging field of German Studies. Defined in the 1988 German Studies Association *Guidelines for Curricular Organization at American Educational Institutions* as "the interdisciplinary study of the contemporary cultural, social, economic, and political life of the German-speaking peoples in their historical and international context," German Studies has been embraced most enthusiastically by scholars trained in the discipline of German literary studies. For literary scholars, German Studies, often loosely associated with British Cultural Studies, has provided an opportunity to import Anglo-American methodologies developed over the past several decades into their own field and to address a wider range of German cultural products than was authorized by the traditional canon of German literature. German Studies has found particular acceptance among younger, U.S.-trained Germanists poised to assume leadership of the field as an older cohort of German emigrés whose intellectual production was oriented towards the Federal Republic now moves towards retirement. To younger Germanists, German Studies seems to represent a new, uniquely U.S.-American perspective on "things German." As Marc Weiner put it in his provocative letter announcing the policies *German Quarterly* would pursue under his editorship: "German Studies has begun to develop an identity different from that of its counterpart, (German) Germanistik, as manifested in a variety of intellectual paradigms that differ from those abroad."

Despite the claims to interdisciplinarity made in the GSA *Guidelines,* then, Germanists have frequently considered German Studies mainly the purview of German Departments, viewing it particularly as a vehicle that would allow them to broaden curricular offerings, teach courses in English, and hence reach larger numbers of students at a time of declining language enrollments. Unlike Germanists, however, proponents of German Studies in fields like history and political science, the other core areas of the GSA, seem much more strongly committed to interdisciplinary cooperation among the multiple disciplines focused on the study of Germany and make no assumptions about the proper methodology or content (or degree of generational conflict) of such projects. To use Russell Berman's metaphors, historians and political scientists (to the degree that they are interested in German Studies at all) are committed to a conception of German Studies as *großdeutsch,* seeking "to bring together German specialists from various fields," while Germanists more often conceive German Studies to be *kleindeutsch,* "revitalizing the language and literature model by using an innovative pedagogy that examines a culture through a range of objects, including but not restricted to canonic literature" (91).

Feminist scholarship, however, has always made a claim to interdisciplinarity: as historian Gisela Bock put it in her opening speech to the first Berlin *Sommeruniversität* in 1976: "Scholarship on women has to be interdisciplinary: for a single scholarly discipline [*Wissenschaft*] or method doesn't suffice to answer our questions" (18). Though feminism's growing acceptability in the academy has meant that feminist approaches have increasingly developed via interchanges with other tendencies within their own discipline rather than merely in dialogue with other feminists, in my observation feminist scholars continue to remain more in touch with developments in other fields than do my other colleagues. This awareness of the vital, exciting feminist research taking place in other fields forms the backdrop to the *Yearbook*'s publication of these three essays by non-Germanists. Grossmann, Ferree, and Cocks were guests of honor at the 1995 Women in German conference, and their essays are revised versions of the talks they gave there. The decision to invite three feminist scholars from disciplines outside our own was made at the 1994 conference after discussions following a panel on "Feminist Theory and (German) Cultural Studies," at which conference participants expressed their eagerness to undertake interdisciplinary feminist research in German Studies and their simultaneous concern that they lacked adequate background in other fields to do so. Our guests were thus asked to take on three functions at the 1995 conference: to provide us with an overview of important trends and directions in current feminist scholarship in their field; to respond from a disciplinary perspective to a German cultural product, the film *Beruf: Neo-Nazi*; and to participate generally in the conference (which last task they carried out most energetically) so that we could see how the optic of their fields might vary from our own. This charge to our guests (which, as co-organizer of the program together with Sara Friedrichsmeyer, I played some part in formulating) suggests to me that feminists' greater familiarity with other fields helps them to recognize how very different even the feminist methodology and content of other fields is from that of literary studies and thus how problematic German Studies in one department might be. Here I would like to look first at these three essays through the eyes of a literary scholar in order to underline what feminist Germanists share with, and how they differ from, feminist historians, sociologists, and political theorists. Then I want to discuss how strikingly those differences were brought home to us in our joint discussion of *Beruf: Neo-Nazi*. Finally I will suggest what conclusions I think can be drawn from WIG's very productive engagement with feminist German Studies across the disciplines.

In her presentation to the WIG conference, Grossmann began by reminding us that "historians tell stories"; that is, they construct narratives (a statement that is itself somewhat contested within the historical profession). In her essay here, she has illustrated her methodology by telling us a story about the stories historians tell. Though, of course, we know better, we literary scholars are still inclined to regard the historical context of textual production as stable and unchanging, though we would maintain that the text opens itself to a variety of changing readings. But Grossmann shows us that historians never produce narratives of the past "wie es eigentlich gewesen," but that instead their stories are always shaped by the particular historical situation in which they find themselves. Some of the forces acting on contemporary feminist historians also influence us as literary scholars: among them, of course, the impact of unification, the shift in feminist attention from women to gender relations, the new feminist concern with race, the impact of postcolonial theory, the emphasis on the heterogeneity rather than unity of our objects of investigation, and the new interest in memory and commemoration. (Grossmann also shows that German history has been at least as resistant to postmodernism as *Germanistik*.) Other influences seem more specific to historians: access to archival material, for instance, or the prominence of gender issues or the rise of xenophobic violence since unification that encourage historians to look for antecedents and causes in the past.

While in literary studies "positionality" is often taken as a description of the standpoint of the individual scholar ("Speaking as a white, heterosexual, lower-middle-class, materialist feminist..."), Grossmann shows how groups of historians and the kind of history they write are much more clearly influenced by structural imperatives: that, for instance, an emphasis on victimhood may derive from a historian's nationality, related to German efforts to redeem some Germans from responsibility for National Socialism, or that feminist historians' interest in *Männergeschichte* may stem from the career advantages of dealing with masculinity within a still highly misogynist profession. As well, Grossmann underlines the many conceptual decisions that shape the description of the past, which is much less foregrounded in literary studies: What *is* the relationship between female agency and victimhood? Of what does modernity consist and how might it have affected women and gender relations? How might the historical process called "rationalization" (a term derived from sociological theory) impact all social experience, including interpersonal relations and subjectivity, and to what degree is it beneficent or malevolent? As is also the case to some degree in literary studies, feminist historians of Germany have moved away from an emphasis on women alone and often focus now on general topics into which a gender analysis is fully integrated. On the other hand, German historians' new comparative emphasis has few parallels in German literary studies, since graduate study in history frequently demands a knowledge of the history of more than one country, while graduate training in German concentrates on the study of German literature alone. Above all, Grossmann's essay shows, historians are more interested than literary scholars in change over time. They examine change as it impacts upon and is produced by groups as well as individuals, interrogate the causes of such change, and at least in some cases endeavor to determine the degree to which it is possible to make general statements about such historical transformations and the people participating in them.

As a sociologist, Ferree's focus is even more emphatically the general and supra-individual: she wants to look at how groups of people are positioned within social structures and at how social structures impinge upon collectivities. Gender she also understands to be a social structure within which individuals are embedded rather than as a quality that inheres in individuals; and in that respect, as she emphasizes, feminist sociologists' understanding of gender displays some affinities to feminist humanists' description of gender as "discursively constructed," since both move gender "outside the arbitrary boundaries of our skins and place it where it can be understood as interactive, collective, dynamic, and contested"—though sociologists insist on identifying the social locations of discourses, while humanists are more inclined to conceive of discourse as amorphous and free-floating. Like feminists in many other fields, Ferree insists on looking at gender as inflected by race and class, and argues that gender and race are not just relevant for individuals and groups disadvantaged by them but also affect access to power and privilege. Her conceptual categories are also influenced by other feminists, including feminist sociologists in Scandinavia, and by Black American feminist theory. She shows that sociology, like history, is also very often comparative, understanding aspects of various societies in terms of their contrast with one another, since via cross-national work "the features of the systems as systems can more readily be seen in the similarities and differences between them."

To illustrate the methodology of feminist sociology and also show how gender functions as social structure, Ferree advances a most provocative analysis comparing the "macro-level gender systems" of East and West Germany before unification. Her investigation of the way in which each German state exercised structural power over women shows the profound effect of the different state systems on women's options and life choices as well as how they influence women's own conception of their self-identities, how women conceive resistance to domination, and why they find it difficult to understand and organize in concert with women from the other Germany. As a sociologist, Ferree, as she stressed in discussion, does not inevitably favor quantitative over qualitative analysis, preferring instead a combination of the two. Nor is she as a sociologist uninterested in the analysis of specific literary texts, but she urges that textual analysis be placed in the context of an understanding of gender as social structure provided by feminist sociology, an undertaking that will simultaneously further illuminate the text and help sociologists to understand how specific individuals respond to structural relations. Though Ferree's essay underlines the immense utility of sociology to literary scholars, it also reveals the huge gap that looms between the methodological apparatus of sociology and that of literature. Perhaps to an even greater degree than with history, the insights of feminist sociology, though clearly of immense utility to literary scholars, are not ones at which we could arrive using the methods of our own field alone.

Of the three disciplines of our visiting scholars, political theory as Cocks presents it may employ a methodology most similar to certain kinds of literary analysis. Reading Arendt in the company of Luxemburg and Fanon, Cocks is not interested in coming to summary conclusions, but in understanding the specific arguments of these three thinkers in very particular texts. Moreover, though she does argue that all three thinkers derived from pariah peoples (an Arendtian term) and lived far from their geographic home, her method is more formalist than that of history or sociology: she is not primarily interested in the conditions of these texts' genesis, the formative influences on these thinkers, the other thinkers with whom they may have been in dialogue, and the historical situation their theory was written to address. Though Cocks concedes that Arendt's present appeal to feminists and others derives from the changed historical circumstances of the post-Cold War era, those conditions are also not ones she explores in any detail. Cocks is, however, concerned to place Arendt in the context of contemporary feminist *theory,* and there she shows that Arendt's texts can speak to feminist questions that have emerged only recently (and that, *mutatis mutandis,* are also issues in Grossmann's and Ferree's essays and in the work of many literary scholars): how to address the tension between sameness and difference, commonality and plurality; how to conceive the relationship of the biological realm, particularly as it involves the female body, to freedom; how to counter essentialist definitions of particular social groups and the insatiable bourgeois appetite for wealth. Cocks can also be understood here as undertaking the kind of analysis Grossmann observed among many recent feminist historians, an investigation of what appears to be a non-feminist topic to which a gender analysis is nonetheless central. Cocks's very subtle reading of the twists and turns in the writings of these three complex thinkers reveals political theory's conception of textual analysis (and, as literary scholars might observe, its limitations as well: Cocks is not interested in the expressive or figurative qualities of the text, nor does she consider the possibility that language may not always be true to an author's intention or may speak behind his/her back). What may also distinguish Cocks's approach here from that of literary scholars is the purpose to which she wishes to put Arendt's thought. She began her WIG presentation by remarking, "Political theory asks how to act with practical wisdom in the world." Unlike literary scholars, then, to a certain degree Cocks is operating at the level of generalization after all: she turns to this theory, as she herself stresses, to answer urgent contemporary questions, "for help in making sense of nationalism and the intellectual's relation to nationalism in the midst of what I see as a contemporary crisis in that relation." One might then argue that political theory, at least as Cocks presents it, is undertaken as a quest for general truths that is largely foreign to literary scholarship.

The differences between our guests' methodologies and our own were brought home most strikingly to us in our discussion of the film *Beruf: Neo-Nazi*. Though our guests adamantly refused to consider themselves representative of their fields, to many of us it seemed that their responses—and our own—were deeply shaped by disciplinary presuppositions. WIG members' discussion of the film after viewing it on Friday evening had, we recognized afterwards, focused to a great degree on questions of aesthetics and representation: How does the filmmaker manipulate camera angles to make the protagonist look sympathetic? How is the protagonist's homoerotic seductiveness related to a fascist aesthetic? How are women represented and why are they relatively absent from the film? Does such a film need a voice-over in order to direct audience response? But during the Saturday evening panel our three visitors raised much different issues. Grossmann did not like the film, which, she argued, had too many subplots, was too idiosyncratic, overly psychologized the protagonist, did not tell her what she wanted to know about the Neo-Nazi movement, was—in summary—a bizarre drama, not a documentary from which historians could learn. As a historian, her interest lay less in the film itself than in the story of the controversy surrounding it, which again raised the question of how Germans confront the legacy of Auschwitz.

Ferree began her response to the film by remarking that she had watched it in a way that seemed "natural" to her, but then realized that she too was viewing it through a disciplinary perspective. She was most interested in what the film told viewers about social movements and she particularly emphasized the relationship between charismatic leadership and formal organization. Cocks was not certain that political theory, concerned to probe such questions as "What is the good society," could address many of the questions this film raises, which seem rather the purview of psychology: Why are certain kinds of people attracted to such movements? The film allowed her, however, to raise questions about the relationship of nationalism and fascism as well as political leadership and democracy. Despite their reluctance to view themselves as exemplary for their disciplines, then, our guests' reactions to the film nonetheless seemed to typify their fields. Grossmann, the historian, looked for satisfying and coherent stories and was not content with the story the film told; Ferree used a framework drawn from Max Weber, the founder of modern sociology, to talk about social structures and charisma (and asked with astonishment if she was the only one in the room for whom the film's title immediately invoked Weber's essay "Politik als Beruf"); Cocks, the political theorist, looked for general maxims explaining political behavior that could be drawn from the film.[1] What might initially have seemed to be "natural" and "spontaneous" responses to the film were, we discovered, deeply informed by our disciplinary assumptions. Though it would be pleasant to think that our various reactions happily complemented each other, it was also not so clear that the conclusions at which our respective disciplines enabled us to arrive were compatible or reconcilable with each other, and it was quite apparent that none of us could have reproduced the responses of disciplines other than our own.

What can we conclude from this very productive cross-disciplinary experiment? We can probably answer the question posed by Frank Trommler—"Is Interdisciplinarity Really So Hard To Do?"—with a resounding "Yes!" (210).[2] The essays that follow this introduction reveal how much the perspectives of feminist historians, sociologists, and political theorists could contribute to our literary and cultural analyses—yet the discussion of *Beruf: Neo-Nazi* showed that it is unlikely that we literary scholars alone will be able to supplement our research with the perspectives of these or other disciplines. Our disciplinary training provides us with optical tools that allow us to examine our object of study more carefully, but it also fits us with blinders that prevent us from seeing that with which our discipline does not concern itself. Moreover, not only do we lack the years of scholarly training that would allow us to see through other disciplines' eyes, but few of us possess the time or capacity to remain abreast of scholarly developments that would be required for serious research integrating the field's newest insights. Too often literary scholars, after reading a few representative books, believe they are qualified to speak as historians, anthropologists, media specialists, or political scientists—but in fact produce shoddy and dilettantish work that is not taken seriously by scholars from those other disciplines. That is not to say, of course, that we should not invest every effort in broadening our horizons, in reading as widely as possible in other fields, in challenging our disciplinary assumptions. In fact, as the "Editorial Introduction" to the *Monatshefte* "Special Survey: German Studies Programs and Courses" noted: "Even a reading of dissertation titles in our annual listings indicates, at least to literary scholars brought up in the 1950s and 1960s, an almost total change in paradigm. Pure study of literature seems to be the exception now, rather than the rule" (360). But what this means is that our *own* discipline has changed, not that we have metamorphosed into historians or ethnologists or musicologists—as scholars from those disciplines, who, when called upon to determine whether a particular work of scholarship should be regarded as contributing to their field, often manifest something of a guild mentality, would be swift to remind us.

What then of German Studies? In my view, our experiment at the Women in German conference argues for a model of multi- and cross-disciplinary cooperation that is *großdeutsch*—though "League of Nations" might be an image less burdened by imperialist overtones. As Grossmann remarked at the conference, it is hard to be "deeply trained" in more than one field, and she is reluctant to forego the benefits of scholarship within the disciplines informed by such training. Since, at least within German Studies, only a few multidisciplinary projects have as yet been launched, it is difficult to predict results: perhaps the insights of our fields complement or supplement each other, but they may also prove incompatible or irrelevant, stressing different elements of the object of study (or even different objects of study), asking different questions about it, and coming to different conclusions. But if this is a project worth undertaking, as our conference experiment suggests, if the study of women indeed *demands* engagement in a range of disciplines, then we need to devise mechanisms to enable that encounter: German Studies cannot continue to mean, as GSA members have frequently quipped, that historians, political scientists, and Germanists meet in neighboring rooms at the annual GSA convention. One important vehicle for such cross-disciplinary encounters might be team-teaching (and disseminating the results, perhaps at future WIG events); others might be joint panels, joint conferences, joint research projects. Participants at the final wrap-up session at the WIG conference urged WIG to continue periodically to invite guests from other disciplines, and to establish contacts and forge coalitions with feminist caucuses in other fields. Since we Germanists are the most enthusiastic proponents of German Studies (historians and social scientists are not, for instance, threatened with enrollment declines), it is likely that the initiative for such encounters and projects must come from us. In the postscript to the 1994 *Yearbook*, "WIG 2000: Feminism and the Future of *Germanistik*," editors Jeanette Clausen and Sara Friedrichsmeyer noted: "We are not the first to recommend that Germanistik become more international, more heterogeneous; but we are the first to suggest that WIG can and should play a leadership role in providing direction for that change..." (269). Precisely because of feminism's long-term commitment to interdisciplinary scholarship, precisely because feminists across the disciplines have more reason to seek each other out and more need of each other's work, we can hope that feminists in German literary studies will also assume a leadership role in promoting a genuinely multi- and cross-disciplinary German Studies.

Notes

[1] My description of the visitors' responses is indebted to Sara Friedrichsmeyer's summary of this session in the Fall 1995 *Women in German Newsletter* (9).

[2] Trommler's question in turn draws on the title of an essay by Stanley Fish, "Being Interdisciplinary Is So Very Hard to Do," in *Profession 89*.

Works Cited

Berman, Russell A. "Global Thinking, Local Teaching: Departments, Curricula, and Culture." *Profession 95*: 89–93.

Bock, Gisela. "Frauenbewegung und Frauenuniversität: Zur politischen Bedeutung der 'Sommeruniversität für Frauen.'" *Frauen und Wissenschaft: Beiträge zur Berliner Sommeruniversität—Juli 1976*. Berlin: Courage Verlag, 1977. 15–22.

Clausen, Jeanette, and Sara Friedrichsmeyer. "WIG 2000: Feminism and the Future of *Germanistik*." *Women in German Yearbook 10*. Ed. Jeanette Clausen and Sara Friedrichsmeyer. Lincoln: U of Nebraska P, 1994. 267–72.

German Studies Association. *Guidelines for Curricular Organization at American Educational Institutions*. [Tempe, AZ], 1987. 4.

"Special Survey: German Studies Programs and Courses." Editorial Introduction. *Monatshefte* 87.3 (1995): 360–66.

Trommler, Frank. "The Future of German Studies or How to Define Interdisciplinarity in the 1990s." *German Studies Review* 15.2 (May 1992): 201–18.

Weiner, Marc A. "Letter from the New Editor of the German Quarterly." *AATG Newsletter* 30.1 (Fall 1994): n.p.

Remarks on Current Trends and Directions in German Women's History

Atina Grossmann

For the benefit of literary scholars curious about recent developments in German women's history, this contribution offers a critical survey of trends in the United States and Germany. Moving beyond its earlier focus on the history of women and feminism, the field now tends to analyze broader topics, i.e., nationalism, as they are inflected by issues of gender. Feminist explorations of the potential of postmodern analysis for the interrogation of historical reality have, however, made few inroads into traditional, mainstream historiography. There have been insightful contributions in, for example, debates about women's status as victims and perpetrators or the situation of women since unification, but xenophobia and antisemitism persist in some German feminist work. (PH)

In both the United States and Germany, the next generation of daughters and younger sisters appears less focused on women or gender *per se* and more committed to integrating women and gender into broader analyses of topics such as the welfare state, racial politics, or popular culture. At the same time, of course, "old-fashioned" work on feminism and women's organizations is still being produced.

The emphasis on gender rather than women's history is perhaps particularly visible in Germany, for example in Ute Frevert's recent volume, *Mann und Weib*. German women's historians embraced that shift with great alacrity; rather overstating the difference between the two genres, many still tend to treat women's history as compensatory and gender history as the radical approach that will shift the paradigm. Ironically, some German feminist historians have rushed to do what has come to be called *Männergeschichte* (men's history); one thinks of recent work on masculine honor and dueling or on Prussian army officers. Interesting and important as such research is—and for sure, there is much for us to learn here—the career and professional rewards of this approach to being a feminist historian are considerable in a country where the profession is still unremittingly male-dominated; there was not a single women's panel at the last *Historikertag* (the major conference of historians in Germany), I am told.

If one looks at the field as a whole, however, some substantively new questions and approaches are emerging—many of them similar to those Women in German members have been thinking about. Since the rupture of 1989, there has been an explosion of work about the post-1945 period, and especially about the history of the Soviet zone and the German Democratic Republic—a result of the changed political context and the quite stunning new availability and openness of archives (and stories). German history (*qua* history, as opposed to *Zeitgeschichte* [contemporary history], political science, or sociology) no longer concludes in 1945, and postwar studies no longer refer primarily to the West. The prominence accorded to gender issues, such as female work force participation, childcare, and especially abortion and Paragraph 218, in the politics of unification has also surely heightened general interest in gender and gendered histories of the postwar half-century.

There has also been an increased attention to race, and not only in the conventional sense of racial hygiene and population policy, and their contested teleologies leading to World War II and the Holocaust. A growing body of research (among graduate students here in the United States certainly, but inspired also by the "coming out"—*Farbe bekennen*—in print and in the women's movement of "Afro-Germans") examines racial politics after World War II, especially relations with French-African and African-American occupation soldiers and their (so-called) mixed-race *Besatzungskinder* (occupation babies). Generally, the gender politics of the occupation period, notably the vexed issue of "fraternization" between German women and Allied troops as well as refugees and displaced persons, are attracting attention.

We see also a burgeoning concern with the history of German colonialism, a topic almost wholly ignored up until now, obscured perhaps by the dominance of National Socialism on our historiographical screens. This new interest obviously is not accidental and correlates not only with broader developments in postmodernist and postcolonial theory, but also with the more obviously multicultural profile of the new united Germany (see, for example, Lora Wildenthal's new work). At the same time, the unification of Germany and its repositioning of the national question on the political agenda—with all the questions it raised about definitions of Germanness and citizenship—has focused attention on notions of the nation and its gendering. Indeed, the interest in colonialism is now extending to research on German expansionism and influence in Eastern Europe. (The two most recent meetings of the Northeast Workshop on German Women's History and Culture reflect this turn.)

At the same time—and again this is surely not accidental—as twentieth-century German history normalizes, the growing preoccupation with the (gendered) nation and the state is accompanied by a very welcome new emphasis on comparative work. German history and identity itself are increasingly perceived as less homogenous than generally posited, continually stressed by political, religious, regional, and migration pattern divisions (see Volker Berghahn's recent interpretation of the *Kaiserreich*). Historians of women and gender are increasingly situating German history in a comparative context, or better, several comparative contexts: 1) within a continuity of West European welfare states, 2) within a continuity of other "authoritarian" states, namely the Stalinist Soviet Union, fascist Italy, and even—very interestingly—Japan, and 3) in comparison with that other always "exceptional" and hypermodern state with a clear "race" problematic, the United States. Fifty or more years after May 1945, there is a growing willingness—and urgency—to pursue German history in a comparative framework, and to move out from under the sense that Germany's uniquely horrific, horrifically unique, history in the twentieth century must necessarily preclude or distort comparisons. This tendency produces, of course, its own anxieties about how to historicize and memorialize the Holocaust.

As these new areas of research open up, certain discussions have proceeded, I think, to an at least temporary closure, signaled by a series of three important conferences on modernity, rationalization, and the welfare state (and gender). Meetings at Columbia University (organized by Molly Nolan, Carola Sachse, Tilla Siegel, and me) in September 1994, in Paris in November 1994 and January 1996 (organized by Helmut Gruber), and in Bad Homburg in February 1995 (organized by Karen Hagemann) marked an initial culmination of ongoing work on gender and modernity (proceedings forthcoming in a special issue of the journal *Social Politics* and in a volume edited by Helmut Gruber and Pamela Graves). All of these discussions, focused on comparisons among Germany, Great Britain, France, Italy, Belgium, the Netherlands, Denmark, Sweden, Norway, the Soviet Union, and the United States, underscored how gender as a historical category seems to have been salient in particularly public and visible ways in the twentieth century, especially perhaps during the interwar period, at least in the West (and probably elsewhere, although that was beyond the scope of our conversation). In the German case, this arena of inquiry has been largely defined by the concept of "rationalization" or "social rationalization" (see, for example, Molly Nolan's and my own recent books or Carola Sachse on company social policy in Weimar).

We have achieved a certain kind of conclusion about the usefulness and limits of the term "rationalization," a concept that has enjoyed more currency in the German context, and that has indeed proven extremely fruitful for analyzing the turbulent and radically shifting history of modern Germany. We have moved from our, by now very well developed, discussions of rationalization and social welfare at home (housework), in the workplace (trade union and company social policy), and in the welfare state (including the impact of socialism and communism) to consider new areas of comparative investigation: race, empire, nation, and citizenship, mass consumption and consumer culture, as well as violence and war (which can, of course, be seen as either the failure or the logical result of rationalization). We concluded that questions regarding inclusion and exclusion, boundary-making and -keeping—perhaps we could call this citizenship—are integral and complementary to any discussion of processes of rationalization and structuring of gender systems.

In order to understand these conclusions, it might be useful to outline the contours of the discussion about "rationalization," and to clarify what German women's historians have meant by the terminology of rationalization. The term, broadly conceived, suggests organized efforts—by the state, by business, by social, political, and labor movements—to order and regulate the chaos of modern societies, to govern behavior and structure social relations, and hence the effects of industrialization and urbanization. It encompasses at least three overlapping discourses: that of business and management about efficiency and division of labor, a Weberian focus on power and bureaucracy that clearly sets out an irrational/rational dichotomy, and a broader discourse on social welfare and population policy and racial hygiene. When the word first came into renewed use in the early 1980s in the context of discussions about Fordism and post-Fordism, it was usually applied in terms of the scientific management of industry.

In the past decade however, social historians of Germany have identified, especially for the 1920s, a broad social phenomenon permeating all areas of everyday life, from sexuality to the assembly line, in which the gospel of rationalization was preached widely by industrialists, social workers, and politicians to workers and others in all social spheres; hence the term "social rationalization" (see the volume on *Rationale Beziehungen,* edited by Reese, et al.). Rationalization efforts, in the United States as well as in Germany, involved not only external discipline but support for the internalization of mores in which rational, planned, efficient behavior was coded as good, and the irrational as bad. In both Europe and the United States, Taylorist attempts to maximize planning and efficiency by minimizing time, labor, and money—be it in the bedroom, kitchen, or workplace—also extended to state policies regulating the economy, public health, or racial policy. But the relative balance of individual initiatives and state intervention differed significantly between Germany and the rest of Europe on the one hand and the United States on the other.

This tension between individual and collective needs, market and state forces, expert control and popular desire, as linked to national, class, race, and gender differences, in the shaping of "modern" "rationalized" gender relationships informed many of our discussions. We repeatedly grappled with a key question, given particular resonance by the term's close association with Germany and its continuities into the Nazi era: must social rationalization always contain elements of coercion, hierarchy, and segregation? If rationalization is inevitably normative and necessarily tied to calculation and control, must those deemed uncontrollable and "irrational" (always in gendered and racialized terms) then be excluded and deemed wasteful or unfit? Is there, in Tilla Siegel's words, an inherently destructive, totalitarian side intrinsic to instrumental reason? Clearly, as the twentieth-century resort to total war and genocide has dramatically shown, technologies of order also produce extreme disorder, and languages of rationalization also encompass extreme irrationalities.

Yet, at the same time, rationalization (like mass consumption, we decided) operates as a trademark of modernity, producing both hope and despair. These are, as has been repeatedly pointed out, highly elastic phenomena, contradictory and ambivalent, both liberating and controlling, expansive and exclusive. They undermine and then reconstruct differences (of class, race, and gender especially), lending themselves to similar rhetorics but different applications at different times in different places under different regimes. Most clearly perhaps for women and marginalized groups, rationalization can create increased prosperity and leisure as well as exacerbate inequality and surveillance. For all modern welfare societies, a paramount challenge was to develop strategies of social rationalization that could accommodate both maternity and modernity, both maternalist and waged work, while also maintaining (easing or exacerbating) class and racial hierarchies.

Germany, of course, offers a particularly dense site for examining various strategies to achieve this delicate balance: Weimar, the Third Reich, and two different postwar regimes. Rationalization (often equated with modernization) did not equal emancipation and certainly reproduced gender hierarchy and inequality. Nonetheless, the push for a rationalized economy and a more interventionist welfare state after World War I did lead to important changes and openings for women, offering both practical and discursive entries into modernity. Social welfare and consumption—privileged female realms—clearly function as prime arenas for examining the ambiguous impact of rationalization.

Feminist historians of Germany have reached, I think, some kind of consensus that arguments about race, citizenship, the state, and popular culture (probably the most undeveloped) are now on the agenda. There is also widespread agreement about deploying notions of "modernity," not in the teleological progressive terms of modernization but in the contested crisis-ridden sense used by Detlev Peukert in his pioneering *The Weimar Republic: The Crisis of Classical Modernity*. But there is still much disagreement about the balance of emphasis when analyzing rationalization or consumption, or, for that matter, women's history in general: between coercion and control versus agency and space, between women as victims and women as actors.

In some ways then, German women's history has been waging its own form of the postmodernist debate about the evils and limits of Enlightenment discourse. One could equally argue, however, that a glance at recent publications and conferences reveals once again that the postmodern or linguistic turn has made few significant inroads into German women's history. Kathleen Canning's important intervention in her *Signs* article, "Feminist History after the Linguistic Turn," as well as Jane Caplan's and Isabel Hull's much earlier reflections in a 1989 special issue of *Central European History* on feminist and gender history "in postmodern times," have not yet had much of an echo. The most dramatic evidence of this is that, astonishingly, during several months of hot (and for the most part not particularly edifying or interesting), virtually entirely male debate about postmodernism and German history on H-Net German last summer and fall, Canning's piece was never even mentioned, much less discussed! There is as yet no counterpart to, for example, Judith Walkowitz's *City of Dreadful Delight* in German women's history, although some may well be in the pipeline.

German history has its own peculiar (and unsurprising) heavy-hitting rationales for rejecting so-called postmodern analysis. They are neatly summarized by Kenneth Barkin in a 1995 *German Studies Review* polemic that attacked postmodernism as being, on the one hand, simply a more incomprehensible, illegible, and elitist version of certain longstanding German intellectual and historiographical traditions of *Begriffsgeschichte* (history of ideas) and hermeneutics, and, on the other hand, inadmissible in a field that, confronted with events bearing the moral and world historical dimension of the Holocaust, could not permit itself the playful interrogations of historical reality associated with postmodern readings. I am sure that as the current generation of graduate students and recent PhDs, feminist or not, but schooled at least to some degree in discursive analysis, enters the field, this condition of "belatedness" (as diagnosed by Michael Geyer and Konrad Jarausch in their controversial response to Barkin) will change.

However pronounced the resistance to postmodernism (or what is understood as postmodernism), German history has clearly not escaped—indeed in many ways serves as a benchmark for—the contemporary intellectual and cultural fascination with memory and history. Consider only the flood of commemorations, publications, films in theaters and television, *Podiumsdiskussionen,* and debates about the proper nature of museums, monuments, and historical writing as we pass the fifty-year anniversary of the end of World War II. There seems to be no obvious gender dimension to these extensive arguments; certainly the split opinions about whether and how to build a Holocaust memorial in Berlin (a project that remains mired in controversy) were about how to remember and think or teach about Auschwitz a half century after its liberation, and not about the particularities of representing female or male experience. And the calls for remembrances of homosexual "victims" also seem to have been very muted (see, however, Schoppmann).

There has, however, been a steady stream of work—scholarly and journalistic—on women's memories of World War II and the immediate postwar period. Never, it would seem, had, as Susanne zur Nieden has pointed out in her excellent study of women's diaries, German women put pen to paper as copiously as they did during the turbulent years at war's end. Key to this trend was Helke Sander's controversial (and long!) 1992 documentary film *BeFreier und Befreite* (*Liberators Take Liberties*) about the rape of German women at war's end, especially (but not only) by Red Army soldiers. The film provoked much response in Germany where it was lavishly praised for opening up a topic supposedly long marked by taboos. It also garnered passionately negative reactions, mostly, but not only, from outside Germany, for once again essentializing universal notions of female victimization and decontextualizing a very specific series of events that took place at a particularly toxic juncture in history: the fact that the final defeat of Nazi Germany (accomplished only by outside conquerors) was accompanied by massive attacks on civilian German women. Interestingly, to the best of my knowledge, the most severe German criticism came from the Frankfurt film scholar Gertrud Koch who identifies herself as Jewish. A special issue of the journal *October* (Spring 1995) documents some of this discussion, including Koch's and my own contribution.

The disputes unleashed by Sander's film referred to related—and ongoing—discussions about women as *Opfer* and *Täter* (victims or, in an interesting language slippage, agents/perpetrators) during the Third Reich. These debates, which have by now earned the title *Historikerinnenstreit,* were highlighted by the virtually uniformly critical German feminist reaction to *Mothers in the Fatherland,* Claudia Koonz's study of middle-class German women's attraction to National Socialism. The vituperative critique by Gisela Bock, one of Germany's few high-profile feminist professors of history, was voiced, although on a less shrill level, by almost all her colleagues—in comparison to the generally positive reception in the United States. No matter whether their research focused on women as *Opfer* of patriarchal fascism or on some women as *Täter* (or in another variant, *Mittäter* [accomplices]) of a murderous regime, German feminist critics of Koonz resented being subsumed in what they perceived as an undifferentiated German collective agency (*Handlungskollektiv Deutschland*). They strenuously resisted a genealogy that mandated Nazi foremothers for all German daughters (see Grossmann, "Feminist Debates"; and Reese and Sachse).

In a sense, the discourse about German female victims of rape (and the preceding and still ongoing debate about *Opfer* and *Täter*) was only the avant-garde, the tip of the iceberg, so to speak, of an avalanche of material on German victimization in the wake of defeat in World War II. Perhaps most dramatic has been the newly respectable discussion (and honoring) of German suffering on the flight west from the eastern territories occupied by the Soviets. This huge migration of over ten million people is increasingly situated as part of the massive resettlement politics of the mid-twentieth century, perpetrated by both Hitler and Stalin (to cite the common shorthand); indeed it is being seen as a forced population movement that some would now define (or redefine) as ethnic cleansing. The gender dimensions of this flight have so far been underplayed in the political debates about how to order this experience in relation to both the Holocaust and German responsibility for the war and war crimes. Certainly, however, as hundreds of memoirs and memories attest, flight and refugee life is "women's work," and it was primarily women and children who made up the vast unhappy refugee treks dragging west (Heineman).

Such an unapologetic focus on German suffering, a topic that has become increasingly socially acceptable (*salonfähig*) since unification, reflects another post-1989 phenomenon: increasingly Germans are writing their own history. The deferential, guilty, and also often resentful bowing to the dominance of Anglo-American historians in the definition and interpretation of modern Germany is over. This is certainly true of women's history as well. Gone is the respectful attention granted to the eager Anglo-American researchers of the 1970s and 1980s, who, in the American case at least, were also often Jewish and had family ties to German-Jewish refugees or Eastern-European Jewish Holocaust survivors. American historians generally had the advantage of perspectives passed on by scholars exiled to the United States by fascism and war. They also had easier access than West Germans to archival sources, for example in the Berlin Document Center and the institutions of the GDR. In recent years, however, as the relatively polarized German and American reactions to Koonz's book and Sander's film demonstrate, German women's historians are no longer taking their cues from their Anglo-American colleagues. In both those cases (and there are more), the German renditions focused on German women as victims—of the Nazi regime, of the war, of occupation, of patriarchy in general—while American interlocutors asked about German women's agency and collaboration in the Third Reich and the war.

Yet, it is important to note that German feminists have also been waging their own internal historians' debate (*Historikerinnenstreit*) about what constitutes a usable past. They too ask how not only daughters but also granddaughters should cope with a past that in some ways seems to grow more vivid in commemoration even as it recedes in years. Alongside the new popularity and respectability of studies in German (especially female) victimization, there has simultaneously been some greater interest in German women as *Täter* (perpetrators in this case) and not as *Opfer* (victims) in National Socialism. This tendency is perhaps best represented by the volume *Nach Osten* edited by Theresa Wobbe and based on an April 1991 conference organized by Wobbe and Gudrun Schwarz. In this category would also belong Brigitte Scheiger's research on women's role in Aryanization, from clerks filling out the forms in the revenue office (*Finanzamt*) to the building caretaker (*Hausmeisterin*) disposing of the remaining property of deported Jews, Ursula Nienhaus's study of women careerists in the postal system, and in particular Gudrun Schwarz's important work on women in the SS. American Claudia Koonz's new work on women's role in Nazi racial hygiene and medicalized killing projects also continues to take up questions of complicity and agency.

Another welcome new direction emerges in Marion Kaplan's research on Jewish women and families in Nazi Germany, and a in spate of very recent work on Jews, displaced persons, and allied occupiers in postwar Germany, as well as the powerful influence of American popular culture (Höhn; Poiger). Here, too, I include my own current project on "Victims, Victors, and Survivors: War's End and Postwar Reconstruction, Berlin 1945-1949." In keeping with the novel interest in colonialism, multiculturalism, and comparison that I have already noted, some studies of German gender and women's history now seek to emphasize the diversity and "non-German" aspects of a history too often told as narrowly national, even *Völkisch* (that is, assuming that German history is only about "Germans").

Finally, it is worth noting that these reflections on the problematics of discussing women in Germany as victims and agents operate in a double context: related, on the one hand, to the amazing resilience of public as well as scholarly attention to National Socialism, the war, and the Holocaust, and, on the other hand, to the dramatic impact of unification and the demise of the German Democratic Republic. Debates about the latter, which focused so much on women's role as the "primary losers" of unification, were invariably shadowed by the historical debates about women's position as "victims" (*Opfer*) or "perpetrators/agents" (*Täter*) in the Third Reich. These debates have, I think, entered a new stage now that we have passed the five-year mark, and the initial uncertainties have cleared. It seems that for many former East Germans, a low point of disappointment and resentment came around 1992-93 when their hopes for democratic renewal had been smashed and their lives remained insecure and in turmoil. Now I have the sense that at least among those we know best—sister academics, intellectuals, professionals, and artists—the situation has somewhat stabilized; people have decided that in many ways their lives have in fact gotten better (travel for work and pleasure, open access to research materials and the international conference circuit, new jobs) but that the country remains divided and that their most significant social and work relationships remain with other former East Germans with whom they feel bonds of memory, socialization, and sensibility. And it is at this point of relative or intermediate stability that the discussion about women's relative status continues, both about the facts and about the political/psychological implications of taking public positions that posit women as "losers" or victims.

There is, in any case, much new comparative work on East and West Germany. We have the opportunity to analyze how postwar family and welfare policy in both Germanies defined itself not only in contrast to National Socialist policies but also in relation to Soviet and or American models, and above all in opposition to the perceived approaches of the respective "other" state. Some feminist scholars (such as Ute Gerhard) have even suggested that, despite the differing models regarding the integration of work and family, when it comes to gender, the two regimes may turn out to be more similar than different in their structures of social inequality and persistent gender divisions and inequity, whether in the workplace, household, or bedroom.

At the same time, altercations about anti-Semitism and xenophobia in parts of the current German feminist movement, which attack especially Jewish and Muslim religious traditions in the name of female liberation, seem to be continuing apace. (See Heschel, who also reported on the attempts of so-called Protestant Christian feminists to use the Old Testament as a prime example of patriarchal oppression at a GSA session in October 1995.) I have also been shocked by references to the supposedly murderous patriarchalism of Islam in issues of one popular German feminist magazine, *Emma* (see Lennox). Whatever else they may signify, such incidents speak, I think, to the continuing uneasiness within Germany and among German feminists about the momentous effects of unification, large-scale immigration of both ethnic Germans and *Ausländer,* and an increasingly multicultural and multinational population—compounded by threatened cutbacks in long taken-for-granted welfare state benefits.

All of these changes affect the ways in which feminist and gender-conscious scholars, both in and outside Germany, write the history and study the culture of Germany. All of us, no matter what field we are trained in, will require all of our deconstructive and critical literary skills, careful and unblinking historical research, and exquisitely calibrated political and ethical good sense.

Works Cited

Barkin, Kenneth. "Bismarck in a Postmodern World." *German Studies Review* 18.2 (May 1995): 241–51.

Berghahn, Volker R. *Imperial Germany 1871–1914: Economy, Society, Culture and Politics.* Providence: Berghahn, 1994.

Bock, Gisela. "Antinatalism, Maternity and Paternity in National Socialist Racism." *Maternity and Gender Policies: Women and the Rise of the European Welfare States 1880–1950.* Ed. Gisela Bock and Pat Thane. New York: Routledge, 1991. 233–55.

Canning, Kathleen. "Feminist History after the Linguistic Turn: Historicizing Discourse and Experience." *Signs* 19.2 (Winter 1994): 368–404.

Caplan, Jane. "Postmodernism, Poststructuralism and Deconstruction: Notes for Historians." *Central European History* 22.3/4 (1989): 119–37.

Frevert, Ute. *Mann und Weib und Weib und Mann: Geschlechter-Differenzen in der Moderne.* München: Beck, 1995.

Gerhard, Ute. "German Women and the Social Costs of Unification." *German Politics and Society* 24/25 (Winter 1991–92): 16–33.

Geyer, Michael, and Konrad H. Jarausch. "Great Men and Postmodern Ruptures: Overcoming the 'Belatedness' of German Historiography." *German Studies Review* 18.2 (May 1995): 253–73.

Grossmann, Atina. "Feminist Debates about Women and National Socialism." *Gender and History* 3.3 (Autumn 1991): 350–58.

———. "A Question of Silence: The Rape of German Women by Occupation Soldiers." *October* 72 (Spring 1995): 43–63.

———. *Reforming Sex: The German Movement for Birth Control and Abortion Reform 1920–1950.* New York: Oxford UP, 1995.

———. "Unfortunate Germany: Rape, Motherhood, and Survival 1945–1950." Center for German and European Studies Conference. University of California at Berkeley, 1995 (forthcoming in volume edited by Gerald Feldman).

Heineman, Elizabeth. "The Hour of the Woman: Memories of Germany's 'Crisis Years' and West German National Identity." *American Historical Review* 101.2 (April 1996): 354–95.

Heschel, Susanne. "From the Bible to Nazism: German Feminists on the Jewish Origins of Patriarchy." *Tel Aviver Jahrbuch für deutsche Geschichte* (1992): 319–33.

Höhn, Maria. "GIs, Veronikas and Lucky Strikes: German Reactions to the American Military Presence in the Rhineland-Palatinate during the 1950s." Diss. U of Pennsylvania, 1995.

Hull, Isabel V. "Feminist and Gender History through the Literary Looking Glass: German Historiography in Postmodern Times." *Central European History* 22.3/4 (1989): 279–300.

Kaplan, Marion. "Jewish Women in Nazi Germany: Daily Life, Daily Struggles, 1933–1939." *Feminist Studies* (Spring 1991): 579–606.
Koch, Gertrud. "Blood, Sperm, and Tears." *October* 72 (Spring 1995): 27–41.
Koonz, Claudia. "Eugenics, Gender, and Ethics in Nazi Germany: The Debate about Involuntary Sterilization, 1933–1936." *Reevaluating the Third Reich*. Ed. Thomas Childers and Jane Caplan. New York: Holmes and Meier, 1993. 66–85.
———. *Mothers in the Fatherland: Women, the Family and Nazi Politics*. New York: St. Martins, 1987.
Lennox, Sara. "Divided Feminism: Women, Racism, and German National Identity." *German Studies Review* 18.3 (1995): 481–502.
Nach Osten: Verdeckte Spuren nationalsozialistischer Verbrechen. Ed. Theresa Wobbe. Frankfurt a.M.: Verlag Neue Kritik, 1992.
Nienhaus, Ursula. "Von der (Ohn)Macht der Frauen: Postbeamtinnen 1933–1945." *TöchterFragen*. 193–210.
Nolan, Mary. *Visions of Modernity: American Business and the Modernization of Germany*. New York: Oxford UP, 1994.
October 72 (Spring 1995). Special issue on "Berlin 1945: War and Rape, 'Liberators Take Liberties.'"
Opitz, May, et al., eds. *Showing Our Colors: Afro-German Women Speak Out*. Trans. Anne v. Adams. Amherst: U of Massachusetts P, 1991.
Peukert, Detlev J.K. *The Weimar Republic: The Crisis of Classical Modernity*. 1987. New York: Hill and Wang, 1992.
Poiger, Uta. "Taming the Wild West: American Popular Culture and the Cold War Battles over East and West German Identities, 1949–1961." Diss. Brown U, 1995.
Reese, Dagmar, and Carola Sachse. "Frauenforschung und Nationalsozialismus." *TöchterFragen*. 73–106.
Reese, Dagmar, Eve Rosenhaft, Carola Sachse, and Tilla Siegel, eds. *Rationale Beziehungen? Geschlechterverhältnisse im Rationalisierungsprozess*. Frankfurt a.M.: Suhrkamp, 1993.
Sachse, Carola. *Siemens, der Nationalsozialismus und die moderne Familie: Eine Untersuchung zur sozialen Rationaliserung in Deutschland im 20. Jahrhundert*. Hamburg: Rasch und Röhring, 1990.
Sander, Helke, and Barbara Johr. *BeFreier und Befreite: Krieg, Vergewaltigung, Kinder*. München: Kunstmann, 1992.
Scheiger, Brigitte. "'Ich bitte um baldige Arisierung der Wohnung...': Zur Funktion von Frauen im bürokratischen System der Verfolgung." *Nach Osten*. 175–96.
Schoppmann, Claudia. *Days of Masquerade: Life Stories of Lesbians during the Third Reich*. New York: Columbia UP, 1996.
Schwarz, Gudrun. "Verdrängte Täterinnen: Frauen im Apparat der SS (1939–1945)." *Nach Osten*. 197–227.

TöchterFragen: NS-Frauengeschichte. Ed. Lerke Gravenhorst and Carmen Tatschmurat. Freiburg i.B.: Kore, 1990.

Walkowitz, Judith R. *City of Dreadful Delight: Narratives of Sexual Danger in Late-Victorian London.* Chicago: U of Chicago P, 1992.

Wildenthal, Lora. "Race, Gender and Citizenship in the German Colonial Empire." *Tensions of Empire: Colonial Cultures in a Bourgeois World.* Ed. Frederick Cooper and Ann Stoler. Berkeley: U of California P, forthcoming.

zur Nieden, Suzanne. *Alltag im Ausnahmezustand: Frauentagebücher im zerstörten Deutschland 1943-1945.* Berlin: Orlanda, 1993.

Additional Suggested Readings in German Women's and Gender History

Allen, Ann Taylor. *Feminism and Motherhood in Germany 1800-1914.* New Brunswick: Rutgers UP, 1991.

Bridenthal, Renate, Atina Grossmann, and Marion Kaplan, eds. *When Biology Became Destiny: Women in Weimar and Nazi Germany.* New York: Monthly Review, 1984.

Burleigh, Michael, and Wolfgang Wippermann. *The Racial State: Germany 1933-1945.* Cambridge: Cambridge UP, 1991.

Canning, Kathleen. "Gender and the Politics of Class Formation: Rethinking German Labor History." *American Historical Review* 97.3 (June 1992): 736-68.

_____. *Languages of Labor and Gender.* Ithaca: Cornell UP, 1996.

Czarnowski, Gabriele. *Das kontrollierte Paar: Ehe und Sexualpolitik im Nationalsozialismus.* Weinheim: Deutscher Studien Verlag, 1991.

Daniel, Ute. "Women's Work in Industry and Family: Germany 1914-18." *The Upheaval of War: Family, Work and Welfare in Europe 1914-1918.* Ed. Richard Wall and Jay Winter. Cambridge: Cambridge UP, 1988.

Davis, Belinda. "Food Scarcity and the Empowerment of the Female Consumer in World War I Germany." *The Sex of Things: Gender and Consumption in Historical Perspective.* Ed. Victoria de Grazia with Ellen Furlough. U of California P, 1996.

Duden, Barbara. *The Woman beneath the Skin: A Doctor's Patients in Eighteenth-Century Germany.* Cambridge: Harvard UP, 1991.

Fehrenbach, Heide. *Cinema in Democratizing Germany: Reconstructing National Identity after Hitler.* Chapel Hill: U of North Carolina P, 1995.

Frevert, Ute. *Women in German History: From Bourgeois Emancipation to Sexual Liberation.* Providence: Berg, 1989.

Grossmann, Atina. "Girlkultur or Thoroughly Rationalized Female: A New Woman in Weimar Germany?" *Women in Culture and Politics.* Ed. J. Friedlander, et al. Bloomington: U of Indiana P, 1986.

Hausen, Karin. "Family and Role Division: The Polarisation of Sexual Stereotypes in the Nineteenth Century—An Aspect of the Dissociation of Work and Family Life." *The German Family*. Ed. Richard Evans and W.R. Lee. London: Croom Helm, 1981. 51-83.

———. "Unemployment Also Hits Women: The New and the Old Woman on the Dark Side of the Golden Twenties in Germany." *Unemployment and the Great Depression in Weimar Germany*. Ed. Peter D. Stachura. London: Macmillan, 1986. 78-120.

Hull, Isabel V. "The Bourgeoisie and its Discontents: Reflections on Nationalism and Respectability." *Journal of Contemporary History* 17.2 (1982): 247-68.

———. *Sexuality, State and Civil Society in Germany, 1700-1815*. Ithaca: Cornell UP, 1996.

Huyssen, Andreas. "Mass Culture as Woman: Modernism's Other." *After the Great Divide: Modernism, Mass Culture, Postmodernism*. Bloomington: Indiana UP, 1986.

Kaplan, Marion. *The Making of the Jewish Middle Class: Women, Family and Identity in Imperial Germany*. New York: Oxford UP, 1993.

Kolinsky, Eva. *Women in Contemporary Germany: Life, Work, and Politics*. 2nd ed. Providence: Berg, 1993.

Lüdtke, Alf. "What Happened to the 'Fiery Red Glow'? Workers' Experiences and German Fascism." *The History of Everyday Life: Reconstructing Historical Experiences and Ways of Life*. Ed. Alf Lüdtke. Princeton: Princeton UP, 1995.

Mamozai, Martha. *Schwarze Frau, Weisse Herrin*. Reinbek bei Hamburg: Rowohlt, 1989.

Moeller, Robert G. *Protecting Motherhood: Women and the Family in the Politics of Postwar West Germany*. Berkeley: U of California P, 1993.

Petro, Patrice. *Joyless Streets: Women and Melodramatic Representation in Weimar Germany*. Princeton: Princeton UP, 1989.

Quataert, Jean. "The Politics of Rural Industrialization: Class, Gender, and Collective Protest in the Saxon Oberlausitz of the Late Nineteenth Century." *Central European History* 20.2 (June 1987): 91-124.

Reagin, Nancy R. *A German Women's Movement: Class and Gender in Hanover, 1880-1933*. Chapel Hill: U of North Carolina P, 1995.

Sachse, Carola. "The National Socialist Maternity Protection Law: A Strategy to Rationalize Labor in the Second World War." *International Journal of Political Economy* 24.4 (Winter 1994-95): 71-94.

Schoppmann, Claudia. *Nationalsozialistische Sexualpolitik und weibliche Homosexualität*. Pfaffenweiler: Centaurus, 1991.

Siegel, Tilla. "It's Only Rational: An Essay on the Logic of Social Rationalization." *International Journal of Political Economy* 24.4 (Winter 1994-95): 35-70.

Theweleit, Klaus. *Male Fantasies: Women, Floods, Bodies, History.* Minneapolis: U of Minnesota P, 1987.

Usborne, Cornelie. *The Politics of the Body in Weimar Germany: Women's Reproductive Rights and Duties.* Ann Arbor: U of Michigan P, 1992.

Weindling, Paul. "Eugenics and the Welfare State during the Weimar Republic." *The State and Social Change in Germany 1880-1980.* Ed. W.R. Lee and Eve Rosenhaft. New York: Berg, 1990. 131-60.

Wildenthal, Lora. "'She is the Victor': Bourgeois Women, Nationalist Identities and the Ideal of the Independent Woman Farmer in German Southwest Africa." *Nations, Colonies and Metropoles* 33. Ed. Daniel A. Segal and Richard Handler. (September 1993): 68-88.

Sociological Perspectives on Gender in Germany

Myra Marx Ferree

Sociological research looks particularly at social structures, that is, persistent patterns of human behavior arising from and impacting on collectivities. Thinking of gender as a social structure rather than an individual trait shifts the analytic focus to include multiple levels of interaction (macro, meso, micro) and the varied processes in which gender is actively produced and contested. This perspective leads me to an analysis of public and private patriarchies as contrasting ways in which the state may organize gender at the macro level. Using the FRG and GDR as examples of public and private patriarchy, I suggest that current conflicts in feminism in unified Germany may partly reflect realistic responses to different past experiences with gender as a social structure. (MMF)

Although many disciplines are currently trying to define what they understand by the concept of gender, the consensus on what it means rarely seems to extend beyond a general sense that it is, somehow, social. I find the most generally useful definition of gender to be that of the historian Joan Scott, who describes it as "a constitutive element of social relationships based on perceived differences between the sexes, and gender is a primary way of signifying relationships of power" ("Gender" 1067). This definition not only distinguishes gender as social from the merely biological realm of "the sexes" but identifies it as a dynamic social force that both constitutes and signifies human relations. This begins to specify the notion of what we mean when we say that gender is social, but as a sociologist I find this definition is no more than a starting point.

My goal in this paper is to offer some background on the distinctive features and contributions of sociology to the study of gender, thus defined, and then focus more narrowly on one element of this perspective that has animated my own comparative research on German and American feminisms.[1] This is, namely, the effort to characterize social systems and state practices in gender terms, and thus also to understand women's responses to injustice in different national contexts as being shaped by the varied and contested structures of gender inequality that women experience. Thus I must begin by better defining what I mean by a social structure.

One premise of sociology is its claim to look at society structurally, that is, in terms of persistent patterns of social relations.[2] Embracing a structural perspective does not mean that sociologists ignore considerations of human agency. Even if the conditions are not of their own choosing, we recognize that people do make history. However, sociological explanations resist reduction to arguments of human agency alone; doing sociology demands attention to forces that arise from and impact on collectivities as such, which is what we call social structure. Such structural forces are understood to exist at all levels of society, from the micro (individuals and their interaction), through the meso (groups and their interaction), to the macro (whole societies or institutional sectors and their interaction). These levels are not equivalent in scope or scale, and each has its distinctive forms of social organization, yet all three can be understood at least in part in terms of their structures.

Feminist sociologists have been insisting for some time now on the importance of understanding gender as a social structure rather than as an individual difference (e.g., Ferree and Hess; Wharton; Lorber). In some ways this is parallel to the trend in the humanities to speak of "discourses," although as sociologists we want to be more concrete about the social location of any discourse: is this speech situated in the interaction of individuals, where the processes of *microlevel interaction,* such as interruptions and tone of voice are relevant; or is it at a *meso* (or group) level, where, for example, one can try to examine the claims that are offered, accepted, or contested; or is this at a *macrolevel,* a cultural framing of issues into particular packages with different resonances and meanings in specific societies? Researchers need to be specific about levels in order actually to examine the structures that make discourse possible and the power relations that constrain and shape it (Huber). However, in both the sociologists' emphasis on structures and the humanities' concern with discourses, I detect a common concern to understand gender as something that operates as a social *process* rather than reducing it to a trait or feature of individuals. Both sociological and literary feminist rethinkings of gender move it outside the arbitrary boundaries of our skins and place it where it can be understood as interactive, collective, dynamic, and contested (cf. Connell).

Nonetheless, it is hard for sociologists, even feminist sociologists, to work through all the implications of looking at gender as a social structure at the group or societal level because we are so accustomed to thinking of it at the individual level alone. When sociologists think of macro-level social structures, we tend to think in terms of social class and the organization of access to economic resources alone. Thus we are comfortable comparing societies in terms of their GNPs or average level of education or form of economic organization; it is still novel to compare countries in terms of their relative rape-proneness, or the degree of male dominance in state policy-making or other institutions, or the control that women can exercise over their reproductive lives. Yet this is in fact the direction in which feminist social science is increasingly moving, and it has exciting implications for doing comparative social studies.[3]

There are two such directions that I want to stress: First, looking at gender as a macro-level system like class implies that we must consider additional dimensions of social stratification; in addition to access to economic resources, important as they are, we also need to look at hierarchies that are centered around *autonomy,* that is, the freedom to make life choices and the freedom of movement, and *power,* that is, participation in the making of decisions concerning the social group as a whole (cf. Agassi). Second, we need to consider race and gender as something more than the devalued attributes of non-white, non-male individuals, and attempt to understand the institutionalization of race preference and gender hierarchy in social organizations and political practices (Anderson; Hess; Omi and Winant). This implies that race and gender are not just about structuring disadvantage but understanding the organizational roots of power and privilege and seeing the links between the social construction of whiteness and masculinity, racial purity, and paternal authority.

This feminist focus on autonomy and power as well as on resources, and on the gender and race of white men as socially meaningful, even fundamental to stratification systems, gives a different angle of vision on comparisons of Germany with the United States and comparisons of the former GDR with the old FRG, for example, asking new questions about how the relative ability of women to gain access to political leadership may reflect different ways in which masculinity is "proven" by men in these different political systems. It widens the considerations of the gains and losses for different groups in the aftermath of German unification and of the continuing integration of the unified Germany into the European Community by counting costs and benefits in political influence and in self-determination as well as economic welfare. And it provides a more systematic basis for linking issues facing women with those of other marginalized groups that are also struggling for greater power and autonomy in *systems* organized around racial preference and gender hierarchy.

Let me turn now to some of my own work as a way of making concrete how one might look at the organization of gender hierarchy as a social system in structural terms.[4] Because one of my central concerns over the years has been the study of feminism, I have been drawn to studying the origins and consequences of the "wall remaining" between the women's movements of the two formerly divided Germanys. I see many current causes for misunderstandings and difficulties in communication that

I won't go into here: experiences of domination, or competition, or recriminations in the period after unification are important, but here I look only at sources that were already there before the wall ever fell, especially differences that arise from the different structures of state policy in each country, and the resulting differences in women's experiences and collective identity. Such collective self-representations link an interpretation of the past—what are women's experiences—to an interpretation of the future—what are women's aspirations (Mansbridge). Collective identity is thus neither just a reflection of past experience nor independent of it, but an actively constructed interpretation of shared history (Melucci; Taylor and Whittier).

My argument is that a discourse situated at the group level—among women concerned about women's issues in the GDR and in the FRG respectively—constructed a collective self-representation of feminism that differs in important ways, in part reflecting the nature of two different macro-level gender systems. I call these macro systems public and private patriarchy, drawing these terms from the growing Scandinavian literature on the gendered welfare state (e.g., Siim; Jónasdóttir and Jones; Hobson and Lindholm). The state socialism of the GDR embodied principles of public patriarchy; the state policies undergirding the social market economy of the FRG are, in contrast, strongly oriented to sustaining private patriarchy. The issue is *not* whether the state is more or less influential in women's lives, but rather the *nature* of the effects that it strives for and accomplishes.

In the GDR, state policy tended to diminish the dependence of women on individual husbands and fathers but to enhance the dependence of women as mothers directly on the state (Ferree "Rise"; Bastian, Labsch, and Müller). In the FRG, state policy follows the principle of subsidiarity and actively encourages private dependencies. In particular, it has a mandate to preserve "the" family, which it understands primarily to be the husband-wife relationship as a context in which children can be raised (Moeller; Ostner). As Scandinavian feminists have defined it, the nature of the state's role in public patriarchy is to emphasize the *direct* relationship of mothers to the state, and the nature of the state's role in private patriarchy is to encourage the dependency of wives on husbands and of children on parents. In turn, this means that in public patriarchy, women experience their oppression as *mothers,* and as more directly connected to the activities of the state as patriarch; in private patriarchy, women experience their oppression as *wives,* and as more directly connected to their individual dependency on their spouses.

The effects that these two differently structured gender systems had on the nature of German women's ordinary life experiences are no doubt familiar.[5] In the former GDR, approximately a third of all babies were born out of wedlock, virtually all women were in the labor force and worked essentially full-time jobs, and women earned 40% of the family income on average. Out-of-home childcare for children under three and kindergartens for older children were universally available at low cost; subsidies from the state for childcare, rent, and other basic necessities reduced differences in standard of living between single mothers and two-parent, two-income families. Divorce was easy to obtain and the divorce rate was exceptionally high. Dependence on an individual husband appears to have been reduced to a minimum in this system.

By contrast, in the old states of the FRG, 90% of babies are born within marriages. Living together is not uncommon, but when the baby comes, so does marriage (87% of cohabiting relationships are childless). Having a child is structurally inconsistent with having a full-time job, given the short and irregular school hours and scarcity of childcare for preschool children, so the percentage of women who never have children is relatively high (15% of women aged 40–50 are childless). There are childcare places for less than 5% of children under 3 years old. Only a third of all women in their prime childbearing years have full-time jobs; given their restricted labor force participation, it is not surprising that West German women provide on average only 18% of the family income. The majority of employed women do not earn enough to support themselves independently, let alone raise a child. Tax subsidies such as income splitting further widen the gulf between the standard of living of two-parent families and single mothers. Dependence on an individual husband is strongly institutionalized in this gender system.

These differences are well known. Yet understanding them as system characteristics should turn our attention to the consequences they have for structurally influencing feminist identity and analysis. Let me outline several distinct areas where I think the differences between public and private patriarchy, and thus the structurally different experiences of dependency and oppression get "expressed in the specifics of feminist politics. First, there is a difference in women's identity that arises in relation to the dominant form of patriarchy in general and how it has been institutionalized. In the West, there is a conceptual package invoked by the phrase "wife-mother"; these two roles are treated as bundled together and virtually inseparable. This conceptualization does not carry over easily to the East where motherhood is not so structurally bound to wifehood. Thinking about mothers in the FRG shades easily into imagining them only as wives; one needs to specify "single mother" and in doing so, one invokes the image of mothers who are politically and culturally deviant as well as impoverished. In the East, on the one hand, the imagery of single mother was not so necessary: women were mothers and workers and they may or may not have chosen to be or stay married. To be a single mother was not to hold an identity that carries a connotation of victimhood, deviance, or struggle. On the other hand, the identity of worker, a central one to the GDR, for women was restricted both symbolically and practically into the specific identity of the "mother-worker" through the institutionalization of *Muttipolitik* (Ferree "Rise").

The structurally organized difference between the lives of the wife-mother and the mother-worker did not go unnoticed on either side of the Wall. Stereotypes that expressed envy of the differently organized patriarchal demands of another gender system and articulated the problems of ones' own system as a contrast with the other emanated from feminists on each side: from the East the stereotype of the Western woman was of a housewife of leisure working on her appearance waiting for her husband to come home; from the West, the stereotype of the Eastern woman was the single mother with a career who has the help and support of the state to do it all. Note that from each side, the dependency of the other is idealized: husbands supported their wives, the state supported "its" mothers, and neither patriarch asked anything in return. From inside either public or private patriarchy, it was never so simple or appealing, of course. Although the grass was always greener on the other side of the *Grenze,* dependency on individual husbands as well as dependency on the state both have their contradictions and limitations.

Neither public nor private patriarchy constitutes liberation for women, but each does tend to shift the focus of women's attention to different aspects of their oppression. In the context of private patriarchy, the family and relations between husbands and wives are initially at the forefront of theorizing (see, for example, Janssen-Jurreit; Millett; Friedan). The feminist idea is that if relationships between individual men and individual women could be put on a different footing, this would lead to structural change and vice versa—the structural changes that are sought are those that would change the balance of power within familial relationships. Power relationships within the family are often problematized and are seen as "spilling over" into the rest of social organization. Rejecting marriage and seeking full-time employment, in the context of private patriarchy, are in reality ways for women to resist individual male dominance and live out a challenge to the status quo.

In the context of public patriarchy, the role of public policy and the state is more immediately central. The male domination of political decision-making in all areas, the role of the state as "guardian," one who speaks for women rather than allowing them to speak for themselves, the felt absence of a collective political voice: these are all aspects of powerlessness that are central to the experience of women's subordination by collective rather than individual male power (see GDR feminist materials from the period of the *Wende* such as Merkel, et al.; Kahlau; Hampele "Frauenverband"). Power relationships within the family, if problematized at all, are seen as stemming from the more fundamental policies and decisions taken at the public political level. Private relationships—whether lesbian or heterosexual—are experienced as irrelevant or secondary in comparison. In the GDR, quitting one's job, home-schooling one's children, and protesting the militarism of the state were in reality ways for women to resist state authority and live out a challenge to the status quo.

Neither of these experientially grounded perceptions is wholly wrong. At a more abstract level, I suspect we would all agree that patriarchal power is both public and private and that both intrafamilial relations and state politics are arenas in which women's subordination is constructed and male domination exercised on a daily basis. However, each form of organization of patriarchy tends to encourage one distinctively one-sided form of analysis or the other because each "fits" and better explains a certain gut-level experiences of oppression. What is particularly interesting and instructive, albeit painful, is the collision between these two understandings (see, e.g., Helwerth and Schwarz; Rohnstock).

Because of German unification, there are two differently grounded feminist identities that arose in these structurally different contexts that now have to share the same political space. Both sides have a tendency to disparage the degree of feminist understanding of the other: backward, hypocritical, arrogant, atheoretical, insensitive, hypersensitive—the charges and countercharges go on and on, unfortunately cast primarily in terms of the individual or collective personalities of the "other." Even though the one-sidedness of unification itself means that the structure of private patriarchy now is the reality for all German women, the contrast between the feminism that arose in response to public patriarchy in the GDR and that of the "old" FRG can still help to connect the structures to the discourses. The contrast between public and private patriarchy is particularly telling, because it binds together a number of common experiences across specific situations.

Among the most interesting of these are the ways in which Black feminist thought has also attempted to come to terms with the greater significance of public patriarchy in African-American women's lives than in the lives of white American women (e.g., Collins). Despite dramatic differences in race and class-based structures of opportunity and oppression, there are some similarities in the gender-based structures and thus also some points where Black feminist thought touches closely on issues that GDR women also have been attempting to express.

First, there has been a tendency for East German feminists to talk more positively about the family, and to see a challenge for feminism in integrating men more fully into family life. In comparison to women under private patriarchy, they did not see men's exclusion from the family as offering a good in itself nor did they define single parenting as freedom from male oppression—but they were also not so willing to marry, unless men met their expectations for family participation. Men's relationship to children was something that women valued and that the state ignored and actively marginalized (cf. analyses of gender, family, and state socialism in Einhorn and in Funk and Mueller). These are experiences that Black American feminists have also had to insist on and that white feminists have been skeptical about.

Second, women's labor force participation is easy to connect to women's liberation in the context of private patriarchy since the extent of a woman's earnings is in practice directly related to her independence from an individual husband. This link is more problematic in public patriarchy, since women's labor is expected, even demanded, in the paid labor force as well as in unpaid domestic chores. For Black American feminists, as well as for East German feminists, paid employment provides a self-evident part of their identity as well as a burden—but it is hard to confuse it with "emancipation." For East German women, after unification, the self-evidentness of paid employment was destroyed, but answering the question of what exclusion from the labor force means is a new issue for them, not a standard part of a feminist repertoire of self-understandings. This continues to amaze Western feminists who have been grappling with such issues all their lives.

Third, within a framework of public patriarchy, it makes little or no sense to talk about doing politics that remains "autonomous" by virtue of keeping its hands out of the affairs of government for fear of being coopted. Insofar as it is the state that is directly usurping the right of women to speak for themselves, there is little alternative to challenging this head-on and pragmatically. That means that women can and must find ways to restructure the state itself to be less patriarchal. This "obsession" with formal politics makes much less experiential sense to women in private patriarchy, who have more of their lives directly shaped by non-state actors and by cultural norms and expectations that are not formally enacted into law. Within the context of private patriarchy the targets for action seem both more diffuse and more personalized. To East German women, accustomed to state-centered public patriarchy, this can look like too much concern with symbolic issues, such as language, that are "trivial" compared to direct confrontations with policy-makers.

Let me move back now from the specific to the general, and attempt to draw a few conclusions. I think that cross-system comparisons between FRG and GDR types of patriarchies, and between GDR and African-American feminist responses to public patriarchy, are especially useful for interdisciplinary work. They situate discourses in their structural context, rather than labeling them as if they were isolated and idiosyncratic expressions of individual needs. I think we need to try to move up from merely descriptive labels like "Black feminism" or even "public patriarchy" toward a more focused analysis of the common and divergent features of macro-level gender systems, not only as they produce and maintain gender hierarchies but also as they intersect with other systems such as class and race. This seems to me to call particularly for cross-national work, where the features of the systems as systems can more readily be seen in the similarities and differences between them (Ferree and Gamson).

It also seems to call for more efforts to understand the gendered nature of politics—not just in terms of the narrow picture of including individual women in formal political representation and decision-making, but in comparing gender systems at a macro-social level at all the institutional locations where power is exercised, including families, labor markets, media and social movements, religion, and law. Although the state's role in maintaining class stratification has always been considered theoretically important (and much debated), the role of the state in expressing and maintaining gender stratification has long been ignored (but see such recent pathbreaking exceptions as Hoskyns; Stetson and Mazur; Sainsbury; Gordon). Yet gender is part of the political process: state practices maintain certain family types as the norm, reallocate resources between men and women based on gendered concepts such as "deservingness" and "dependency," "freedom" and "responsibility," and respond to organized expressions of gender interests (Fraser and Gordon; Skocpol). This perspective demands that we compare the role of states vis-à-vis major institutions in terms of their gendered practices: for example in organizing schools or credentialling work in terms of a more or less rigidly age-structured "normal" lifecourse that is gendered male, or placing healthcare demands to a greater or lesser extent on unpaid family caregiving that is gendered female. These are fruitful questions not only for researchers but also for comparative cultural studies classes, since they allow students to understand politics and compare systems in terms of features of their own lives.

Interdisciplinary work, in my view, will benefit from the inclusion of a sociological understanding of gender as a social structure. Textual analysis that rests on such a model can then broaden and enrich the understanding of social scientists for the operations and meanings of these structural relations as individuals interpret and respond to them. Such analysis can be found in materials that are defined as literature as well as in many types of non-literary texts and accounts. I suggest that such analysis allows us truly to locate and ground the individual or groups whose understanding of reality we in turn wish to understand. Perhaps if we can do this, we can avoid placing all the differences or similarities we observe solely inside the skins of individuals, while also giving serious weight to our real diversity when articulating and finding meaning for our own experiences.

Notes

[1] See, for example, my 1994 article, "'The Time of Chaos Was the Best.'"

[2] Many of the differences between a structural and an individual perspective on gender are developed and illustrated more extensively in my forthcoming article with Elaine Hall.

[3] A venue for much of the most interesting crossnational work on gender processes and systems is the new journal *Social Politics,* which links this structural perspective on gender to analyses of class, race, and citizenship as well.

[4] The following discussion extensively quotes and summarizes an argument I presented in more detail in "Patriarchies and Feminisms."

[5] For details and statistics on the status of women in the GDR, see Einhorn; Helwig and Nickel; Maier; for a history of policy that discusses its objectives and how it has secured these outcomes, see Penrose. For more extensive and detailed data on the status of women in the pre-unification Federal Republic of Germany, see Helwig and Nickel; Maier; Kolinsky; for a history of policy that suggests how these outcomes were sought and institutionalized, see Moeller; Ostner.

Works Cited

Agassi, Judith Buber. "Theories of Gender Equality: Lessons from the Israeli Kibbutz." *Gender & Society* 3 (1989): 160–86.

Andersen, Margaret. "Denying Differences: The Continuing Bases for Exclusion in Curriculum." *Working Paper Series.* Memphis State University Center for Research on Women, 1988.

Bastian, Katrin, Evi Labsch, and Sylvia Müller. "Zur Situation von Frauen als Arbeitskraft in der Geschichte der DDR." Originally published in *Zaunreiterin* (Leipzig c. 1989), reprinted in *Streit* 2 (1990): 59–67.

Collins, Patricia Hill. *Black Feminist Thought: Knowledge, Consciousness, and the Politics of Empowerment.* Boston: Unwin Hyman, 1990.

Connell, R. W. *Gender & Power.* Stanford: Stanford UP, 1987.

Einhorn, Barbara. *Cinderella Goes to Market: Citizenship, Gender and Women's Movements in East Central Europe.* New York: Verso, 1993.

Ferree, Myra Marx. "Patriarchies and Feminisms: The Two Women's Movements of Post-Unification Germany." *Social Politics* 2.1 (1995): 10–24.

———. "The Rise and Fall of 'Mommy Politics': Feminism and Unification in (East) Germany." *Feminist Studies* 19 (1993): 89–115.

———. "'The Time of Chaos was the Best': The Mobilization and Demobilization of a Women's Movement in East Germany." *Gender & Society* 8 (1994): 597–623.

Ferree, Myra Marx, and William A. Gamson. "The Gendering of Abortion Discourse: Assessing Global Feminist Influence in the United States and

Germany, 1972-94." *Social Movements in a Globalizing World.* Ed. Dieter Rucht, et al., forthcoming 1996.

Ferree, Myra Marx, and Elaine J. Hall. "Rethinking Stratification from a Feminist Perspective: Gender, Race and Class in Mainstream Textbooks." *American Sociological Review,* forthcoming.

Ferree, Myra Marx, and Beth Hess. "Introduction." *Analyzing Gender: A Handbook of Social Science Research.* Ed. Beth Hess and Myra Marx Ferree. Newbury Park, CA: Sage, 1987. 9-30.

Fraser, Nancy, and Linda Gordon. "A Genealogy of Dependency: Tracing a Keyword of the U.S. Welfare State." *Signs* 19 (1993): 309-36.

Friedan, Betty. *The Feminine Mystique.* New York: Dell, 1963.

Funk, Nanette, and Magda Mueller. *Gender Politics and Post-Communism.* New York: Routledge, 1993.

Gordon, Linda. *Women, the State and Welfare.* Madison: U of Wisconsin P, 1990.

Hampele, Anne. "Der unabhängige Frauenverband." *Von der Illegalität ins Parlament.* Ed. Helmut Müller-Enbergs, Marianne Schulz, and Jan Wielgohs. Berlin: LinksDruck Verlag, 1991.

Helwerth, Ulrike, and Gislinde Schwarz. "Drei Jahre nach der Wende: Zum Stand der Ost-West-Beziehungen in der Frauenbewegung." Paper presented at the Goethe Institute, New York, 1993.

Helwig, Gisela, and Hildegard Maria Nickel, eds. *Frauen in Deutschland, 1945-1992.* Studien zur Geschichte und Politik. Vol. 318. Bonn: Bundeszentrale für politische Bildung, 1993.

Hess, Beth B. "Beyond Dichotomy: Drawing Distinctions and Embracing Differences." *Sociological Forum* 5 (1990): 75-93.

Hobson, Barbara, and Marika Lindholm. "Collective Identities, Women's Power Resources and the Making of Welfare States." Paper presented at the Tenth International Conference of Europeanists, Chicago, March 1996.

Hoskyns, Catherine. *Integrating Gender: Women, Law and Politics in the European Union.* New York: Verso, 1996.

Huber, Joan. "Macro-Micro Links in Gender Stratification." *Macro-Micro Linkages in Sociology.* Ed. Joan Huber. Newbury Park, CA: Sage, 1991. 11-25.

Janssen-Jurreit, Marielouise. *Sexismus.* München: Hanser, 1976.

Jónasdóttir, Anna G., and Kathleen Jones, eds. *The Political Interests of Gender: Developing Theory and Research with a Feminist Face.* London: Sage, 1988.

Kahlau, Cordula, ed. *Aufbruch! Frauenbewegung in der DDR.* München: Frauenoffensive, 1990.

Kolinsky, Eva. *Women in East Germany: Life, Work and Politics.* Oxford: Berg, 1989.

Lorber, Judith. *Paradoxes of Gender.* New Haven, CT: Yale UP, 1994.

Maier, Friederike. "Frauenerwerbstätigkeit in der DDR and BRD: Gemeinsamkeiten und Unterschiede." *Ein Deutschland—Zwei Patriarchate?* Ed. Gudrun-Axeli Knapp and Ursula Müller. Bielefeld: U of Bielefeld, 1992.

Mansbridge, Jane. "What is Feminism?" *Feminist Organizations: Harvest of the New Women's Movement.* Ed. Myra Marx Ferree and Patricia Yancey Martin. Philadelphia: Temple UP, 1995.

Melucci, Alberto. "Getting Involved: Identity and Mobilization in Social Movements." *From Structure to Action: Comparing Social Movement Research across Cultures.* Ed. Bert Klandermans, et al. Greenwich, CT: JAI Press, 1988.

Merkel, Ina, et al., eds. *Ohne Frauen ist kein Staat zu machen.* Hamburg: Argument, 1990.

Millett, Kate. *Sexual Politics.* Garden City, NY: Doubleday, 1970.

Moeller, Robert. *Protecting Motherhood: Women and the Family in the Politics of Postwar West Germany.* Berkeley: U of California P, 1993.

Omi, Michael, and Howard Winant. *Racial Formation in the United States: From the 1960s to the 1980s.* New York: Routledge, 1994.

Ostner, Ilona. "Back to the Fifties: Gender and Welfare in Unified Germany." *Social Politics* 1 (1994): 32-59.

Penrose, Virginia. "Vierzig Jahre SED-Frauenpolitik: Ziele, Strategien, Ergebnisse." *IFG: Frauenforschung* 4 (1994): 60-77.

Rohnstock Katrin. *Stiefschwestern: Was Ost-Frauen und West-Frauen voneinander denken.* Frankfurt a.M.: Fischer, 1994.

Sainsbury, Diane. *Gendering Welfare States.* Thousands Oaks, CA: Sage, 1994.

Scott, Joan. "Gender: A Useful Category of Historical Analysis." *American Historical Review* 91 (1986): 1053-75.

Siim, Birte. "The Scandinavian Welfare States: Toward Sexual Equality or a New Kind of Male Domination." *Acta Sociologica* 3-4 (1987): 255-70.

Skocpol, Theda. *Protecting Soldiers and Mothers: The Political Origins of Social Policy in the United States.* Cambridge, MA: Harvard UP, 1992.

Stetson, Dorothy McBride, and Amy Mazur. *Comparative State Feminism.* Thousand Oaks, CA: Sage, 1995.

Taylor, Verta, and Nancy Whittaker. "Collective Identity in Social Movement Communities: Lesbian Feminist Mobilization." *Frontiers of Social Movement Theory.* Ed. Aldon Morris and Carol McClurg Mueller. New Haven, CT: Yale UP, 1992.

Wharton, Amy. "Structure and Agency in Socialist-Feminist Theory." *Gender & Society* 5 (1991): 373-89.

On Commonality, Nationalism, and Violence: Hannah Arendt, Rosa Luxemburg, and Frantz Fanon

Joan Cocks

In this essay I briefly discuss the reasons why feminist theory, which twenty years ago had repudiated Hannah Arendt, now embraces her. I then present my own embrace of Arendt as an illustration. I examine how Arendt, in the company of Frantz Fanon and Rosa Luxemburg, illuminates nationalism as an especially explosive form of "identity politics." I argue that all three thinkers press feminists to consider the dangers of political solidarities based on "being," not "thinking and doing." In addition, Fanon and Arendt press feminists to reconsider the significance and value of violence in politics. (JC)

Introduction

For the past decade Hannah Arendt has enjoyed a resurgence of interest among intellectuals that is almost smothering in its intensity. The buzzing in book reviews about Arendt's love affair with Martin Heidegger is only the latest and most salacious expression of that interest. What accounts for Arendt's current popularity? She is brilliant, but it is impossible for her to be more brilliant now than she was at her death twenty years ago, when she was highly respected but hardly universally adored. It must be the spirit of the age that has changed. Judith Shulevitz makes this point in her 1 October 1995 *New York Times* "Bookend" piece, when she traces Arendt's appeal to "the intellectual demands of the post-cold war era." Shulevitz also quotes Seyla Benhabib as saying that "Thinkers without camps are interesting right now, because camps have played themselves out." I think Shulevitz is right that Arendt is suited to an era in which all certainties seem to have dissolved except the certainty of the triumph of capital, but I don't share Benhabib's sigh of relief that "camps" are over and done with.

Political camps—that is, solidarities based, not on ethnic or racial or sexual being, but on shared beliefs, values, and ends for social life—do have their drawbacks, among them, a susceptibility to dogmatic thought and roughshod action. But they also provide individuals who otherwise would think and will in isolation with the company of others, and they turn the relatively ineffectual actions of singular selves into collective, public strength. Indeed, the collapse of camps no less than the rise of uncertainty must be counted as contributing to the political paralysis of critical thinkers today. I will return to this problem of political paralysis later on. Now I need only say that while in the West, at least, political camps may have played themselves out, intellectual camps surely have not. Remarkably, almost every intellectual camp in political theory— Habermasian, post-modernist, radical democratic, communitarian—has claimed Hannah Arendt as one of its own.

Feminist political theorists are locked in a tight embrace with Arendt these days too, and they also come to her from Habermasian, post-modernist, democratic, and communitarian directions. In part, this is because feminist intellectuals are as modish as everyone else and gravitate to fashionable thinkers and thoughts. But feminism's attraction to Hannah Arendt has its own special features. Most peculiarly, the feminist attraction to Arendt grows out of a prior repulsion toward Arendt for her disdain of bodily life, and for her celebration of politics as the struggle for individual greatness, glory, and fame. Least peculiarly, feminist attraction to Arendt is political in a way that non-feminist attraction typically is not. Certainly Arendt is a tempting figure for anyone with a political interest, for unlike Western thinkers from Plato to Marx, she conceives of politics as an activity irreducible to any other activity and as worthy for its own sake, rather than as significant or worthy because it serves or protects philosophical contemplation, religious truths, social needs, or economic functions. But how is Arendt a tempting figure for anyone with a feminist political interest? The essays in *Feminist Interpretations of Hannah Arendt,* a recently published collection edited by Bonnie Honig, provide the following clues.

First, Arendt conceives of politics and the public sphere as an association of equals in a world shared in common. At the same time, she insists on the plurality of persons in that association, on the distinctness and uniqueness of individual "speakers of words and doers of deeds" (Dietz 31). As Honig puts it, Arendt conceives of "action in concert that is also always a site of struggle...with *and* against one's peers" (Honig 159). In linking, but not merging, the values of association and uniqueness, commonality and plurality, Arendt offers feminism a way of recognizing and preserving the tension between identity and difference as a political good.

Second, Arendt severs the idea of freedom from the idea of self-determination, tying "freedom" instead to the possibility of beginning something new, and to the spontaneity, creativity, and unpredictability of such beginnings. She insists on the importance, for both human freedom and human pleasure, of participating in a public sphere where individuals can set off new chains of events in the world through speech and action. Conversely, she exposes the unfreedom of lives chained entirely to the repetitive cycles of the biological life process. While drawing on Arendt's *conception* of freedom to critique women's enslavement to domestic toil, feminists extend Arendt's *topography* of freedom by posing the body as a site of secret "new beginnings" on which gender identity and sexual desire can take creative, unpredictable turns.

Third, Arendt charts the progress of two different kinds of corrupting pressures on political freedom. One of these pressures is the bourgeois appetite for private wealth. That appetite destroys the possibility of politics by transforming the public sphere into a "housekeeping" state that normalizes social behavior to serve the economic processes of production and consumption. The other, almost opposite corrupting pressure on political freedom is the ascription of fixed characteristics to individuals on the basis of their membership in social groups. Arendt highlights the special dangers, in an age of political equality, of defining selves in terms of the "whatness of being," which prevents individuals from disclosing themselves through the "whoness of acting." She also counters that essentialist definition by investigating collective identities as they are determined in specific socio-historical relations with other identities, fractured by a variety of distinctions within the collective group, and transfigured from one region and age to the next as a consequence of particular constellations of conditions and events.

To provide a concrete example of how contemporary feminism works with these Arendtian ideas, I will focus on a few sample arguments from my own essay in Honig's collection, which, while not about sex and gender, is informed by and relevant to feminist concerns.[1] In this essay, I turn to Hannah Arendt in the company of Frantz Fanon and Rosa Luxemburg, for help in making sense of nationalism and the intellectual's relation to nationalism in the midst of what I see as a contemporary crisis in that relation—a crisis in which feminist intellectuals play their part.

While Fanon, Luxemburg, and Arendt probably would protest "against being gathered into a common room" (*Dark Times* vii), they are well worth considering as a trio, for several reasons.

First, they all speak about the national question with a depth, a sharpness, and a passion that testify to their intellectual detachment from the world in order to make critical sense of it, and to their political engagement in the world in order to press it in one direction rather than another, or, as in Arendt's case, in order to reveal the wreckage that followed from the world's having been pressed in one direction rather than another. Second, their intelligences span the first three quarters of our century. Thus they might cast light from the recent past on predicaments of collective identity in the present. Third, all three belong to pariah peoples, are at ease in polycultural settings, are multi-lingual, and move back and forth among geographical regions, no one of which can be called their true home. That is, all three instantiate the kind of fracture, plurality, and fluidity in identity that make them problematic figures from a nationalist point of view, and make nationalism problematic for them and us in turn. Fourth and finally, Fanon's, Luxemburg's, and Arendt's ideas on the national question are neither harmonious with nor disconnected from one another. They are just incongruous enough to produce good sparks.

To fan a few sparks our way, let me first turn to Arendt's and Fanon's considerations on violence as a means to national emancipation.

Arendt and Fanon

In her little volume *On Violence,* Arendt argues that violence is antipolitical even though it belongs to "the political realm of human affairs"(82). This combination of "anti-political" and "political" is less peculiar than it seems, for Arendt can charge violence with being antipolitical—that is, at odds with argument and persuasion, and destructive of "the company of our fellow-men"—only if she also can establish that violence belongs to the realm of human contingency and artifice, not the realm of biological necessity and natural forces, where charges against anything are beside the point (67). Arendt denies that violence has an instinctual or organic origin in part by fiat, stipulating that human violence occurs in the socio-political realm, and that biological factors never can explain anything there. But she also denies that violence is instinctual or "vital" by tracing violence to rage, and rage not to unreason but to an offended sense of justice or a reaction against the hypocrisy of lying speech.[2] In addition, Arendt rejects the equation of violence with automatic impulses or bodily reflexes by defining violence as strategic or "instrumental by nature," so that it is assimilated to rational calculation.[3] Finally, she states that violence does not repeat some natural cycle but brings into being something new, even though what this type of action brings into being is most probably only "a more violent world" (80).

One of Arendt's aims in *On Violence* is to discredit thinkers, and above all Fanon, who embrace bloodshed as either an inescapable element of politics or a positive good. But what must be said at once on Fanon's behalf is that his representation of both violence and nationalism in *The Wretched of the Earth* is not at all fixed and flattering. Indeed, Fanon continuously revises that representation to reflect changes wrought by the explosive effects of decolonization on the entire social environment, the instability of every aspect of life during "a program of complete disorder" (36). For Fanon, the sudden thawing out of a world that had been previously frozen requires a corresponding fluidity in the conception and assessment of that world's constitutive elements.

Thus, Fanon calibrates his judgment of violence to suit torrential changes in the political landscape. In his first essay he condemns the colonial order for speaking "the language of pure force" (38) but declares that against such an order, the "'thing' which has been colonized" must exert a counter-force in order to become "man" (36–37). In his second essay, he insists that spontaneous, violent uprisings must give way to thought and action tempered by political education, if a popular movement against tyranny is not to become either tyrannical itself or vulnerable to a new kind of tyranny through having too naive a notion of the world. Fanon's startling final essay exhibits the psychiatric case studies of torturers, soldiers, resistance fighters, and civilian victims of brutality, all suffering the after-shocks of anti-colonial war. In their psychological disintegration, these figures reach an eerie equality with one another, being most clearly distinguishable not as Algerian or French, and not as the active agents or passive targets of violence, but rather as individuals plagued by this or that nightmarish neurosis or psychosis.

In "Concerning Violence," Fanon praises violence for making subjects out of human objects. In "Colonial War and Mental Disorders," he reveals that violence shatters human subjectivity. The two essays together confirm the following truth: that the slave who "at the moment he realizes his humanity...begins to sharpen the weapons with which he will secure its victory," can win freedom from the master/slave relation with those weapons but not freedom from the reverberations of his own acts (43).

If Fanon treats the question of violence with greater complexity than Arendt admits, he also treats it with greater complexity than Arendt musters.

First, Fanon represents violence in the colonial context as anti-political in its original thesis but as pre-political in the antithesis to that. The imposition of colonial rule by "bayonets and cannons" (36) and its maintenance by "the policeman and the soldier" (38) are anti-political because, as Arendt would put it, they prohibit the emergence of a sphere for public speech and action. The rebellion of the colonized against colonial rule is pre-political because, as Fanon does put it, it catapults those who are oppressed from the position of "spectators crushed with their inessentiality into privileged actors" (36). This is not to say that he is sanguine about whether these newly privileged actors can make their way from violence to politics. That depends, for a start, on whether they manage to escape being psychologically "crushed with" the horror of what they have violently done and what has been violently done to them.

Second, Fanon conceives of violence as expressive of somatic feelings no less than ideas about injustice or intentions to achieve specific ends. Fanon highlights the bodily aspects of violence not because he sees violence as belonging to a biological rather than socio-political zone, but because he does not ever divide off the body from socio-political life, and also because he believes the bodily aspects of violence loom large in the colonial setting. The world into which the colonizer herds the popular masses is not so much ideologically mystified—or, as we would say today, discursively constituted—as it is physically claustrophobic, a "narrow world, strewn with prohibitions" (37), in which "[t]he first thing which the native learns is to stay in his place, and not to go beyond certain limits" (52). Because colonial power operates on the masses by brute force and physical containment; because the native's sense "that his life, his breath, his beating heart are the same as those of the settler" (45) fuels a resentment in him that is as visceral as it is cerebral; and because the muscles of the native are "always tensed" (53), violence against the colonizer offers the colonized a physiological as well as psychological release from the effects of servitude.

Is Arendt right, or wrong, to find Fanon politically irresponsible for advocating violence as a part of national liberation? The answer depends in part on whether Fanon is right or wrong that the colonized cannot escape either the external rule of the colonizer or his own internal situation of being permanently "tensed" without a physical explosion. But the answer just as centrally depends on whether Arendt is right or wrong that violence is anti-political because the language of politics is exclusively verbal, never physical; and on whether Arendt is right or wrong that violence belongs to the political, not biological, realm because no somatic experience ever pressures a subject to act with physical force.

Arendt's belief that it always is possible and almost always desirable to forswear the "use" of violence makes her highly congenial to contemporary critical and especially feminist sensibilities. Fanon disturbs those same sensibilities because he does not bristle at the thought of spilling blood. Still, Fanon has much in his favor to recommend to us. Fanon is unprejudiced against the body and consequently is not compelled to pry the realm of the body and the realm of speech and action apart. Thus he can see violence as a feature simultaneously of visceral and political experience, as a means of detonating the master/slave relation, and so as a provider of one crucial pre-condition of a democratic public sphere. Fanon would find it perverse to call "anti-political" a conversation in which "[t]he violence of the colonial regime and the counter-violence of the native...respond to each other in an extraordinary reciprocal homogeneity" (88). Through that conversation, the native achieves the status of an active subject in history that a monologue of violence had precluded before. Nonetheless, Fanon shows us that the violence that emancipates the self socially can destroy the self "humanly." In that case, the free self will be too tormented to enjoy politics or any other human pleasure.

Luxemburg and Arendt

For another spark for feminist thought, let us turn to Luxemburg and Arendt. Writing from a European rather than an African vantage point, both women make a strong case against nationalism by showing how it is a product of the bourgeoisie, which eventually bursts beyond the boundaries of the nation-state in its search for endless wealth, using the right of national self-determination to justify capitalist overseas expansion. That expansion, in turn, precludes the possibility of national self-determination in non-European regions and hence negates the universality of that "so-called" right.

Here, however, I want to focus on a second way nationalism becomes, for both Luxemburg and Arendt, "anti-national." In Luxemburg's eyes, national self-determination turns into national oppression in any social context characterized by the mingling of peoples—which in the modern age is synonymous with the human context. For as a result of a long history in which, as Luxemburg puts it, nationalities "were constantly moving about geographically... joining, merging, fragmenting, and trampling one another," nationalities have become everywhere an entangled intermixture (Davis 124), an entanglement only intensified by modern capital.[4] Given the fact that a melange of peoples inhabits the same geographical space, the bid for national self-determination on the part of any one of them will be a bid to consign the rest to a fate on that continuum of unhappy fates ranging all the way from political inconsequence and social discrimination to persecution, expulsion, and genocide.

What makes movements for ethnonational self-determination so decentralizing and democratic vis-à-vis the political unities they are moving against, and so centrist and tyrannical toward their own ethnic and racial minorities? Part of the answer lies in the logic of "self-determination," whenever the "self" is particular, not universal, and possesses the material means to try to impose its will on the world.[5] Hegel exposes this logic when he states that the self-determining self must seek to determine everything outside itself that otherwise would determine it. It is because the quest for self-determination inevitably degenerates into a quest for domination that Arendt refuses to equate freedom with self-determination at all. She conceives of freedom instead as the ability of the self to begin something new in the world, setting off a chain of other unpredictable and uncontrollable actions on the part of other selves, so that all selves are, in their very freedom, radically un-self-determining.[6] Alas, it is the nature of every ethnonational movement to understand freedom in Hegelian, not Arendtian, terms: to view its own identity as made not through a process of creative self-composition and self-combustion with other identities, but through the assertion of a rigidly separate substance over against all other substances.

If Hegel assures us that the struggle for domination is not the final resolution of the search for subjective freedom, Luxemburg warns us that the reciprocal recognition of equally independent and self-determining subjects is not either, at least not when those subjects are ethnic nationalities. The equal independence and self-determination of ethnonational subjects is exactly what the geographical intermixture of peoples rules out. Not mutual recognition on the part of autonomous peoples, each fortified inside its own territorial nation-state, but a community's composition of itself as an ethnoculturally multiple political identity is for Luxemburg the only democratic path that modern polities can take. She supports political identity against political separation out of a realistic assessment of the tendency towards the economic integration of larger and larger geographical areas in the modern age, and out of an idealistic faith in the potentially universal expansion of human identification, as well as the belief that, once class domination has been brought to an end, human identification should expand until it reaches the limits of the whole human race. She supports ethnic difference against ethnic domination not out of a respect for difference but rather out of a repugnance for domination, as well as out of an appreciation for specific traditional cultures that are, in comparison with capitalist society, cooperative and unexploitative.

As appealing as Luxemburg's formula of a unity of political identity and ethnic difference may be, it is easy to suspect it of hinging on the substitution of a dream of ethnic harmony for the reality of ethnic conflict. It is also easy to suspect it of hinging on a presumption that ethnic differences in the long run will not be very great. Certainly the spread of bourgeois political liberties and the eventual triumph of social democracy which Luxemburg views as the road to inter-ethnic peace and understanding, she also portrays as part and parcel of the general shift in the world from traditional cultural particularities to the universal characteristics of modern social life. Then, too, from the perspective of minority peoples, any attempt to extend the ties of solidarity to cover the entire human race is likely to appear as a threatening move by a large and morally arrogant but still particular people dressed up in universal-culture disguise. Her passionate hatred of all forms of subjugation notwithstanding, even Luxemburg cannot escape suspicion on this last count.

Arendt makes her case against the "anti-nationalism" of nationalism when she details the nineteenth- and twentieth-century pan-movements in Europe and their devastating impact on modern history. These pan-movements are born out of the situation of oppressed minorities in Central and Eastern European multinational states and give rise to what Arendt terms "continental imperialism." Unlike overseas imperialism, continental imperialism is the work not of capital but primarily of the "mob"—the déclassé, the unemployed, the criminal elements at the top and bottom of society—and secondarily of the intelligentsia. Its principle of expansion is not economic gain but an "enlarged tribal consciousness" with a commitment to unify all individuals of the same "blood" or "spiritual" origin and to elevate this distinctive "folk" above all other people. It threatens the established European nation-states through its disregard for settled political borders; its elaboration of a compensatory myth in the absence of a real state, a real territory, a real public life; and its location of the criteria for belonging to a people in "being," not "acting." Still, as Arendt warns us in her chapter on "Continental Imperialism," the tribal or ethnonational idea of the people is not utterly at odds with the republican idea, which implies through its own hyphenation of "nation" and "state" that before acquiring an artificial state, the people had a naturalistic existence (*Origins* 222–66).

Moreover, while in theory republican nationalism is unlike ethnonationalism in extending the possibility of citizenship to individuals of any origin who accept the nation's law and public life as their own, in practice the republican nation-state is twice capable of ethnic persecution. In the service of insuring the national identity and equality of its citizens, that state is driven to suppress public signs of ethnocultural difference, which in effect means the suppression of ethnic minority difference. In the service of limiting its citizen body to a particular sub-segment of the whole human race, that state also will resort to exclusionary policies as soon as it is besieged by refugees from elsewhere *en masse*. The peoples whom ethnonational states select out to despise and expel will be treated as stateless and rightless by republican nation-states, so that those republican states end up reiterating the racial judgements of ethnonational states.[7] In Arendt's somber words, "Those whom the persecutor singles out as scum of the earth...will be received as scum...everywhere" (*Origins* 269).

A gloom pervades Arendt's account of the outcome of nationalism in politics that Luxemburg and Fanon never even distantly match. Luxemburg and Fanon manage to preserve their optimism partly as a consequence of their own engagement in revolutionary movements. These movements spare them the isolation and impotence Arendt describes in *The Origins of Totalitarianism* and the regrets she expresses on behalf of herself and others like her in her personal letters. Certainly, too, the times are more hopeful for Luxemburg and Fanon than for Arendt. In comparison with the 1930s and 1940s, the two decades leading up to the Russian Revolution are open-ended enough that barbarism *or* socialism can strike Luxemburg as equally possible. In turn, the two decades after the defeat of Nazism have something heartening about them, in that each year transports one part of the world further and further away from the collapse of its own civilization, and another part closer and closer to independence from that civilization's rule.

Yet Arendt is also bleak about the national question because, unlike our other two thinkers, she sees it as a riddle with no solution. More than her alienation from collective political action and the extraordinary darkness of her times, it is her view of the national question as a conundrum that makes Arendt so well-suited a thinker for us. She warns us that once modern rootlessness undermines the organic homogeneity of peoples in every region, all answers to the national question are bad.[8] In a world that is socially an intermixture of peoples and politically all sewn up by established nation-states, the very worst answer to the national question is the fine-sounding conviction that "true freedom, true emancipation, and true popular sovereignty [can] be attained only with full national emancipation..." (*Origins* 272). That conviction, in that setting, is a recipe for claustrophobia: not Fanon's colony-claustrophobia, in which native populations are restricted from moving beyond narrow limits, but a world-claustrophobia, in which peoples turned by the politics of national self-determination into "natives of nowhere" can find nowhere on earth to go to be free without setting off a new chain of discriminations, coercions, and exclusions.

Conclusion

So salient in the first half of the century, nationalism became a matter of relative indifference to many intellectuals until almost the last decade of the second half. One obvious reason why is that the most explosive political faultline from the end of World War II to the late 1980s was the single "difference" between capitalism and communism, not the multiple differences among ethno-nationalities or nation-states. The intellectual uninterest in nationalism except when it dovetailed with decolonization (and even then, the interest in it was a subsidiary of the question "capitalism or communism?") was overdetermined in the feminist case. Feminism repudiated the synonymity of politics with the public life of nation-states, proclaimed the division between the sexes to be more fundamental than national or ethnonational divisions, and alienated itself in practice from the affairs of nation-states as entities organized and ruled by men.

The sheer strength of ethnic and communal passions at the end of our century has compelled critical thinkers to turn to the national question once again. Here, too, feminism's own turn has been doubly compelled. For the national question currently is posed in terms feminism likes best: not in the external, institutional terms of state formation but in the internal, psycho-cultural terms of identity and difference. As our three authors intimate, however, feminists and other critical thinkers are naive to tout multiculturalism as the happy resolution of the latter antinomy. Multiculturalism seeks to mesh a respect for difference with a value on multiplicity and heterogeneity in identity. But a respect for difference induces an anxiety about judging how different identities see the world and what they do in it, and thus a nervousness about attacking identities that refuse to see multiplicity and heterogeneity as positive goods. The paralysis of political judgment and action that can set in just at the crucial moment, while troubling in any context, is tragic in the nationalist context, where identities have or are out to acquire a legal-military apparatus to enforce the singularity and homogeneity of a people in a territory, a culture, a society. This paralysis is ironic as well as tragic when intellectuals in one place happily chatter away about multicultural community, while in another place, as if separated from the chatterers by a universe instead of an ocean, a people actually defining itself in multiple terms is left to withstand on its own an ethnonationalist drive to wipe it off the face of the earth.

Especially when a people is persecuted for its very being, our authors would find incomprehensible a squeamishness on the part of intellectuals before the need for fighting words and deeds. Their personal temperaments—Fanon's compassionate anger, Luxemburg's fiery impetuousness, Arendt's arrogance—help explain why, but so do their theoretical dispositions. Fanon and Luxemburg can judge and act with self-certainty because they see situations as having an underlying truth to them, because they have a concept of humanity that overarches all particular identities, and because they make clear-cut distinctions between the forces of oppression and the forces of emancipation. Arendt presents us with a more complicated case. On the one hand, she is contemptuous of the idea of a single good that it is the task of history or politics to realize, and she champions the idea of a plurality of ends in human life. On the other hand, she insists that identities are made through the inter-relations of selves rather than being the foundational ground of selves, so that no holy essence stands in the way of judging and acting with some selves and against others. Moreover, she affirms a truth not of ends but of beginnings, by insisting that plurality can flourish only under particular conditions, including the condition that plural selves share a love of the world. Consequently, Arendt can and does make imperious pronouncements about the worth of different social orders on the basis of whether they secure those conditions or not.

I want to conclude with a lesson Fanon has to teach. The same importance that many of us accord today to the bodily components of gender identity and sexual desire, and to the sensuous pains and pleasures of intimate life, also must be accorded to the bodily component of resentment, indignation, and rage, and the visceral pressures to violence against a social order that is felt to be unjust. Moreover, against power that works through physical coercion and deprivation rather than through the manufacture of consent or the normalization of selves, violent rebellion is one suitable if problematic response. To admit to the visceral aspect of the fury at injustice and the physicality of certain forms of domination is also to admit that the lack of a desire to lash out against domination may itself be a domination-effect. When it is, the absence of the impulse to violence must be counted as a political problem, not a moral virtue. At the same time that Fanon teaches us this lesson, however, Arendt reminds us to learn it with the utmost delicacy and caution. For she shows us that if violence should be judged in context (is it the violence of the persecutor or the persecuted?), it also threatens all contexts by shattering the common world.

Notes

[1] The remainder of this article is exerpted from my essay "On Nationalism: Frantz Fanon, Rosa Luxemburg, and Hannah Arendt." *Feminist Interpretations of Hannah Arendt*. Ed. Bonnie Honig. University Park: Pennsylvania State UP, 1995. 221–45. Reprinted with permission of the press.

[2] Arendt even defends the limited use of enraged violence: "...under certain circumstances violence—acting without argument or speech without counting the consequences—is the only way to set the scales of justice right again" (64).

[3] And violence is rational "to the extent that it is effective in reaching the end that must justify it" (79). This is the end of "multiplying natural strength," which she defines in turn as "the property inherent in an object or person," belonging "to its character, which may prove itself in relation to other things or persons, but is essentially independent of them" (46, 44).

[4] Modern capital knits small, parochial communities into large, highly integrated units. We would have to stress other factors leading to the intermingling of peoples as well, among them two world wars, colonization and its aftermath, global labor migrations, the breakdown of multinational empires, and the rise of ethnonationalism itself, with its production of new refugees, exiles, and stateless persons.

[5] Marxism can avoid the authoritarian logic of its own ideal of the self-determination of the proletariat only by representing the proletariat as a universal class.

[6] As for Luxemburg—although she rejects the idea of freedom as national self-determination, she does not reject the idea of freedom as self-determination *per se*. Indeed, her greatest grudge against both capitalism and Bolshevism is that they deny self-determination to most people inside the nation and, in the case of capitalism, outside.

[7] Thus republican states consign peoples condemned by ethnonationalism as non-national to the extra-legal authority of their own police forces and the extra-territorial limbo of their own concentration camps.

[8] These answers include the nation as a society of heterogeneous strangers joined only by the same central state, or the nation as a unified culture created and imposed by state authority; the formal distinction and protection of ethnic

minorities, or the disappearance of minorities through their cultural assimilation or physical liquidation; the exclusion of "non-nationals" by the nation-state, or its indiscriminate inclusion of them until "the nation" swells up to universal size; the domination of a minority people by a national majority, or the minority's acquisition of its own separate nation-state, with the domination of some new minority people and the further political fracturing of the human race as inescapable results.

Works Cited

Arendt, Hannah. *Men in Dark Times*. New York: Harcourt Brace Jovanovich, 1983.
———. *On Violence*. New York: Harcourt Brace Jovanovich, 1969.
———. *The Origins of Totalitarianism*. 2nd. ed. New York: Harcourt Brace Jovanovich, 1973.
Davis, Horace, ed. *The National Question: Selected Writings by Rosa Luxemburg*. New York: Monthly Review, 1976.
Dietz, Mary. "Feminist Receptions of Hannah Arendt." *Feminist Interpretations of Hannah Arendt*. 17–50.
Fanon, Frantz. *The Wretched of the Earth*. New York: Grove, 1963.
Feminist Interpretations of Hannah Arendt. Ed. Bonnie Honig. University Park: Pennsylvania State UP, 1995.
Honig, Bonnie. "Toward an Agonistic Feminism: Hannah Arendt and the Politics of Identity." *Feminist Interpretations of Hannah Arendt*. 135–66.
Shulevitz, Judith. "Arendt and Heidegger: An Affair to Forget?" *New York Times Book Review* 1 October 1995: 39.

Gender-Bending in the Biedermeier

Todd Kontje

This essay complicates the notion that the German Wars of Liberation brought about renewed conservatism regarding the gender stereotypes that restricted women to their "natural" calling in the domestic realm. An examination of homosocial bonding in Theodor Körner's patriotic poetry leads to an analysis of Caroline de la Motte Fouqué's novels about the French Revolution, and Henriette Frölich's *Virginia, oder die Kolonie von Kentucky.* Although the two women writers differ sharply in their political viewpoints, both use their fiction to explore the limits of permissible behavior for women and to intervene into the public sphere. (TK)

My goal in this essay is to counter—or at least complicate—the notion that the German Wars of Liberation brought about renewed conservatism regarding gender stereotypes, i.e., the belief that only men should have access to the public sphere, while women are to fulfill their "natural" calling as mothers, wives, and managers of the household economy. "The Napoleonic Wars brought with them a new frenzy of masculinity [*Männlichkeitsrausch*]," summarizes Gerhard Schulz in a recent literary history, "through which the bourgeois family was eventually consolidated in its conservative form" (76).[1] Without meaning to deny the power of an ideology that found its most influential proponent in Jean-Jacques Rousseau and which displays continued resilience in today's climate of anti-feminist backlash, I would like to stress how often it has been necessary to renegotiate these conservative values in the changing historical contexts of the past two centuries. In the place of a monolithic norm we see instead the sort of ebb and flow that Susan Faludi has charted in her history of American feminist movements, where even the semblance of progress triggers a vigorous reaction. It is precisely in moments of revolutionary turmoil that efforts to define sexual difference become most intense, and when the outcome of those efforts is most uncertain.

The initial stages of the French Revolution touched off just such a crisis in gender definition. Joan B. Landes has shown how women played an active role in the early years of the Revolution, beginning with the march to Versailles to bring the royal family back to Paris in October 1789 and continuing through the founding of the Society of Revolutionary Republican Women in February 1793 (93-94, 122-23). For a brief period it seemed as though the *Declaration of the Rights of Man* would yield equal progress in the rights of women. Such hopes were short-lived. By October 1793, the French government declared all women's clubs illegal, and women were henceforth excluded from participation in the revolutionary regime. Republican mothers were to fulfill their duties in the home, while their sons and husbands took care of the fraternal order of the state (cf. Hunt, Landes, Laqueur).

German reactions to the early Revolution, and its consequences for women, were mixed. Most notorious is Schiller's reference to French women as "hyenas" in "Das Lied von der Glocke" ("The Song of the Bell" 440), but we can find a similarly anxious reassertion of traditional values against the unsettling backdrop of revolutionary change in Johann Heinrich Campe's pedagogical treatise *Väterliche Rath für meine Tochter* (Paternal Advice for My Daughter, 1789),[2] in Wilhelm von Humboldt's essays on sexual difference (1794 and 1795), and in Caroline von Wolzogen's novel *Agnes von Lilien* (1798). At the opposite extreme we find the early Romantics doubled over with laughter upon reading Schiller's "Glocke,"[3] Theodor Gottlieb von Hippel's arguments for women's rights in *Über die bürgerliche Verbesserung der Weiber* (On Improving the Status of Women, 1792), and open sympathy for the Revolution in Caroline Schlegel-Schelling's letters, Sophie Mereau's *Das Blüthenalter der Empfindung* (The Springtime of Feeling, 1794), and Therese Huber's *Die Familie Seldorf* (The Seldorf Family, 1795-96). As this brief overview suggests, any attempt to identify a single German response to the Revolution is inherently misguided. We should speak instead of an intensification of debate regarding both political alternatives and sexual politics in an era of unprecedented social change.

Symptomatic of this turbulent state of affairs is the persistent fascination with androgyny, cross-dressing, and sexual deviance in German literature around 1800.[4] Goethe's Mignon fascinated his contemporaries, to judge by the number of romantic imitations inspired by the hoydenish preteen. Huber's Sara Seldorf spends some time in the Republican armies while disguised as a man, and Sophie Mereau allows the courtesan Ninon Lenclos to defend her sexual promiscuity by insisting that she be judged by male standards of conduct. Karl Philipp Moritz's Anton Reiser feels a strong pull toward members of his own sex and an aversion to women (Tobin), while Friederike Helene Unger's Julchen Grünthal has a brief encounter with a lesbian countess.

Another example of the way in which authors experimented with gender roles around 1800 is what Madeleine Kahn has termed narrative transvestism, in which a male author ventriloquizes a female persona, as in the case of Goethe's "Bekenntnisse einer schönen Seele" ("Confessions of a Beautiful Soul," 1795–96), or vice versa, as in Dorothea Veit-Schlegel's *Florentin* (1801). Kahn stresses the asymmetry of the technique: the male writer asserts control over imaginary women, while the female writer usurps male authority. I suspect that there is also a desire on the part of both male and female writers to exploit the ambiguity of a narrative situation that uncouples gender from a biological subject and turns it into a cultural performance. Sophie Mereau, for instance, published *Das Blüthenalter der Empfindung* anonymously, but signed the preface as "The Authoress" (*Die Verfasserin*). A first-person narrative follows; eventually the narrator turns out to be a man, but Mereau keeps her readers guessing for quite a while. "At first a young creature appears who is flooded with every possible purple passion," wrote an annoyed Friedrich Schlegel to his brother. "It sits there completely placidly in the grass. I say "it," because I was certain it was a girl; but it is supposed to be a boy."[5]

All this uncertainty allegedly changed when the Germans rallied to defeat Napoleon two decades later. "Dear Edmund, the new world will need men," writes a character to the hero of Caroline de la Motte Fouqué's *Edmunds Wege und Irrwege* (Edmund's Ways and Byways 3: 77) as he stands poised to battle the French. To judge by the patriotic literature written in the years immediately before Napoleon's defeat, women were to play only a peripheral role in the formation of the German nation. In Theodor Körner's *Leier und Schwert* (Lyre and Sword, 1814), an extremely popular collection of patriotic poems, the primary focus is on male bonding in the effort to expel the French from German soil.

> Doch *Brüder* sind wir allzusamm,
>   Und das schwellt unsern Mut.
> Uns knüpft der Sprache heilig Band,
> Uns knüpft *ein* Gott, *ein* Vaterland,
>   *Ein* treues deutsches Blut (92).[6]

Virtuous German women feature as the moral backbone of the Fatherland that their sons defend:

> Und Frauenunschuld, Frauenlieb'
>   Steht noch als höchstes Gut,
> Wo deutscher Ahnen Sitte blieb
>   Und deutscher Jünglingsmut (85).[7]

This sort of patriotism in the name of God, family, and Fatherland is fairly predictable for inspirational verse written in war. What gives Körner's poetry a macabre fascination is the extent to which he eroticizes war and death[8]:

> Was weint ihr, Mädchen, warum klagt ihr, Weiber,
> Für die der Herr die Schwerter nicht gestählt,
> Wenn wir entzückt die jugendlichen Leiber
> Hinwerfen in die Scharen eurer Räuber,
> Daß euch des Kampfes kühne Wollust fehlt?
> Ihr könnt ja froh zu Gottes Altar treten!
> Für Wunden gab er zarte Sorgsamkeit,
> Gab euch in euren herzlichen Gebeten
> Den schönen, reinen Sieg der Frömmigkeit! (89)[9]

Although Körner praises nursing and religion as the peculiarly feminine contributions to the war effort, they seem poor substitutes for the ecstatic passion of death in battle. The fight for the Fatherland is not just a defense of virtuous women; it is itself an erotic act. This becomes particularly evident in the final poem of the collection, which is nothing less than a love song dedicated to the poet-soldier's sword:

> Ja, gutes Schwert, frei bin ich
> Und liebe dich herzinnig,
>   Als wärst du mir getraut
>   Als eine liebe Braut!
> Hurra! (112)[10]

In a logical culmination of this imagery, Körner urges his fellow soldiers to exchange passionate kisses with their weapons before plunging into battle:

> Drum drückt den liebeheißen
> Bräutlichen Mund von Eisen
>   An eure Lippen fest!
>   Fluch! wer die Braut verläßt!
> Hurrah! (114)[11]

At this point it becomes clear that Körner's rigidly heterosexual division of labor in the war effort serves the primary purpose of celebrating homosocial bonding.[12] This is not to suggest that either Körner or his Prussian comrades were homosexuals. It is rather to demonstrate that the seemingly bipolar gender division between male and female is actually triangular in Körner's vision. At first, women serve to solidify bonds between men, as soldiers unite on the battlefield to defend their families at home. In the final poem, however, women drop out of the picture altogether, as the men make love to their swords. To put it as bluntly as Körner does in this poem, men get more satisfaction from kissing phallic symbols than they do from embracing their brides.

The work of Caroline de la Motte Fouqué (1775–1831) offers the perspective of a woman writer on gender and the Revolution. Like Sophie Mereau-Brentano, Caroline Schlegel-Schelling, and Dorothea

Veit-Schlegel, Fouqué made her way into literary history primarily as a footnote to the career of her more famous husband. Yet she was a prolific author in her own right, publishing some twenty novels and several volumes of stories in a career that stretched over nearly three decades.[13] The daughter of a Prussian nobleman, Caroline was actually married twice: first to Friedrich von Rochow, who died in 1799, and then in 1803 to Friedrich de la Motte Fouqué, the popular romantic author of the novella *Undine* (1811) and another dozen tales of chivalry set in an idealized medieval world. Her early work also shows the influence of the Romantic period, but the theme that captures her sustained interest is the French Revolution[14]; a series of novels written between 1812 and 1824 provide an ongoing commentary on recent and current events in France and Germany from the perspective of a conservative German noblewoman.

In *Magie der Natur: Eine Revolutions-Geschichte* (The Magic of Nature: A Story of the Revolution, 1812), Fouqué paints a sympathetic portrait of French aristocrats forced into exile by the Revolution.[15] Fouqué makes no secret of her anti-revolutionary sentiments, reserving particular scorn for the revolting masses: "[T]hey are the dirty scum spewn out by fermenting thoughts" (55). From the opening image of the quiet Rhone river flowing through a land convulsed with political chaos, Fouqué suggests that the Revolution perverts the natural order of things and creates "vulgar people, who sully the earth with their shame" (101). The mob forces the Marquis de Villeroi out of his ancestral home and sends him fleeing with his twin daughters Marie and Antonie into Switzerland and Germany, where they meet other family members and acquaintances. Much of the novel concentrates on the romantic entanglements that arise in the group of exiled aristocrats, while Fouqué also uses the Marquis's obsession with mesmerism and the occult to explore this familiar romantic topos. In the end, however, the revised French constitution of 1795 enables the aristocrats to return to France. The Marquis finds a country that has grown calmer, but even more alienating, in that the new social order has been ratified by law. The result is a profound sense of disorientation in the old aristocrat: "The Marquis felt the push of time's forward progress, but he could not remember where he himself was standing!" (219). With this insight into time's relentless advance, Fouqué identifies an ambivalence that will remain at the heart of her subsequent treatments of the Revolution and its aftermath: while she condemns the Revolution as an unnatural aberration in the order of things, she nevertheless accepts historical change as inevitable and irrevocable: "That which is old will not return" (*Das Alte kommt nicht wieder* (80). The question for the conservative aristocrat, then, will be how to preserve or rejuvenate old values in a new era, neither clinging rigidly to an outmoded vision of the past, nor surrendering completely to the fashion of the present.[16]

Where do women fit into Fouqué's political novels of contemporary events? Most of her work focuses on male protagonists who play an active role in the public sphere, as we might expect from a woman whose work deals with the traditionally masculine concerns of war and politics. Men, in turn, need women, but only as foils to their own development. *Magie der Natur*, *Edmunds Wege und Irrwege*, and *Die beiden Freunde* (The Two Friends) all end with marriages that promise peace to their exhausted heroes. "The old miracles had disappeared from the earth," writes Fouqué in conclusion to *Magie der Natur*, "but love created new ones every day. The magic of Marie's family heritage blossomed in her in such a strange way that it tied her husband's heart to hers with ever tighter bonds" (234–35). Edmund seals the German victory over France by marrying young Agnes, and Graf Dominique marries another woman named Agnes at the end of *Die beiden Freunde*. Yet before the conclusions to these novels other women play decidedly less conventional roles. "Antonie stands alone, distant from me and her sister too" (38), warns the abbess when her father comes to pick her up at the beginning of *Magie der Natur*; and the passionate visionary does indeed stand apart from her fellow exiled aristocrats until she commits suicide with a dagger on a riverbank—an allusion to Karoline von Günderrode?—in the novel's final pages. In *Die beiden Freunde* the demise of the tragic Marquis Alphonse undermines the health of one woman and the sanity of another. Before Edmund settles down with his adolescent bride he incurs lasting guilt by refusing to trust the love of Alinde, a woman trapped in a marriage of convenience to an older Italian Duke. Edmund's moral failure, in other words, arises from the fact that he chooses *not* to continue his affair with a married woman, hardly the sentiment we might expect from a Biedermeier author.

Even less conventional in the light of the extreme gender polarization we noted in Körner's popular lyrics is the extent to which Fouqué defends the direct participation of women in politics and war. In an important discussion among the exiles in *Magie der Natur,* one of the men insists that women have no place in the public sphere: "indeed, they have no other Fatherland than the narrow space enclosed by the four walls of their household activities...they will never understand politics" (174). Two of the women disagree sharply, pointing out that any number of women have ruled wisely in the past, and insisting that there is no reason to assume that women are biologically incapable of any social skill: "'Never,' retorted Viktorine, 'will I be convinced that we are excluded from any sphere of human activity'" (177). Fouqué leaves the argument unresolved in this novel, but Frau Norbert of *Edmunds Wege und Irrwege* provides a good example of a woman whose political activities extend far beyond the narrow confines of her domestic duty. She not only utters some of the central ideological statements that rally the Germans against Napoleon, but personally organizes the underground resistance. Certainly her aristocratic status gives her access to a much wider range of activity than that of a bourgeois women. In addition, she remains loyal to her family, whose members fight together for the German cause. It is presumably Frau von Harville's disregard for her own daughter in the name of a higher cause that discredits her political activity in *Die beiden Freunde,* and not her engagement in the Royalist cause itself.

The most intriguing case of a politically engaged woman in Fouqué's fiction appears as the title figure of *Das Heldenmädchen aus der Vendée* (The Heroic Maiden of the Vendée, 1816). Elisabeth Rochefoucault—pale, shy, blond, and beautiful—disguises herself as a man to fight with the Royalist armies of the Vendée against the Revolution. In doing so she goes far beyond Frau Norbert's discreet efforts to organize future soldiers in an all-male army, venturing into a realm that Sara Seldorf's father had already discredited as "unnatural" for a woman (Huber 26). The topos of the young woman disguised as a soldier recurred frequently in fiction of the Napoleonic era, most famously in the Russian Nadezhda Durova's *The Cavalry Maiden* (1836), but also in Germany (cf. Mosse 101). As Mosse observes, woman's entry into the male domain "was not necessarily seen as blurring the distinction between the sexes" (101). Yet Fouqué's fictional representations of male and female cross-dressing during the French Revolution *does* seem to reflect considerable cultural anxiety about the "natural" distinctions between the genders. In the slightly later novella entitled "Laura: Eine Begebenheit aus der französischen Revolution" (Laura: An Occurrence from the French Revolution, 1821), Fouqué includes a vivid description of the women who marched from Paris to Versailles, deriding them as a "repulsive group of drunken, reeling wenches" (207). Still more shocking is the fact that "men are disguised in women's clothing so that they can commit their crimes all the more safely under this cover" (208). If, from Fouqué's conservative perspective, the Revolution itself is a violation of the natural order of things that causes women to act like men, it is still more perverse to find men dressing up like women in order to participate in criminal acts.

How, then, can Fouqué condemn revolutionary "perverts" and glorify her cross-dressing heroine? Most obviously, Elisabeth Rochefoucault fights for the just cause; what for the Revolutionaries is a manifestation of an unnatural madness is for the Royalists a heroic response to a time that is out of joint. Even so, the female soldier is an exceptional individual, something that troubles Elisabeth in one of her few introspective moments: "[W]hy has the unnaturalness of the age [*die Unnatur der Zeit*] thrust me, of all people, alone, onto this steep resisting path?" (2: 41). Just this resistance to her potentially unnatural role as Amazon testifies to her mental health, in terms of the gender stereotypes of the period, and Fouqué goes out of her way to emphasize that Elisabeth does not enjoy dressing up like a man: "She wrapped the horse's reins around a low, half-burned branch, and, with trembling fingers and with loud, almost suffocating heartbeats, began the unaccustomed, frequently repellant, change of clothes" (1: 88). Once in battle she remains painfully conscious of the potentially transgressive status of her military adventure. "What," calls an outraged Elisabeth to her fellow Royalist soldiers as they begin to retreat, "are you men, and afraid of danger. I am a girl...is nature so upside-down that France's men crawl away from women?" (2: 195). Another factor that permits Elisabeth's military heroism is her largely personal motivation, a product of her passionate admiration for her cousin Prince Talmont. In addition, Elisabeth does not act like the "repulsive wenches" of the lower class. Even in the heat of battle she remains smart in her attractively fitting uniform, and her "fighting" itself seems to consist largely in waving the flag and cheering others into battle.

One interesting question remains in assessing this heroine: why does her relationship with Prince Talmont remain unconsummated? The modern reader might assume that their relationship as first cousins would prohibit any romantic entanglement, but this proves no obstacle in many novels of the period. Fouqué gives every indication, moreover, that we are to regard the cousins as potential lovers. Elisabeth is captivated by Talmont's charm at their first meeting, follows him unswervingly into battle, and shares a quiet moment with him after the fight that seals their union: "A ray of higher life shot through them both, and they belonged to one another for all eternity" (1: 133). Unfortunately for both, Talmont is captured at the end of part one and executed by a firing squad, leaving Elisabeth to mourn him for the entire second volume. But Fouqué could have had the two lovers marry immediately after they declared their love. I suspect she does not because she needs her heroine to remain a virgin. In this way Elisabeth can be freed from her duties as a woman to a specific man to fulfill the role of a saint for the Royalist cause. As one fellow soldier puts it on the battlefield, she represents "France's virginal honor!!" (2: 199).

Thus Fouqué's depiction of gender roles displays an unexpected complexity that parallels the occasional subtlety of her political views. As a conservative monarchist she often vilifies revolutionaries and glorifies German patriots and French Royalists, but she also recognizes the inevitability of historical change. In reflective moments when her characters are not busy purging their native soil of revolutionary "scum," they often seem uprooted, disoriented, and uncertain of their role in a post-revolutionary world. Perhaps it is Fouqué's recognition of the fundamental instability of the social order that enables her to free certain female characters from the fetters that bind them to their "natural" supporting roles. Fouqué is, of course, hardly the sort of feminist activist who demands equal rights for all women at all times. Yet she does allow a few exceptional women to bend the rules in exceptional circumstances, provided that they remain loyal to their families, act with decorum, and—as in the case of Elisabeth—do not particularly enjoy masquerading as a man.

At the opposite end of the political spectrum from the aristocratic Fouqué stands the revolutionary Republican Henriette Frölich (1768–1833). The heroine of her only novel, *Virginia, oder die Kolonie von Kentucky: Mehr Wahrheit als Dichtung* (Virginia, or The Colony in Kentucky: More Truth than Poetry, 1820), is born on Bastille Day and grows up as an enthusiastic supporter of the French Revolution (cf. Brandes; Steiner; Vollmer, *Roman* 98–102). She remains in France until Napoleon's defeat in 1814, whereupon she sails to America and establishes a utopian colony in Kentucky. Here she hopes to continue the pursuit of liberty, equality, and fraternity that would soon be crushed in the European Restoration. Given Frölich's uncompromising support for the ideals of the Revolution, it is not surprising that this novel attracted attention in the former German Democratic Republic, where it was republished in 1963. In an enthusiastic afterword to this edition, Gerhard Steiner celebrates Frölich's vision of an early socialist community, and counters the possible charge of escapism to America by pointing out that the proletarian movement in Europe was not yet fully enough developed to permit radical political action at home (231). Yet in his effort to claim Frölich's novel as an early ally in the movement that led to the formation of a German socialist state, Steiner obscures certain aspects of the novel that do not quite fit the mold. If we reverse the historical perspective and view Frölich's novel as growing out of the tradition of German domestic fiction,[17] we see surprising affinities to the conservative ideals of a previous generation in a novel that offers outspoken support of the Revolution.

Virginia's father is Leo von Montorin, a member of the landed aristocracy who abandons his studies in law to fight for the American colonies against England. After returning to France he manages to avoid the efforts of his uncle, a duke, to place him in a position at court, and retires instead to a small estate that he has inherited from his mother. Here he distributes land to the peasants, removes all signs of servitude, and relates to his subjects as friend and advisor: "The highly educated man, whose scintillating conversation was admired by courtiers, was as simple as these children of nature when he was with them.... Thus he strode like a demigod among these oppressed, neglected people, and a new morning broke in this little friendly valley" (20). As the language of this passage indicates, Leo von Montorin rules as a benevolent patriarch, and not as a member of a revolutionary band of brothers. The feudal lord grants favors to his "children," who in turn worship him as a minor deity. When the Revolution breaks out, Leo von Montorin voluntarily gives up all privileges of his estate, and as a result his little valley remains an island of peace while France is wracked with blood and turmoil. For all her support for the Revolution, Frölich suggests that if there had been more nobles like Montorin, the Revolution might never have been necessary in the first place.

In accordance with his liberal beliefs, Montorin marries for love across class lines, and Virginia insists in her letters to her friend Adele that her parents enjoyed an exceptionally happy marriage. Yet she also acknowledges that the relationship was not completely free of tension: when Leo von Montorin's wife forbids him to enlist in the revolutionary armies, he keeps a stiff upper lip in her presence, but confides his dissatisfaction to his daughter. While he chafes at his enforced inaction, she understands. Even as a small girl Virginia rejects her mother's puppets in favor of her father's illustrated world history. In Virginia, Montorin finds a malleable subject whom he can mold into his own image, and she responds with boundless love for him and the Republican Fatherland.

At this point it is useful to recall Lynn Hunt's study of *The Family Romance of the French Revolution*. In Hunt's view, the Revolution involved killing the father-king and replacing him with a band of brothers, a process that was scripted in advance by popular fiction. Frölich's novel *Virginia* offers the seemingly contradictory combination of faith in the benefits of enlighted patriarchal rule and open sympathy for the fraternal Republican order. The source of this paradoxical blend, in my opinion, lies in the double standard central to Republican ideology: the man enters the public sphere as an equal member of the band of brothers, but he becomes king of the castle when he returns home to his family. Just this tension between public fraternity and private patriarchy stands at the center of *Die Familie Seldorf* (Kontje). Like Therese Huber before her, Henriette Frölich begins from a position of sympathy for the Revolution, but goes on to explore the inherent contradictions of Republican beliefs from what we today would call a feminist perspective.

To a certain extent, Frölich makes her heroine into a tomboy. Virginia identifies more with her father than her mother and has a "manly" appreciation of martial valor. As her proud father puts it, "[T]here is more Roman spirit and masculine strength in this girl's soul than in many of our comrades in arms" (95). Identification with the father allows Virginia to experience at least vicarious participation in the revolutionary struggle. Moreover, Virginia laments the fact that women are remembered in history only as passive sacrifices, not active participants: "Unfortunate woman! The man fights for his opinion and clears a path for himself; the women is not supposed to have an opinion" (11). Virginia *does* have opinions, most notably about the "masculine" spheres of history and politics, yet she stops short of following the example of Sara Seldorf or Elisabeth Rochefoucault in actually joining the army. "'Women do not belong in battle,'" admonishes her father, "'their participation in martial events is unnatural, and can only be excused when they are forced to do so against their will'" (89). Virginia reluctantly accepts her father's advice, and remains behind when he enlists. The fact that she is a woman excludes her from the political party that promises equal rights for all citizens.

Virginia's deference to her father's authority carries over to her boundless admiration of Napoleon. She astonishes her family by cutting off all her hair when she hears that Napoleon is in Egypt, vowing to remain shorn until he safely returns. She then surprises herself with an involuntary gesture of obeisance when he passes through her village: "I, the born Republican and proud of freedom, equality, and the value of human life, knelt before him, unaware of what I was doing, and laid the little basket with wreaths at his feet" (47). Napoleon leaves her in a state of dazed reverence: "My imagination was silent, but I felt myself penetrated by a submissiveness that, with my liberal education, I did not even feel for my father" (48). In other words, Virginia's Napoleon-worship is a heightened form of her father-fixation. She transfers the ambivalence that surrounds her "feminism" in the private sphere into her attitude toward public politics, and as a result, the staunch believer in human equality finds herself in awe of an emperor.

While Fouqué grants selected aristocratic women limited access to the public sphere in the fight against the Revolution, Frölich refuses to let her pro-revolutionary heroine enter the fray. Virginia remains torn between her desire to play an active role in the new republic and deference to the "natural" limitations of her sex; she is at once patriotic citizen and obedient daughter. A similar ambivalence characterizes her activities in America. Here she travels independently, resists the advances of an eligible bachelor out of loyalty to her presumably dead fiancé—whom she rather implausibly rediscovers at Niagara Falls—and becomes a founding member of an egalitarian community in Kentucky. Equality goes only so far, however: children receive the same education only until they are twelve, whereupon the boys go on to learn ancient languages and the girls take up sewing; adult women each receive one-half of a vote in the communal assembly.

* * *

Theodor Körner, Caroline de la Motte Fouqué, and Henriette Frölich are only three authors of a period in German literary history that is currently undergoing a substantial reassessment.[18] While the early Restoration was previously known for a handful of canonical texts,[19] recent studies have unearthed a wealth of long-forgotten literature. Hartmut Vollmer's survey of the German novel between 1815 and 1820 gives one example of the effort required to gain an overview of even one genre in a limited time-frame, and I make no claims to comprehensiveness in this brief essay. Indeed, the current state of research cautions against sweeping generalizations about the Biedermeier period while we explore uncharted territory. The recovery of novels by such authors as Caroline de la Motte Fouqué and Henriette Frölich—in addition to works in the same period by Therese Huber, Johanna Schopenhauer, Karoline von Woltmann, and Caroline Pichler—presents a particularly welcome opportunity to redress an imbalance in the history of German women and the novel that has tended to focus either on the period around 1800 or on the authors of the *Vormärz* (Möhrmann).[20]

For the time being, at least, local knowledge should replace global theorizing, and it is in this spirit that I have focused on a few works by the above writers. Even this brief survey suggests that the reputed conservatism of the period regarding both public policy and sexual politics is at best an oversimplification. Of particular interest is the disjunction between political allegiance and attitudes toward gender on the part of these authors. Fouqué may be a political conservative in her opposition to the Revolution, but she proves relatively liberal in the range of public activism she grants her heroines; on the other hand, Frölich's liberal political credentials do not prevent her from half-heartedly affirming conservative gender stereotypes. Körner's patriotic fervor seems to rest on an absolute distinction between masculine valor and feminine domesticity, yet in moments of greatest ecstasy heterosexual love fades behind the passion of homosocial bonding unto death. Far from espousing a common certainty about the proper division of labor between the sexes, these authors explore the limits of the permissable and bend the edges of the acceptable. No doubt the bourgeoise family eventually did consolidate itself in its conservative form for some, once the dust of the Revolution and its immediate aftermath settled, as Schulz suggests; yet here again closer attention to specific works of the 1820s would be necessary before proclaiming the universality of connubial bliss in the Biedermeier. In the literature of the early Restoration, at least, naturalized gender roles were as contested as they had been in the opening years of the Revolution.

Notes

All translations from the German are my own.

[1] See also Mosse: "In the midst of the wars of liberation, nationalism and respectability were thus linked, and the restricted, passive role of women legitimized" (96).

[2] Campe's treatise was republished in 1790, 1793, 1809, 1819, and 1829.

[3] Reported in Caroline Schlegel-Schelling's letter to her daughter Auguste, 21 October 1799 (230).

[4] See Friedrichsmeyer on the androgyne as an ideal of wholeness in early German Romanticism. The German examples of gender-bending I explore in this essay generate the sort of "category crisis" that Garber finds typical of transvestite figures from the Renaissance to contemporary popular culture.

[5] Cited from Moens, "Nachwort" 23.

[6] But we are all *brothers* / And that inspires our courage / We are united by the holy bonds of language / *One* God, *one* Fatherland / *One* true German blood.

[7] And women's innocence, women's love / Still stand as our most valued possession / Where the custom of German forefathers remained / And the courage of German youth.

[8] On Körner's preoccupation with death and his traditional view of women see Schulz (69–76).

[9] What are you crying about, girls, why do you complain, women / You for whom the Lord did not forge swords / When we cast our youthful bodies with rapture / Into the hordes of your predators / Because you lack the bold passion of battle? / You can step up happily to God's altar, after all! / For wounds he gave tender care / He gave you in your heartfelt prayers / The beautiful, pure victory of piety.

[10] Yes, good sword, I am free / And love you dearly / As if you were engaged to me / As a beloved bride / Hurrah!

[11] Therefore press the love-hot / Bridely mouth of iron / Tightly to your lips / Accursed he who abandons the bride! / Hurrah!

[12] See Sedgwick for a seminal discussion of male homosocial desire in English literature. Joeres applies Sedgwick's concept of the homosocial experience in a recent study of women's friendship around 1800, arguing persuasively that, in their correspondence, women such as Rahel Varnhagen and Bettina von Arnim created an alternative public sphere. To this I would add the significant number of female novelists of the period, whose works can also be seen as an intervention into a public sphere otherwise denied them by virtue of their gender.

[13] See Wilde for a general overview of Fouqué's life and works.

[14] See Vollmer's "Die Wahrheit" for a recent, informative introduction to Fouqué's historical fiction.

[15] See Hoffmeister's detailed introduction to the modern reprint of this novel.

[16] This sense of crisis is particularly evident in *Fragmente aus dem Leben der heutigen Welt* (1820) and *Die beiden Freunde* (1824).

[17] I borrow this term from Nancy Armstrong's study of English women writers in order to avoid the pejorative connotations of the German term *Frauenroman*.

[18] See Schöwerling and Steinecke; Vollmer (*Der Roman*); Eke and Steinecke; Eke and Eke; and Schöwerling, Steinecke, and Tiggesbäumker. Of particular interest is the work being carried out at the Universität-Gesamthochschule Paderborn, where investigation of the extensive collection of nineteenth-century

novels housed at the nearby *Fürstliche Bibliothethek* Corvey has yielded a far more comprehensive view of the genre than had previously been possible. I am grateful to the director of the project, Hartmut Steinecke, and the DAAD for allowing me to spend the summer of 1995 reading novels from the Corvey Library in Paderborn.

[19] Despite its monumental scale, Sengle's study of the *Biedermeierzeit* remains focused on traditional genres and canonical texts, and the same is true of Schulz's more recent literary history.

[20] Blackwell provides an important exception to this trend, with chapters on both Schopenhauer's *Gabriele* and Huber's *Hannah, der Herrnhuterin Deborah Findling* (1821).

Works Cited

Armstrong, Nancy. *Desire and Domestic Fiction: A Political History of the Novel*. New York: Oxford UP, 1987.

Blackwell, Jeannine. "*Bildungsroman mit Dame*: The Heroine in the German Bildungsroman from 1770 to 1900." Diss. Indiana University, 1982.

Brandes, Ute. "Escape to America: Social Reality and Utopian Schemes in German Women's Novels Around 1800." *In the Shadow of Olympus: German Women Writers Around 1800*. Ed. Katherine R. Goodman and Edith Waldstein. Albany: State U of New York P, 1992. 157–71.

Campe, Joachim Heinrich. *Väterliche Rath für meine Tochter: Ein Gegenstück zum Theophron*. 1789. Ed. Ruth Bleckwenn. Paderborn: Hüttenmann, 1988.

Durova, Nadezhda. *The Cavalry Maiden: Journals of a Russian Officer in the Napoleonic Wars*. Trans., Intro., and Notes Mary Fleming Zirin. Bloomington: Indiana UP, 1988.

Eke, Norbert Otto, and Dagmar Olasz-Eke. *Bibliographie: Der deutsche Roman 1815–1830. Standortnachweise, Rezensionen, Forschungsüberblick*. München: Fink, 1994.

Eke, Norbert Otto, and Hartmut Steinecke, eds. *Geschichten aus (der) Geschichte: Zum Stand des historischen Erzählens im Deutschland der frühen Restaurationszeit*. München: Fink, 1994.

Faludi, Susan. *Backlash: The Undeclared War Against American Women*. New York: Doubleday, 1991.

Fouqué, Caroline de la Motte. *Die beiden Freunde: Ein Roman*. Berlin: Schlesinger, 1824.

———. *Edmund's Wege und Irrwege: Ein Roman aus der nächsten Vergangenheit*. 3 vols. Leipzig: Fleischer, 1815.

———. *Fragmente aus dem Leben der heutigen Welt*. Berlin: Schlesinger, 1820.

———. *Das Heldenmädchen aus der Vendée: Ein Roman*. Leipzig: Fleischer, 1816.

———. "Laura: Eine Begebenheit aus der französischen Revolution." *Erzählungen*. Jena: Schmid, 1821. 2: 169–235.

———. *Magie der Natur: Eine Revolutions-Geschichte*. 1812. Ed. Gerhart Hoffmeister. Bern: Lang, 1989.

Friedrichsmeyer, Sara. *The Androgyne in Early German Romanticism: Friedrich Schlegel, Novalis and the Metaphysics of Love*. Bern: Lang, 1983.

Frölich, Henriette [Jerta]. *Virginia oder Die Kolonie von Kentucky*. 1820. Ed. Gerhard Steiner. Berlin: Aufbau, 1963.

Garber, Marjorie. *Vested Interests: Cross-Dressing and Cultural Anxiety*. New York: Routledge, 1992.

Goethe, Johann Wolfgang. "Bekenntnisse einer schönen Seele." 1795–96. *Goethes Werke*. Hamburg: Wegner, 1950. 7: 358–463.

Hippel, Theodor Gottlieb von. *Über die bürgerliche Verbesserung der Weiber*. 1792. "Nachwort" Ralph-Rainer Wuthenow. Frankfurt a.M.: Syndikat, 1977.

Hoffmeister, Gerhart. "Einführung." Fouqué. *Magie der Natur*. 5–46.

Huber, Therese. *Die Familie Seldorf*. 1795–96. *Frühe Frauenliteratur in Deutschland* 10. Ed. Magdalene Heuser. Hildesheim: Olms, 1989.

Humboldt, Wilhelm von. "Über den Geschlechtsunterschied und dessen Einfluß auf die organische Natur." 1794. *Gesammelte Schriften*. Berlin: de Gruyter, 1968. 1: 311–34.

———. "Über die männliche und weibliche Form." 1795. *Gesammelte Schriften*. Berlin: de Gruyter, 1968. 1: 335–69.

Hunt, Lynn. *The Family Romance of the French Revolution*. Berkeley: U of California P, 1992.

Joeres, Ruth-Ellen B. "'We are adjacent to human society': German Women Writers, the Homosocial Experience, and a challenge to the Public/Domestic Dichotomy." *Women in German Yearbook 10*. Ed. Jeanette Clausen and Sara Friedrichsmeyer. Lincoln: U of Nebraska P, 1995. 39–57.

Kahn, Madeleine. *Narrative Transvestism: Rhetoric and Gender in the Eighteenth-Century English Novel*. Ithaca: Cornell UP, 1991.

Kontje, Todd. "Under the Father's Spell: Patriarchy versus Patriotism in Therese Huber's *Die Familie Seldorf*." *Seminar* 28 (1992): 17–32.

Körner, Theodor. *Leier und Schwert*. 1814. *Körners Werke*. Ed. Hans Zimmer. Leipzig: Bibliographisches Institut, 1893. 1: 65–121.

Landes, Joan B. *Women and the Public Sphere in the Age of the French Revolution*. Ithaca: Cornell UP, 1988.

Laqueur, Thomas. *Making Sex: Body and Gender from the Greeks to Freud*. Cambridge: Harvard UP, 1990.

Mereau, Sopie. *Das Blüthenalter der Empfindung*. 1794. Ed. Hans-Dieter Moens. Stuttgart: Akademischer Verlag, 1982.

———. "Ninon Lenclos." *Kalathiskos*. 1801–02. Afterword Peter Schmidt. Heidelberg: Lambert Schneider, 1968. 52–126.

Moens, Hans-Dieter. "Nachwort." Sophie Mereau. *Das Blüthenalter der Empfindung*. 1–37.

Möhrmann, Renate. *Die andere Frau: Emanzipationsansätze deutscher Schriftstellerinnen im Vorfeld der Achtundvierziger-Revolution*. Stuttgart: Metzler: 1977.

Moritz, Karl Philipp. *Anton Reiser: Ein psychologischer Roman*. 1785. *Werke in zwei Bänden*. Ed. Jürgen Jahn. Berlin: Aufbau, 1981. Vol. 2.

Mosse, George L. *Nationalism and Sexuality: Respectability and Abnormal Sexuality in Modern Europe*. New York: Howard Fertig, 1985.

Schiller, Friedrich. "Das Lied von der Glocke." 1800. *Sämtliche Werke*. Ed. Gerhard Fricke and Herbert G. Göpfert. München: Hanser, 1980. 1: 429–42.

Schlegel, Dorothea [Veit]. *Florentin: Roman Fragmente Varianten*. 1801. Ed. and Afterword Liliane Weissberg. Frankfurt a.M.: Ullstein, 1987.

Schlegel-Schelling, Caroline. *"Lieber Freund, ich komme weit her schon an diesem frühen Morgen": Briefe*. Ed. Sigrid Damm. Darmstadt: Luchterhand, 1988.

Schöwerling, Rainer, and Hartmut Steinecke, eds. *Die Fürstliche Bibliothek Corvey: Ihre Bedeutung für eine neue Sicht der Literatur des frühen 19. Jahrhunderts*. München: Fink, 1992.

Schöwlerling, Rainer, Hartmut Steinecke and Günther Tiggesbäumker, eds. *Literatur und Erfahrungswandel im frühen 19. Jahrhundert*. München: Fink, 1995.

Schulz, Gerhard. *Die deutsche Literatur zwischen französischer Revolution und Restauration: Das Zeitalter der napoleonischen Kriege und der Restauration 1806-1830*. Vol. 7, part 2 of *Geschichte der deutschen Literatur von den Anfängen bis zur Gegenwart*. München: Beck, 1989.

Sedgwick, Eve Kosofsky. *Between Men: English Literature and Male Homosocial Desire*. New York: Columbia UP, 1985.

Sengle, Friedrich. *Biedermeierzeit: deutsche Literatur im Spannungsfeld zwischen Restauration und Revolution 1815-1848*. 2 vols. Stuttgart: Metzler, 1971.

Steiner, Gerhard. "Nachwort." Frölich. *Virginia*. 1963. 205–33.

Tobin, Robert. "Healthy Families: Medicine, Patriarchy, and Heterosexuality in 18th-Century German Novels." *Impure Reason: Dialectic of Enlightenment in Germany*. Ed. W. Daniel Wilson and Robert C. Holub. Detroit: Wayne State UP, 1993. 242–59.

Unger, Friederike Helene. *Julchen Grünthal*. 2 vols. *Frühe Frauenliteratur in Deutschland* 11. Ed. Susanne Zantop. Hildesheim: Olms, 1991.

Vollmer, Hartmut. *Der deutschsprachige Roman 1815-1820: Bestand, Entwicklung, Gattungen, Rolle und Bedeutung in der Literatur und in der Zeit*. München: Fink, 1993.

———. "'Die Wahrheit bleibt das Höchste': Die historischen Romane Caroline de la Motte Fouqués." Ed. Eke and Steinecke. *Geschichten aus (der) Geschichte*. 109–41.

Wilde, Jean T. *The Romantic Realist: Caroline de la Motte Fouqué*. New York: Bookman, 1955.

Wolzogen, Caroline von. *Agnes von Lilien*. 1798. Ed. Peter Boerner. Hildesheim: Olms, 1988.

Epistemological Asymmetries and Erotic Stagings: Father-Daughter Incest in Heinrich von Kleist's *The Marquise of O...*

Irmela Marei Krüger-Fürhoff

Focusing on the scene of reconciliation between the heroine and her father, the article traces the epistemological, erotic, and aesthetic impact of father-daughter intimacy in Kleist's *Die Marquise von O....* While the protagonists rely on bourgeois notions of sexuality, daughterhood, and family bonds that allow them to ignore the libidinal dynamics at home, the reader is asked to reflect on the difficulties of distinguishing between emotions and eroticism within an intimate early nineteenth-century family. This epistemological asymmetry is paralleled by aesthetic ambiguities. By presenting father-daughter desire in the scene of reconciliation as a quotation from contemporary theater and *tableaux vivants*, the novel not only parodies dramatic traditions, but also reveals the erotic impact of successful theatricality. (IMKF)

In 1992, the young German painter Alissa Walser made her writing debut by winning the prestigious "Ingeborg-Bachmann-Preis" with a story about an intimate father-daughter relationship. While some journals praised Walser's novelette "Geschenkt" for its literary qualities and others speculated on the autobiographical aspects of a story written by a daughter of well-known author Martin Walser, the Swiss newspaper *Neue Zürcher Zeitung* wondered "where a father's love ends and incest begins."[1] This seemingly simple question not only reveals the difficulties of demarcating different forms of intimacy; it also suggests that paternal love, filial tenderness, and sexual desire may be intertwined to such a degree that they can be denoted by a single, highly suggestive term: the German expression *Vaterliebe*. It is precisely this ambiguity that I would like to explore in my reading of Heinrich von Kleist's nineteenth-century novella *Die Marquise von O....*[2]

Kleist's story relates a young widow's unconscious impregnation—veiling the sexual act in German literature's most famous dash—,[3] her violent expulsion from and later return to her family, and her scandalous but successful attempt to find her child's father by means of a newspaper ad. Secondary literature on the *Marquise* has focused primarily on the heroine's impregnation, often reducing the erotically charged scene of reconciliation between the young woman and her father to a substitute for her sexual encounter with the Russian count. I propose a reading that concentrates on the father-daughter relationship in order to trace its epistemological and erotic impact. In analyzing the intersecting conceptions of knowledge, sexuality, femininity, and family bonds in the *Marquise*, my article pursues two questions: First, it examines how the protagonists' attempts to seek or evade knowledge engage the reader in a hermeneutics of suspicion; second, it traces how Kleist's novella uses and parodies theatrical *topoi* from bourgeois theater and *tableaux vivants* in order to represent incest as an aesthetic event. Both readings show that the *Marquise* problematizes the epistemology and representation of taboo sexuality.

Epistemological Asymmetries

Kleist's *Marquise* contains two sexual encounters: the first one initiates the entire plot, the second seems to predict the longed-for happy end. Psychoanalytic readings of the novella have repeatedly argued that both scenes mirror each other: hence, the father's passionate caress of his pregnant daughter is seen as a belated graphic representation of the rapist's grasp.[4] Such an interpretation discusses neither the structural connection between latent incest and manifest rape nor the implications of a twofold representation of female passivity vis-à-vis male pleasure. I understand the scenes as two transgressions of sexual taboos outside and inside the family, transgressions whose *tertium comparationis* is less erotic than epistemological. Whereas the Marquise's enigmatic pregnancy incites the family's quest for knowledge, the eroticized embrace between father and daughter—although witnessed in full detail—does not provoke any verbal response from the story's characters. This epistemological asymmetry can be traced back to the nexes between different discourses displayed in Kleist's *Marquise*: first, a traditional theological and a late eighteenth- and early nineteenth-century medical debate on sexuality that concentrates on the morals and physiology of reproduction; and second, the emerging bourgeois idea of close family ties that situates the home as a private refuge of virtue and chastity over and against a dangerous and sexually seductive public sphere, while at the same time ignoring the sexual dynamics within the family.

In the *Marquise*, the heroine's search for enlightenment stems neither from philosophical interest nor from erotic curiosity, but is dictated by physical changes: turning to a medical doctor and to a midwife, the young woman seeks gynecological knowledge. The question of whether the "unheard-of event"[5] of her enigmatic impregnation is sexual in terms of desire, pleasure, or loathing might be the reader's or the literary critic's concern, but it is not the Marquise's. She wants to obtain biological knowledge dissociated from sexual sensations and their moral stigmata. In accordance with those broader social movements that Michel Foucault has shown to be inherent in nineteenth-century constructions of sexuality, the Marquise and her family focus their "immense will to knowledge" on the "physiology of reproduction" while at the same time ignoring with a "stubborn will to nonknowledge" the "medicine of sex" that would force them to confront their own libidinal fears and fantasies (54–55). However, the Marquise's attempts to acknowledge her pregnancy, but disregard the moment of conception and its potentially erotic implications, conflict with more traditional medical and legal discourses that also inform the novella. Thomas Laqueur and Anke Meyer-Knees have described how until the late eighteenth and early nineteenth centuries, conception was believed to depend on female pleasure. Since orgasmic experience was supposed to occur even during rape or a woman's loss of consciousness, pregnancy served as evidence for enjoyment, regardless of the circumstances. In this context, the midwife's mention of "the light-hearted buccaneer who had landed in the night" (102) alludes not only to a passionate embrace under cover of the night, but also to female conception during the nighttime of cognition. In a similar move, the father hints at the Marquise's sexual complicity by conflating her mental absence with her body's activity: "Oh,...she's innocent....She *did* it in her sleep." (110, emphasis added). This ironic outburst anticipates the indignant reaction of a fictive reader who claims to know that women who are faced with erotic events only feign loss of consciousness. Thus, Kleist's epigraph for his own novella, which mocks both the reader's and the critic's sensationalistic delicacy, reads: "This novel is not for you, my daughter. Fainting! / A shameless farce. I know she just held her eyes closed" (1:22). However, even a genuine fainting fit would not have proven the woman's innocence; since—according to contemporary medical knowledge—*con*-ception always supposes a pleasurable *re*ception, at least on a physical level, the Marquise's pregnant body reveals her erotic entanglement.

As my reference to medical history shows, the Marquise's effort to cleanse her pregnant self from sexual experience and moral liability is doomed to fail—nor is it successful on a theological level. The young widow's attempt to obtain a second maidenhood by posing as a virgin mother who conceived her (third) child "in the purest innocence" (105) meets at best indulgent smiles (103) or is dismissed as a blasphemous "fairy tale about a revolution in nature" (101). Reflecting on the post-biblical probability of an unknowing conception (103),[6] the Marquise does not realize that her request to understand her physical state is always already eroticized, no matter how heavenly her pregnancy might be. Ever since Eve's fall from grace through her desire to know and Mary's redemption through her sexual and spiritual ignorance, knowledge—and even any quest for knowledge—connotes sexuality. In a religious paradigm that conflates cognitive and carnal knowledge, the epistemological and sexual spheres cannot be distinguished from one another. Since neither an Immaculate Conception nor an Immaculate Cognition are possible explanations of her condition within early nineteenth-century discourses, the Marquise, who must either discredit her virtue or close her eyes to all enlightenment, shuns the desire to know with the outcry: "I *don't want* to know *anything*!" (108, original emphasis, translation modified).

While the Marquise and her parents pursue gynecological knowledge, they do not recognize the presence of sexuality within the family. Focusing on the public facts of rape, impregnation, and wedding proposals, they ignore the libidinal dynamics at home and understand their own family as a refuge of virtue, chastity, and pure tenderness. The father is portrayed as a man "who respected his daughter's feeling" (84); thus no family member seems puzzled by his passionate caress of his daughter:

> [The mother] tiptoed to the Marquise's room to hear what was going on. As she listened with her ear against the door, she heard a soft whisper that subsided into silence at that very moment; it seemed to have come from the Marquise; and as she was able to see through the keyhole, her daughter was sitting on the Commandant's lap, something he never in his life had allowed her to do. Finally she opened the door and peered in—and her heart leaped for joy: her daughter lay motionless in her father's arms, her head thrown back and her eyes closed, while he sat in the armchair, with tear-chocked, glistening eyes, and pressed long, warm and avid kisses on her mouth: just as if he were her lover! Her daughter did not speak, her husband did not speak; he hung over her as if she were his first love and held her mouth and kissed it. The mother's delight was indescribable; standing unobserved behind the chair, she hesitated to disturb the joy of reconciliation that had come to her home (118–19).

Although the mother hails and hallows their embrace, Kleist's phrasing talks more sex than sacredness. By depicting father and daughter both as family members and lovers, the passage deliberately wavers between familiarity and offense. This ambiguity asks the reader to reflect on the epistemological difficulty of distinguishing between emotions and eroticism within an intimate early nineteenth-century family. While the protagonists continue to regard the family as a refuge from a seductive public sphere, Kleist's reader is—long before Freud—invited to realize that "love begins at home" (Gay 178).[7] Where the characters' quest for knowledge comes to a halt, the reader's epistemological adventure is just beginning.[8] Following the clues that situate the sentimental reconciliation of father and daughter on the threshold between familial intimacy and eroticism, the reader might discover the sexual undercurrent of family life at the Marquise's.

A reading that stresses the libidinal contents of Kleist's father-daughter intimacy is not a post-Freudian *idée fixe*. In a contemporary review of the *Marquise* in March 1808, Karl August Böttiger—obviously out of breath from the scandalous text he has had to endure—comments on this passage as follows:

> And then finally on page 28 the way in which the returning mother finds the father reconciled with his daughter.... If something like this appears in a journal declaring to enjoy *Goethe's* special patronage, then either the editor must be joking, or he himself—or Goethe—let's drop the subject (182).[9]

I am less interested in the alleged morality of German Classicism than in the relation between speech and silence as it is displayed in Kleist's text and its early critique: between the reviewer's remarks, the story's expression, and the total lack of any verbal comment by the protagonists. On the one hand, Böttiger's avoidance of any detailed reflections on the scene resembles the protagonists' attitude; on the other hand, contrary to the story's characters, the critic argues as if he knew *that*—and *where*—decency had been offended. His eagerness to drop the subject interdicts speech and representation at exactly the point where the novella sets out to transgress a taboo. Böttiger's indignant ellipsis at the end of his article mirrors Kleist's earlier dash; this not so frank contributor to the journal *Der Freimüthige* obviously would have preferred another omission within the story's second sexual scene.

I would like to argue that it is the notion of daughterhood that leads to the eroticization of the family. At first sight, the Marquise seems to belong to all those female literary characters who embody a dichotomy of sexual virtue and debauchery. According to eighteenth- and nineteenth-century bourgeois conceptions, a daughter is either good, i.e., chaste, or sexually active and expelled from her parents' home, hence no longer a daughter. Focusing on the Marquise's alleged sexual experience, her parents act within this paradigm and call her either a saint (115) or a whore (103, 111). Since sexuality and daughterhood seem to be incompatible concepts, the father understands the Marquise's attempt to be accepted as both fallen woman and daughter as a sham:

> She wants to carry her contemptible pretense to the bitter end.... She has already learned by heart the story that the two of them, he and she, intend to tell us here at eleven o'clock in the morning of the third. "*My dear little daughter,*" I am supposed to say, "I didn't realize that, who could have believed it, I beg you pardon, receive my blessing, all is forgiven" (111, emphasis added).

Even the father's two passionate outbursts—both his missed pistol shot (104) and his embrace—follow this logic: a sexual daughter has to endure pedagogic aggression, while a virtuous one may rejoice in her father's caresses. However, Kleist's novella reveals that a good daughter may be highly eroticized as long as her charms remain inside the family. At the outset of the story, the Marquise is introduced as an attentive mother and an ardent daughter herself, who as a widow returns to her parents and cares for them with exemplary loyalty. Although her decision to come back to her childhood home follows her mother's wish, it is presented as a return to her father:

> After his [her husband's] death, yielding to the wishes of Madam G..., her worthy mother, she left the estate near V... where she had lived until then and returned to the Commandant's house, to her father, with her two children (81–82, translation modified).

Whereas the mother wishes her daughter to marry again (95), the father opposes such an idea (88, 93). He is backed by the Marquise's contention: "I really shouldn't want to put my happiness at stake a second time" (95). The Marquise locates her precarious happiness in single life and being a good daughter to her father. Hence, the novella contrasts the two parents with a second couple, here the father and his daughter. According to bourgeois conceptions of femininity, a good daughter's qualities are synonymous with the features of a desirable bride. This correspondence between two ideals of feminine adolescence inside and outside the family tends to fuse father and lover into a single role; as Lynda Zwinger has argued, all men long for a "daughter of sentiment" (4).[10] Since the Marquise's return to daughterhood cannot efface the fact that she has been and soon will be desired as a woman, she figures as a "liminal person" whose presence "resexualizes" the family space (Boose 33, 64). Moreover, the young woman is not only the fusion of a good girl and a beloved, but also a widow, i.e., a woman who has obtained sexual experience and may take advantage of her post-marital freedom.[11] Embodying these conceptions of femininity that represent shifting degrees of sexual innocence and availability, the Marquise is a perfect screen for male fantasies and projections.

The father's jealous aversion to the young intruder reveals that he prefers a daughter to a son-in-law, and incestuous ties to exchange, exogamy, and kinship alliances: Having succumbed to the double force of military and erotic penetration that was directed first at the family citadel near M... and then at the Marquise, he angrily comments on the succeeding wedding proposal: "Here I am, surrendering to this Russian a second time!" (96). On the one hand, this double surrender presents parent and suitor as rivals; on the other hand, the daughter's and father's twofold submission to the Count, as shown in the similarity of their bodily responses, reveals their intimacy. During the battle, both the Marquise and her father sink down in a lack of strength or consciousness (83) and recover as *Geschwächte* in a sexual and military sense. As an abused woman, the daughter is sexually and legally *geschwächt*[12]; the father who delivers his dagger to the Count is compromised militarily, but since his capitulation evokes an emasculation, his weakness has sexual connotations as well (Politzer 112). Furthermore, the accord between father and daughter is illustrated on a discursive level. When faced with the return of the presumably dead Count, father and daughter are so emotionally close to each other that they do not only talk in unison, but speak grammatically as a single person: "'Count F...!' gasped father and daughter together" (87).[13] Bodily and linguistic parallelism display a union that comes close to sexual intimacy.

A malicious reading might argue that the text proves the count's paternity as little as the father's continence. Although some critics mention the "remarkably prolonged period of gestation" between the dash and the Marquise's deliverance (Swales 145) and claim that the Count's rape is less confirmed by the text than constructed by the reader,[14] in most scholarly analyses the Marquise's father remains beyond suspicion and is not suggested as a possible rapist. However, the mother herself sexualizes her husband's relationship to the Marquise by introducing both him and the child's imaginary begetter with the same disconnected "He—he himself" (114, 116, translation modified).[15] Finally, whereas the protagonists ignore the liminality of sexuality at home, Kleist's novella counters the paradigmatic equation of family and virtue with an extremely ironic turn. In the *Marquise*, the reconstitution of the young widow's precarious daughterhood is presented as the result of her erotic devotion on her father's lap. Drawing on the passionate father-daughter embrace in Rousseau's *Julie ou la Nouvelle Héloïse* (part I letter 63),[16] Kleist's scene of reconciliation overlays intra-familial chastity with extra-familial sensuality, hence creating an image of filial duty that is at the same time highly sexualized.

Erotic Stagings

As I argued above, the Marquise's multilayered femininity is open to various projections that foreclose all judgment about her emotions. Whereas the father's libidinal interest in his daughter is manifest, the novella does not reveal the Marquise's perspective, leaving the reader to speculate whether she feels rapture, disgust, or agony. Since the question "what does a daughter want?"[17] lies beyond the reader's epistemological grasp, the Marquise's desire is more of a mystery than the identity of the rapist or even the father's forbidden passion. Her apparent emptiness intersects with the physical plenitude of her pregnant body; although the Marquise has been sexually penetrated, she is impenetrable to the reader's desire to know. This epistemological impenetrability works on two levels: on the level of the plot it illustrates the ambiguity of *Vaterliebe*; on the level of representation it both draws on and problematizes literary and theatrical conventions that rely on the figure of a passive woman who remains open to interpretation. By quoting aesthetic *topoi*, Kleist makes scandalous family intimacy presentable while at the same time ironically revealing the erotic impact of successful theatricality.

Since Emil Staiger's analysis of style in the 1940s, references to the dramatic elements in Kleist's prose have become a commonplace. According to Erika Swales, the frequent "family exits" and "curtain lines" within the *Marquise* seem to follow stage directions, thus lending the novella theatrical qualities (147). A reading that focuses on the melodramatic representation of the protagonists can well be applied to the story's central scene of reconciliation. Popular dramatic art in both the eighteenth and nineteenth centuries, from the German bourgeois *Trauerspiel* to the English sentimental comedy as well as French *comédie larmoyante*, indulges in touching scenes of recognition, repentance, and reconciliation among devoted children and tender parents, often celebrating a father's blessing for his dying or penitent daughter.[18] A historic late-comer, Kleist's *Marquise* draws on a rich tradition of (melo)dramatic plots and styles from Diderot and Gellert to Lessing, Iffland, and Kotzebue (Pfeiffer 48). Mimicking the scenery of a *Guckkastenbühne* (proscenium stage)[19] with backdrops, frameworks, and curtains, the scene of reconciliation is framed repeatedly, first by walls that the mother seeks to penetrate "with her ear against the door" (118), then by a keyhole she peeps through, and finally by an opening door that fully displays the father-daughter embrace: "her daughter lay motionless in her father's arms, her head thrown back and her eyes closed" (119). The text continues:

> At last [the mother] moved nearer and, peering around one side of the chair, she saw her husband again take his daughter's face between his hands and with unspeakable delight bend down and press his lips against her mouth. On catching sight of her, the Commandant looked away with a frown and was about to say something; but calling out, "Oh, what a face!" she kissed him in her turn so that his frown went away, and with a joke dispelled the intense emotion filling the hushed room. She invited them both to supper, and they followed her to the table like a pair of newlyweds; the Commandant, to be sure, seemed quite cheerful during the meal, but he ate and spoke little, fom time to time a sob escaped him, and he stared down at his plate and played with his daughter's hand (119).

In short, the sequence of family conflict, solution, and passionate rejoicing constitutes a miniature melodrama. However, as Kleist's *Marquise* does not reveal whether the speechless and gazeless young woman shares her parents' delight, the reader may wonder whether this paradigmatic family union is comic or tragic. Exposing the scene of reconciliation as a dramatic *passe partout*, Kleist criticizes both dramatic highbrow culture and popular amusement, *Trauerspiel* and *Rührstück*.

A mute and motionless object on her father's lap, the Marquise evokes not only melodrama but also a late eighteenth-century hybrid genre that was performed as a popular party game in noble and bourgeois parlors: the *tableau vivant*. Situated between theater and the pictorial arts, and imitating scenes from sculpture and painting, such living pictures not only illustrate society's interest in antique art, but also duplicate the moral poses that complete contemporary novels and plays (Holmström, Langen, Miller). Goethe's novel *Die Wahlverwandtschaften* (*Elective Affinities*), which was published one year after the *Marquise*, presents the staging of several paintings, among them the German engraving of a mid-seventeenth-century Dutch painting known as "Paternal Admonition" ("Väterliche Ermahnung"). Stressing the moral contents of both Gerard ter Borch's original canvas and Johann Georg Wille's eighteenth-century print, Goethe's narrator recounts that a "noble and chivalrous-looking father" is addressing his daughter "with what seems to be the utmost seriousness" while her mother "seems to be hiding a slight embarrassment by gazing into a wine glass which she is about to empty" (148). However, the Goethean audience that witnessed the "Paternal Admonition" as a *tableau vivant* was less interested in pathetic gestures or the gravity of family instructions than in the posed beauty of the young woman's—e.g., the lay actress Luciane's—neck. Faced with a female body frozen in a dramatic posture, erotic connoisseurship cancels out all allusions to pedagogy and the fine arts.[20]

Twentieth-century art history suggests that the erotic reception of ter Borch's canvas in Goethe's *Wahlverwandtschaften* is more to the point than the novelist or his contemporary reader might have known. Iconographical analyses argue that the painting does not present a daughter listening to her father but a courtesan meeting a client in the presence of a procuress. Although scholars still discuss whether the young man originally held a golden coin between his fingers—a monetary reward for sex that later may have been removed by irritated owners who relied on the painting's title—today the painting's *sujet* is generally understood as a bordello scene (Gudlaugsson, Guépin, Kettering). My reading of Goethe and Kleist need not discuss how explicit or debauched the painting really is; it simply stresses the fact that in the late eighteenth and early nineteenth centuries, the representation of a seventeenth-century sexual encounter could pass as a family *tableau,* while at the same time preserving its erotic appeal to the viewer. Even though efforts to understand the painting as narrating a domestic event have been successful, attempts to desexualize it apparently have not; the ambiguity of ter Borch's painting

Gerard ter Borch, "Väterliche Ermahnung" ("Paternal Admonition"), oil on canvas, around 1654, Staatliche Museen zu Berlin, Preußischer Kulturbesitz, Gemäldegalerie (photo: Jörg P. Anders)

pervades its staging in the *Wahlverwandtschaften* and echoes Kleist's precarious family scene.

Within the novella's scene of reconciliation, the detailed description of the protagonists' bodies, their aestheticized eroticism, and the mother's enthusiastic reaction recall the production and reception of a *tableau vivant*. Following the mother's look and thus forcing the reader to see with her eyes, Kleist's description fuses two audiences into a single gaze. This double look through a keyhole, drawing on a rich tradition of erotic literature, transforms the bourgeois living room into a boudoir and is saturated with voyeuristic delight. The mother's obvious pleasure in an embrace that might also have provoked her jealousy and the swell of her heart that not only recalls an arousal but even leads to orgasmic bliss are stumbling blocks that the novella leaves undiscussed. Madam G... seems to be both a counterimage to the Marquise and a successor to her husband: on the one hand she provides a contrast to her daughter's apathy by joyfully dancing around the couple, on the other hand she mimics her husband's objectifying caress by kissing his face "in her turn" (119). As the paragraph that introduces the scene of reconciliation shows, the Marquise's mother figures not only as a spectator to the living picture, but also as its manager who arranges room and board backstage, preparing soothing dishes and warming the bed for her exhausted husband:

> Once outside, she wiped her own tears away, and wondered if the violent agitation of feeling to which she had exposed him might not be a danger to his health and if it were perhaps advisable to send for a doctor. For the evening meal, she prepared everything that she could think of that had a fortifying and soothing effect, turned back the coverlets of his bed and warmed the sheets so that she could tuck him in as soon as he appeared on his daughter's arm, and, when he still did not come and the table was already laid, tiptoed to the Marquise's room to hear what was going on (118).

In a parodistic move, the text plays with the burlesque of an impotent old man who is coddled and coached for a nuptial night with his daughter. Kleist's scene of reconciliation transitorily unsettles gender and family roles: the mother is both stage manager and applauding witness of a primal scene of family reunion; the father appears as loving hero, senile wooer, and speechless *infans* who becomes silent after his excess of "*unspeakable* delight" (119, emphasis added); and the death-like body of their daughter under his caresses both accomplishes and parodies the idea of an erotic and aesthetic *living* picture.

It may go without saying that Kleist's parodies of bourgeois drama and *tableaux vivants* are not addressed to the protagonists but to the reader. Referring to recognized works of art and playing with the reader's expectations, the novella's references depend not only on the audience's education but also on a certain willingness to pursue both the text's aesthetic and erotic clues. While the literary persiflage displays Kleist's wit and sense of humor, the use of aesthetic *topoi* also paves the way for uttering the unspeakable; in the guise of theatrical and pictorial conventions, the scandal of father-daughter desire can be veiled and displayed at the same time. The reader who understands both the ironic and the erotic undercurrent of Kleist's allusions witnesses the veiled transgression of a taboo: reading Kleist's *Marquise*, she—or rather he?—is invited to participate in the staging of father-daughter incest.

It is thus evident that the novella's two sexual encounters can be linked through their epistemological and theatrical effects: both provoke efforts to obtain or circumvent sexual enlightenment. Moreover, both scenes problematize the relationship between discursive and body language. While the corporeality of rape is hidden in a punctuation mark, yet open to comprehensive discussions, the erotic transport of reconciliation is graphically displayed, while passed over in silence. Extra-familial sexuality is veiled, intra-familial eroticism lavishly represented; the first scandal can be articulated by the protagonists, the second is beyond their discursive reach. Heinrich von Kleist's *Die Marquise von O...* confronts speech about unillustrated sexuality with images of speechless eroticism; in this chiasmus, rape and incest represent sexual taboos as transgressions of the limits of (un)knowability.

Notes

An earlier version of this paper was presented at the 1994 Convention of the Modern Language Association in San Diego. I am indebted to Eleanor Courtemanche, Cathy Gelbin, Rahel L.C. Hahn, and Jeffrey A. Schneider, who volunteered as critical readers and native speakers and who made the English translations of Kleist and Goethe available to me. Apart from the *Marquise* and the *Wahlverwandtschaften*, translations are mine.

[1] The original German phrasing "wo die Vaterliebe endet und der Inzest anfängt" is more ambiguous than the English translation might suggest, since it does not explain who desires whom: "Vaterliebe" means both "a father's love" and "loving one's father."

[2] The English passages from the novella are taken from Martin Greenberg's 1960 translation. I have, however, changed Greenberg's use of dashs in the abbreviations of the family names into the more Kleistian use of periods; hence, in both the English and the German quotations I will use "Marquise of/von O..." instead of "Marquise of/von O—."

[3] Since Greenberg's translation does not employ the dash at the critical point in the narrative, one of the novella's central clues is omitted (83).

⁴ Weiss, Politzer, and Swales were among the first to engage in a psychoanalytic reading of the novella's characters.

⁵ Goethe's famous 1827 dictum on the novella reads: "denn was ist eine Novelle anders als eine sich ereignete unerhörte Begebenheit" (6: 744-45). Following this definition, Kleist's *Marquise* can be understood as the novella *par excellence*.

⁶ See Cohn for a more detailed reading of the religious and erotic connotations of "Erkenntnis" and "Empfängnis" (133-34).

⁷ See Gay for a Freudian reading of incestuous relationships in nineteenth-century novels (177-92).

⁸ According to Grathoff, the *Marquise* is structured by the question "wie kann ich meinen Lesern eine Geschichte erzählen, die die beteiligten Gestalten in der Geschichte einander nicht erzählen können und dürfen?" (206).

⁹ For a more accessible, but condensed version of Böttiger's text see Sembdner (194).

¹⁰ Zwinger's study provides a convincing reading of the interstices between the constructions of femininity and daughterhood.

¹¹ The Grimm Brothers seem to refute the contemporary myth of the merry widow with the help of statistics: "gegenüber der ernsten, unglücklichen erscheint die leicht betörbare, sittenlockere oder lebenslustige witwe im schrifttum seltener" (Vol. 14.2, columns 834-44).

¹² Around 1800, the German verb *schwächen*, "to weaken," and its adjective *geschwächt* have three different meanings that stem from 1) physical, 2) military, and 3) sexual, moral, and legal discourses. In the most common sense, *geschwächt* signifies any state of bodily weakness; in a military setting it refers to an enemy who has been defeated; in a legal context it characterizes a women who has been raped and/or impregnated out of wedlock. While the female *Geschwächte* is quite prominent in the statute book *Allgemeines Landrecht für die Preußischen Staaten von 1794* (part II. 20, §901-16), contemporary dictionaries by Adelung (vol. 3, columns 1701-02) and Grimm (vol. 9, columns 2157-58) state that the word's sexual meaning is becoming obsolete. I argue that by drawing on the gendered parallelism of male and female states of weakness, Kleist's *Marquise* puts to work the overlapping meanings of these different discourses.

¹³ By inserting—or overlooking—a grammatical mistake, the German original even stresses the protagonists' intimacy: "Der Graf F...! *sagte* der Vater und die Tochter zugleich" (109, emphasis added).

¹⁴ "Kleists Text ist...so geführt, daß von dem ominösen Gedankenstrich an die Vorstellung, es habe tatsächlich eine Vergewaltigung stattgefunden, zunehmend die Einbildungskraft des Lesers *penetriert*—so der Leser das zuläßt. ...der Schock, den man sich in der Rezeption dieses Textes zuziehen *kann* (und sich zugezogen hat), ist das genaue Pendant zu der vom Leser selbst rekonstruierten Vergewaltigung auf der Ebene des Plots: In ihm macht sich der ohnmächtige Leser zur Sache" (Reuß 17).

[15] Greenberg's translation does not render the stammered staccato of the mother's account.

[16] For a recent discussion of Kleist's reading of Rousseau see Vinken and Haverkamp (139-40).

[17] This inquiry rephrases Freud's famous reflections in a letter to Marie Bonaparte: "The great question that has never been answered and which I have not been able to answer, despite my thirty years of research into the feminine soul, is 'What does a woman want?'" Quoted in Ernest Jones' biography on Freud, this query is meant to illustrate both the psychoanalyst's scholarly vigor and his high esteem for the women in his professional and private life (Jones 2: 468). See also Gelus's comments on gender and sexuality in Kleist.

[18] On *Rührstück* and *bürgerliches Trauerspiel* see Glaser and Szondi; for a discussion of the daughter's part in eighteenth- and nineteenth-century drama see Stephan.

[19] For a similar reading see Neumann (174).

[20] On the eroticized body of the female actress performing *tableaux vivants* see von Hoff and Meise.

Works Cited

Adelung, Johann Christoph. *Grammatisch-kritisches Wörterbuch der Hochdeutschen Mundart*. 4 vols. Leipzig: Breitkopf und Härtel, 1793-1801.

Allgemeines Landrecht für die Preußischen Staaten von 1794. Frankfurt a.M.: Metzner, 1970.

Boose, Lynda E. "The Father's House and the Daughter in It: The Structures of Western Culture's Daughter-Father Relationship." *Daughters and Fathers*. Eds. Lynda E. Boose and Betty S. Flowers. Baltimore: Johns Hopkins UP, 1989. 19-74.

Böttiger, Karl August. "Neue Zeitschriften." *Der Freimüthige oder Berlinisches Unterhaltungsblatt für gebildete, unbefangene Leser* 46 (1808): 181-82.

Cohn, Dorrit. "Kleist's 'Marquise von O...': The Problem of Knowledge." *Monatshefte* 67.2 (1975): 129-44.

Foucault, Michel. *The History of Sexuality*. Vol. 1: *An Introduction*. Trans. Robert Hurley. New York: Random House, 1978.

Gay, Peter. *The Bourgeois Experience: Victoria to Freud*. Vol. 2: *The Tender Passion*. New York: Oxford UP, 1986.

Gelus, Marjorie. "Patriarchy's Fragile Boundaries under Siege: Three Stories of Heinrich von Kleist." *Women in German Yearbook 10*. Ed. Jeanette Clausen and Sara Friedrichsmeyer. Lincoln: U of Nebraska P, 1995. 59-82.

Glaser, Horst Albert. *Das bürgerliche Rührstück*. Stuttgart: Metzler, 1969.

Goethe, Johann Wolfgang von. *Elective Affinities: A Novel*. Trans. David Constantine. Oxford: Oxford UP, 1994.

———. *Werke: Hamburger Ausgabe.* 14 vols. Ed. Erich Trunz. München: Beck, 1988.

Grathoff, Dirk. "Die Zeichen der Marquise: Das Schweigen, die Sprache und die Schriften. Drei Annäherungsversuche an eine komplexe Textstruktur." *Heinrich von Kleist: Studien zu Werk und Wirkung.* Ed. Dirk Grathoff. Opladen: Westdeutscher Verlag, 1988. 204–29.

Grimm, Jacob, and Wilhelm Grimm. *Deutsches Wörterbuch.* 33 vols. Ed. Deutsche Akademie der Wissenschaften zu Berlin. Leipzig: Hirzel, 1854–1971.

Gudlaugsson, S.J. *Katalog der Gemälde Gerard ter Borchs sowie biographisches Material.* 2 vols. The Hague: Nijhoff, 1959–1960. 2: 116–17.

Guépin, J.P. "Die Rückenfigur ohne Vorderteil." *Gerard ter Borch: Zwolle 1617–Deventer 1681.* Münster: Landesmuseum für Kunst und Kulturgeschichte, 1974. 31–38.

Heinrich von Kleist: Kriegsfall—Rechtsfall—Sündenfall. Ed. Gerhard Neumann. Freiburg i.B.: Rombach, 1994.

Hoff, Dagmar von, and Helga Meise. "Tableaux vivants: Die Kunst- und Kulturform der Attitüden und lebenden Bilder." *Weiblichkeit und Tod in der Literatur.* Eds. Renate Berger and Inge Stephan. Köln: Böhlau, 1987. 69–86.

Holmström, Kirsten Gram. *Monodrama, Attitudes, Tableaux Vivants: Studies on Some Trends of Theatrical Fashion 1770–1815.* Stockholm: Almqvist and Wiksells, 1967.

Jones, Ernest. *Sigmund Freud, Life and Work.* 3 vols. London: Hogarth, 1954–1957.

Kettering, Alison McNeil. "Ter Borch's Ladies in Satin." *Art History* 16.1 (1993): 95–124.

Kleist, Heinrich von. "The Marquise of O—." Trans. Martin Greenberg. *The Marquise of O—: Film by Eric Rohmer—Novella by Heinrich von Kleist.* New York: Ungar, 1985. 81–124.

———. *Sämtliche Werke und Briefe.* 2 vols. Ed. Helmut Sembdner. München: Hanser, 1984.

Langen, August. "Attitüde und Tableau in der Goethezeit." *Jahrbuch der Deutschen Schillergesellschaft* 12 (1968): 194–258.

Laqueur, Thomas Walter. *Making Sex: Body and Gender from the Greeks to Freud.* Cambridge: Harvard UP, 1990.

Meyer-Knees, Anke. *Verführung und sexuelle Gewalt: Untersuchungen zum medizinischen und juristischen Diskurs im 18. Jahrhundert.* Tübingen: Stauffenberg, 1992.

Miller, Norbert. "Mutmaßungen über lebende Bilder, Attitüden und 'Tableaux vivants' als Ausdrucksformen des 19. Jahrhunderts." *Das Triviale in Literatur, Musik und bildender Kunst.* Ed. Helga de la Motte-Haber. Frankfurt a.M: Klostermann, 1972. 106–30.

Neue Zürcher Zeitung. "An der Schmerzgrenze: Zum 16. Ingeborg-Bachmann-Wettbewerb in Klagenfurt." 30 June 1992: 25.

Neumann, Gerhard. "Skandalon: Geschlechterrolle und soziale Identität in Kleists 'Marquise von O...' und in Cervantes' Novelle 'La fuerza de la sangre.'" *Heinrich von Kleist: Kriegsfall—Rechtsfall—Sündenfall.* 149–92.

Pfeiffer, Joachim. "Die wiedergefundene Ordnung: Literaturpsychologische Anmerkungen zu Kleists 'Die Marquise von O....'" *Jahrbuch für internationale Germanistik* 19.1 (1987): 36–53.

Politzer, Heinz. "Der Fall der Frau Marquise: Betrachtungen zu Kleists 'Die Marquise von O....'" *Deutsche Vierteljahresschrift* 51 (1977): 98–128.

Reuß, Roland. "Was ist das Kritische an einer kritischen Ausgabe? Erste Gedanken anläßlich der Edition von Kleists Erzählung 'Die Marquise von O....'" *Berliner Kleist Blätter* 2 (1989): 3–20 (supplement to Heinrich von Kleist. *Die Marquise von O....: Sämtliche Werke, Berliner Ausgabe.* Eds. Roland Reuß and Peter Staengle. Vol. II.2. Basel/Frankfurt a.M.: Stroemfeld/Roter Stern, 1989).

Rousseau, Jean-Jacques. *Julie, ou La Nouvelle Héloïse: Oeuvres complètes.* Ed. Bernard Gagnebin and Marcel Raymond. Vol. 2. Paris: Gallimard, 1964.

Sembdner, Helmut, ed. *Heinrich von Kleists Lebensspuren.* 2nd ed. Frankfurt a.M.: Insel, 1992.

Staiger, Emil. "Heinrich von Kleist 'Das Bettelweib von Locarno': Zum Problem des dramatischen Stils." *Meisterwerke deutscher Sprache aus dem 19. Jahrhundert.* 3rd ed. Zürich: Atlantis, 1957. 100–17.

Stephan, Inge. "'So ist die Tugend ein Gespenst': Frauenbild und Tugendbegriff im bürgerlichen Trauerspiel bei Lessing und Schiller." *Lessing Yearbook 17.* Ed. Richard Schade. Detroit: Wayne State UP, 1985. 1–20.

Swales, Erika. "The Beleaguered Citadel: A Study of Kleist's 'Die Marquise von O....'" *Deutsche Vierteljahresschrift* 51 (1977): 129–47.

Szondi, Peter. *Theorie des bürgerlichen Trauerspiels im 18. Jahrhundert.* Frankfurt a.M.: Suhrkamp, 1973.

Vinken, Barbara, and Anselm Haverkamp. "Die zurechtgelegte Frau: Gottesbegehren und transzendentale Familie in Kleists 'Marquise von O....'" *Heinrich von Kleist: Kriegsfall—Rechtsfall—Sündenfall.* 127–47.

Walser, Alissa. "Geschenkt." *Dies ist nicht meine ganze Geschichte.* Reinbek: Rowohlt, 1994. 7–20.

Weiss, Hermann F. "Precarious Idylls: The Relationship between Father and Daughter in Heinrich von Kleist's 'Die Marquise von O....'" *Modern Language Notes* 91 (1976): 538–42.

Zwinger, Lynda Marie. *Daughters, Fathers, and the Novel: The Sentimental Romance of Heterosexuality.* Madison: U of Wisconsin P, 1991.

Not "until Earth Is Paradise": Louise Otto's Refracted Feminine Ideal

Helen G. Morris-Keitel

Typically, analyses of Louise Otto's novel *Schloß und Fabrik* (1846) have focused on the issues surrounding the factory and the unique way Otto involves her female characters in exposing and combatting a new form of poverty. In contrast, this reading of the novel emphasizes the role the question of class or social status plays in delineating and constraining Otto's feminine ideal. Structural elements of the text, such as representative figures and redundancies, are re-examined in light of the "cultural work" the novel was intended to do. (HGM-K)

> *I have always taken great pains not to make this intention obvious, but I have always thought no one could possibly have read even one of my novels without getting the impression that, for the author, a true and noble femininity would be unthinkable without* inner independence *in feelings, thought and purpose and without the conviction that it must be the human right of every woman to strive for the achievement, the confirmation, and the preservation of this independence*—Otto, "Frauenfrage" 212

Louise Otto (1819–95) clearly believed that her contemporaries were able to extract multiple discourses from fictional prose. A key discourse in her own prose was the delineation of the feminine ideal. Otto integrated it with the other issues she addressed in her novels, such as the social question (a term that referred to growing concerns about the living conditions and potential revolutionary strength of a nascent proletariat in the pre-1848 period), the role of art and education in society, as well as national identity and the meaning of citizenship; she was convinced that these issues should not be treated in isolation. In *Schloß und Fabrik* (Castle and Factory, 1846), the social question is inflected with a gender perspective as Otto focuses her readers' attention on the inability of working-class women to fulfill their roles as mothers. Maternal love could not counterbalance starvation, long hours of child labor, and disease

(Morris-Keitel). Equally important in *Schloß und Fabrik* and especially for this reading of the novel is the way in which Otto inflects her advocacy for women's rights, as described in the opening quotation, with the social question. For although Otto constructed a single ideal for all women, she was aware that the inclusive attainment of this "human right" entailed overcoming a myriad of factors, such as wealth and education, which were to a large extent dependent on the social situation of the individual female. Thus, Otto saw her fiction as what Jane Tompkins has described as "an agent of cultural formation," a vehicle for "providing men and women with a means of ordering the world they inhabited" (xvii, xiii).

Such agency entails an attentiveness on the part of the author to the "heuristic and didactic" impulses inscribed in a narrative, perhaps at the sacrifice of aesthetic sophistication (Tompkins xvii). Indeed, Otto's novels have been criticized for a tendency towards "wordiness and overstatement" (Joeres, "Introduction" 113) or because "the fiery tone of her polemical writings stands in contrast to the milder, accommodating and conciliatory prose of the fictional text[s]" (Joeres, "Frauenfrage" 23). Such an assessment of a work of mid-nineteenth-century women's fiction is not uniquely applicable to Otto nor to German-speaking women writers. Twentieth-century readers of nineteenth-century women's fiction often tend to categorize it as "trivial," "formulaic," "sensational," "sentimental" (Tompkins; Harris), or "conciliatory to patriarchal notions of women" (Joeres, "Frauenfrage" 212). One must ask, however, whether preoccupation with aesthetics and/or resistance to nineteenth-century feminist ideologies that subtly reinterpret traditional roles for women as wives, mothers, and moral pillars of society may blind us to textual features of narratives that "serve the purpose of highlighting the problematic nature of the feminine ideal" (Dobson 228).[1]

In particular, the conscious use of "stereotypical" characters (often associated with predictable fates), antithetical to theoretical approaches that privilege the individual either as reader or fictional subject, has caused literary critics, including feminists, to either ignore popular women's fiction or see it as "defective" (Tompkins xii). But Tompkins reminds us that stereotypes "convey enormous amounts of cultural information in an extremely condensed form and can 'operate as instruments of cultural definition'" (Tompkins xvi). Especially in a time of perceived social upheaval and change, as was the case in the pre-1848 period in the German states, stereotypical, or to avoid the negative connotations associated with this term, representative characters were used to understand and define differences and relations between social groups. What for twentieth-century readers may seem to be reified stereotypes may not have been interpreted as such in their time. Certain social groups, such as bourgeois industrialists and factory workers, emerged in this period as a result of the onset of industrialization, a process that did not begin in any significant way in the German states until approximately 1840. Such changes in the social spectrum forced the aristocracy and the educated bourgeoisie to (re)assess and, in some cases, redefine themselves in keeping with the evolving class-based social structure. Representative figures can thus function as means of elucidating the constraints that prohibit individuals from realizing theoretically universal ideals such as equality, democracy, or citizenship, as well as those pertaining to gender roles.

Otto's *Schloß und Fabrik,* not unlike Bettina Brentano-von Arnim's *Dies Buch gehört dem König* (The King's Book, 1843), is often cited as an example of the way in which, during the 1840s, educated bourgeois and aristocratic women began overtly demonstrating political and social activism in their *oeuvres*. Unlike *Dies Buch gehört dem König*, however, Otto's novel has received little critical attention. Those who have examined it more closely have done so in the context of *Vormärz* social prose (Adler; Morris-Keitel). Arising in response to a growing concern with the new pauperism associated with the onset of industrialization, in contrast to "natural" poverty (Pankoke; Jantke and Hilger; Kuczynski), the genre was influenced by French and English writers such as Eugène Sue, George Sand, and Charles Dickens.

Otto's fictional representation of the social question challenged the traditional role of women on two discursive levels, one extrinsic and one intrinsic to the text. As a female author of social prose, Otto was, to paraphrase the mother of one of the characters in *Schloß und Fabrik,* "showing interest in a very unfeminine way in matters only suitable for males" (III: 49). Otto clearly does not share this opinion since she did not publish *Schloss und Fabrik* anonymously or under the pseudonym that she had used in the past, Otto Stern. This demonstrates Otto's conviction that women, especially educated bourgeois women, had the right if not the duty to participate in public discourse (Joeres "Introduction"). Within the novel, this idea is underscored by the central role Otto assigns the educated women Elisabeth von Hohenthal and Pauline Felchner in her depiction of the social question and its possible solutions. This active role for women in social and political issues distinguishes *Schloß und Fabrik* from works in the same genre by male authors of the period such as Ernst Willkomm, Ernst Dronke, or Georg Weerth (Joeres, "Otto-Peters" 297–98; Morris-Keitel).

The new role Otto depicted for upper-class women as the angels of and advocates for the poor has been considered *the* paradigm for understanding the way she demonstrated the inexorable link between the "woman question" and the social question in *Schloß und Fabrik*. Because of the emphasis on what has been seen as the more dominant question of the period, the issues surrounding the factory, critics have failed to ask how the social question functions in *Schloß und Fabrik* when the women's question is considered as equally important. Such a shift is not merely a change in theoretical perspective, it restores the equilibrium between the two questions that is inherent in the structural design of *Schloß und Fabrik*.

Of utmost importance to this reading of her novel is the fact that Otto's ideal of womanhood included not only the notion of responsible citizenship in the public sphere, but also that of the active and equal partner in the private sphere (Koepcke 11). Heterosexual love and partnership was, in Otto's mind, a goal common to women in all social categories. In this novel, she shows that the reality of this experience was closely linked to social factors that determined women's status in society and their ability to control their own lives. Representative female figures, primarily defined by their class or social status, are thus used to articulate a feminist ideal. More importantly, they expose the constraints placed on a woman's ability to realize this ideal. It was Otto's hope—in the spirit of pre-1848 liberalism—that when the various barriers to female self-fulfillment were revealed, society would take steps to tear them down. The nature of these barriers will be explicated in the following section before their significance in Otto's overall narrative strategy is discussed—a strategy most aptly described as variations on a theme. And while this theme—heterosexual love and partnership—was not new to her readers, Otto's reinscriptions of it most certainly were.

Financial, intellectual, or emotional dependence on a male was not commensurate with Otto's ideal of heterosexual love. This is illustrated in *Schloß und Fabrik* most succinctly in the petit-bourgeois figure of Amalie Thalheim. Although one might debate whether Amalie belongs to the petit bourgeoisie or the working class, in the context of the novel a clear distinction is made between Amalie and Lise, for example, who represents what Otto considers the working class or industrial proletariat. The most overt indicator of Amalie's status is that she can read and write. Without a male provider, however, she and her mother must spend most of their time and energy doing fine embroidery and other forms of needlework to support themselves.

Amalie encounters Jaromir von Szariny shortly after he has been exiled from Poland and before he regains access to his family's wealth. In financial matters, the two seem to be equals. However, Jaromir's background and gender mean that he is much more educated than Amalie. Amalie, while enthralled with Jaromir's poetic genius, is aware of her own limitations: "Oh how handsome, how intelligent he was and how insignificant I felt myself to be beside him" (I: 27). This intellectual imbalance leads to Amalie's insane jealousy, reinforced when the two must separate and maintain contact only through correspondence with one another. Amalie attempts to arouse similar feelings in Jaromir by engaging herself to Gustav Thalheim, a teacher to whom she and her mother have rented a room. This attempt fails and Jaromir rejects her completely. When her mother suddenly dies, Amalie is forced to honor her commitment to Gustav, a man whom she does not love.

Amalie survives at the cost of financial dependence on a male. Otto, however, rejected such a basis for marriage. Thus, this fictional marriage must fail, despite Gustav's attentiveness and the birth of their child. For Amalie, Gustav's presence is a constant reminder of her own limitations—intellectual, emotional, and financial: "I admired your magnanimity, your sacrifices, your constant gentleness, but it always seemed to me that you stood on a cold, clear summit that I could never scale" (I: 29). Thus, for Otto, Amalie represents a woman unable to escape the confines of her limited education and weak economic position.

Amalie entered into this marriage because of a lack of alternatives. As a typical, single, petit-bourgeois female of the 1840s, she lacked the education and job skills that would have allowed her to live independently. This message is further reinforced in the novel when, after the couple separates, Amalie begins working as a maid, a position that will provide her not only with a salary, but also with lodging and meals. Only such an occupation can replace the "home" Gustav had provided for her.

In contrast to Amalie, Bella, Jaromir's second lover, is financially independent as an opera singer and actress. In this case Otto is very explicit about the attraction Jaromir, by now a young poet, feels for Bella. He is enthralled and, at first, deceived by her great acting abilities: "It was not her beauty or her charming features that attracted Jaromir, but rather the tremendous artistic talent that allowed him to recognize a related genius who shared his enthusiasm for the theater" (II: 53). Jaromir quickly learns, however, that although Bella understands her craft very well, success has turned her into a *prima donna*. As is typical of "the belle" (Baym xxxviii-ix), she becomes ever more "conceited, proud and at the same time more thoughtless and defiant" (I: 54). Even so, Otto does not totally vilify Bella or depict her career as the first step towards prostitution, a motif common in other works of social prose.[2] Instead, Bella is depicted as a product of her circumstances: "The praise with which the enthusiastic Berliners lauded her did not fail to have its effect" (I: 54).

When Jaromir realizes that it is the performer Bella and the characters she portrays, and not Bella herself, that he idolizes, he offers her his lasting friendship. In this scene (I: 181-89), distinctions are made between passion and love. In addition, the two discuss what effect marriage might have on Bella's career. Bella, as a mouthpiece for Otto's views on this issue, asserts:

> I will never marry. You know, a married actress is a kind of amphibian—she must be a member of the watery element of marriage and

concurrently live on the land of the stage. She will want to be neglected neither by her husband nor her public—and perhaps she will be ignored by both. No, no! No one can serve two masters, I would be a very bad wife and at the same time I would also have perhaps the prospect of becoming a bad singer (I: 185).

Again, what is noteworthy about this characterization of Bella is that Otto does not degrade her because of her choice to pursue a career. Like Jaromir, Otto has a great appreciation for actresses and opera singers who, on stage, can make the audience forget their surroundings and who can transform themselves into the persons they are portraying (I: 183-84). Otto is, however, emphatic that such women are ill-cast in the role of wife or mother because of the time commitment both careers demand.

Interestingly, however, the excellence of Bella's art is cast into doubt in a scene in which Jaromir hears Elisabeth sing for the first time.[3] The reader is privy to Jaromir's thoughts as he compares the two singers. Bella's "tones" are described as "bewitching," "a language of glowing, often wild passion"; her sound of "sirens" aroused in him feelings of "lust" and a "glowing desire" but left him "destroyed, sober, and level-headed." In contrast, Elisabeth's melody, a simple love song, is likened to "a chorus of angels, a holy prayer in which all of creation joins in peaceful jubilation" (III: 10). The pathos of this page-long comparison might be dismissed by the modern reader as overly sentimental, but within the context of Otto's feminine ideal, the scene is most appropriate and revealing.

Taken out of context, the true love of Elisabeth's song may seem to reflect patriarchal notions of the heterosexual bond: "My heart, I ask of thee / What is love?—Pray, tell! / Two souls, one thought, / Two hearts, one beat" (III: 9). Scenes in the novel, however, demonstrate that Otto's conception of "one thought" is not to be equated with the notion of male intellectual dominance. Jaromir's love for Elisabeth is cemented by his appreciation of her ability to think for herself. He explicitly reveals his love for her only after she, in a manner totally uncharacteristic for her class and much to the dismay of her parents, expresses in a discussion about a railroad strike her opinion about the causes for immorality and indecency among the lower classes. His confession of love begins with the words: "Now I can tell you how loudly I rejoiced to myself as I heard your words—that proved to me that you thought differently than—well, than one usually thinks when one is raised in a castle under the eye of venerable, proud ancestral portraits" (II: 171). It is a similarity of perspective on issues, derived independently, that bonds Elisabeth and Jaromir.

Elisabeth represents a new type of woman, one who does not hide her education, who makes her own decisions, and who is not afraid to have opinions about substantive issues in society. She is the woman Jaromir describes in his poem "To the Women" in which "women and freedom are used as synonyms and women are challenged not to lag behind in worthy service to the new age" (III: 45). In the years leading up to 1848, Otto, like many liberal thinkers of the period, was becoming ever more convinced that a new form of government and a reform of many social institutions, among them marriage, was imminent. Women, according to Otto, should be active participants in these changes both beyond and within the walls of their own homes. Elisabeth further embodies this ideal when she rejects the promise of marriage her parents have given to another suitor and declares her love for Jaromir. She argues "that a heart that loves like mine cannot step before the altar with another [man] and therefore without a heart—this disgrace, this misery, this crime you would not want to burden me with and never would I be willing to commit it!" (III: 65). As a woman who does not regard herself as a peripheral or trivial object of admiration, Elisabeth asserts herself as a subject. Equally significant is that Jaromir is attracted by and supportive of Elisabeth in her assertion. Their relationship is the ideal to which Otto subscribes throughout *Schloß und Fabrik* and against which all other heterosexual love relationships are measured.

Elisabeth's ability to realize such a relationship is linked to her privileged position as a wealthy and educated noblewoman. In contrast to Amalie and Bella, Elisabeth is enabled by her social position to attain the "inner independence" central to Otto's concept of emancipation. She is not financially dependent on Jaromir, she does not seek from him the constant affirmation of her abilities, nor does she rely on him to think and act for her. Her identity is not dominated by a male figure, neither by her father nor her prospective husband.

To the modern reader this message may seem trivial. In mid-nineteenth-century Germany, however, where marital status was a primary source of female identity, Otto was signaling that women had the right and the duty to take an active role in decisions that directly affected them. Thus, for Otto, refusing to take an active role in this decision, as was typical of the older generation who did not question the tradition of arranged marriages or denying one's own feelings in matters of love and marriage, as Amalie was forced to do, was tantamount to a "crime against and abasement of the feminine" (Otto, "Frauenfrage" 213). Nevertheless, Otto was aware that a woman's desire and her capabilities—intellectual, financial, or moral—to take an active role did not ensure her an opportunity to do so in the social reality of the 1840s. To illustrate this, Otto invites the reader to contrast the fates of her dual heroines, Elisabeth and Pauline.

Parallels between Elisabeth and Pauline are drawn on two discursive levels in the novel. Both attend the same boarding school and share a reverence for their teacher, Gustav Thalheim. His parting words challenge them to take an active role in society: to befriend the poor and downtrodden, to maintain their friendship despite antagonism between the nobility and the bourgeoisie, and to remain true to their individual characters (I: 97–100). On a descriptive level, both are often depicted in terms likening them to angels or with splendid nature imagery. These images distinguish them from the factory workers who—with the notable exception of Gustav's brother Franz Thalheim, who represents the possibility of the educated factory worker—are described as animal-like and instinctual. Such dichotomous imagery is common for social prose and, as Klaus-Michael Bogdal has shown, it is still prevalent in naturalistic works at the end of the nineteenth century.

The similarity between the two heroines continues when they return to their homes in neighboring estates and are forced to confront the prejudices of their parents' generation. From these confrontations, however, the differences between the two women's situations emerge. Elisabeth's battles center around her right to choose her own partner, whereas Pauline's conflicts with her father, a bourgeois industrialist, have as their focal point the social question. Yet this focus is linked to questions of love and partnership between Pauline and Franz Thalheim, and therefore serves as a contrast to the relationship between Jaromir and Elisabeth.

The emphasis in the delineation of Jaromir's and Elisabeth's love for one another is on "common thoughts." Pauline's and Franz's love, on the other hand, is inflamed by their joint actions against a common adversary, Pauline's father, "a tyrant for all those who were dependent on him because of the ambition to be the richest and most advanced industrialist in his fatherland" (III: 21). Pauline and Franz function as a team in their efforts to relieve the suffering among Felchner's workers. Franz has intimate knowledge of their problems and Pauline, to a limited extent, has the resources needed to combat hunger and physical distress. Thus Pauline's confrontations with her father, in contrast to Elisabeth's, do not primarily concern herself, but rather the moral and ethical responsibility of an entire social group in a period of dynamic social change.

Pauline's belief that her father must become a "benevolent father" to his workers rather than a tyrant represents Otto's answer to the social question and the role the industrial and educated bourgeoisie should play in resolving this question in the German states. Otto described the desired relationship between the bourgeoisie and the emerging working class as a nurturing parent-child relationship that contained the possibility for the "child" to mature into an adult. More importantly for this analysis, through Pauline's and Franz's interactions, Otto exemplified the active role women could play as advocates and "angels" of the poor. Why then must Pauline and Franz die at the end of *Schloß und Fabrik* if they symbolize Otto's positive ideal of responsible citizenship?

Pauline's and Franz's love for one another is, until their death, described as their joint love for a common cause, a "sympathy with the poor and [a belief] in the equality of human beings" (III: 36). Such a love, crossing class boundaries in an unthinkable direction, given that the man, "the provider," was of a lower social standing, was much more radical and threatening to social norms than a love such as Elisabeth's and Jaromir's, which challenged the "normal" way of constituting marriages within a single social class (III: 141-42).

Although both love relationships are based on mutual respect, interests, and intelligence, Elisabeth's and Jaromir's actions serve to reform a class that Otto depicts in a state of decline. This is underscored throughout the novel in various scenes in which Felchner's aristocratic neighbors are forced to sell him their land and through his pejorative references to them as "country squires" (*Krautjunker* I: 173). Pauline's and Franz's love is intricately intertwined with their desires to be recognized as participating, educated citizens in a society that denies them both this right—Pauline because of her gender, Franz because of his social status. Pauline's father represents this point of view throughout most of the novel: He views Pauline as a child (III: 21, 136) and Franz as simply an anomaly, an excellent worker who, because he has had more education, chooses to write in his free time instead of getting into trouble (II: 205-08). However, the potential of their partnership to usurp Felchner's newly gained power poses a serious threat to Felchner as a male, as a father, and as a bourgeois industrialist.

Pauline and Franz, as much as they both want to improve society, are not proponents of revolutionary change. They seek to persuade men in positions of power, such as Felchner, to exercise their authority more humanely, but they do not reject a social hierarchy as such. This is underscored in *Schloß und Fabrik* in long passages in which Otto carefully distances herself and her protagonists from communism (II: 79-96, 179-95; III: 35-42). On a personal level, both Pauline and Franz painfully accept the fact that "until earth is paradise, it is not always possible to realize the feelings of our hearts" (III: 142). If Pauline were to act on her love, she would have to betray her father, still an unthinkable act for her: "she wanted to honor him because a child is not meant to pass judgment on her father" (III: 162). Franz finds himself in an analogous situation. Although he is given the opportunity to flee and establish himself as a writer (with money donated by Elisabeth who hopes to enable Pauline and Franz to experience the happiness she and Jaromir share), he cannot leave his fellow workers at the moment when they are in the greatest danger because of their uprising against Felchner. Although he does not support their revengeful and destructive revolt, Franz feels compelled to "stand and fall with them, triumph and be ruined, or die" (III: 156).

Both Pauline and Franz value principles of kinship even higher than their own personal happiness. Thus, self-assertiveness, as was the case in Elisabeth's conflict with her parents, is not sufficient to overcome the constraints, external and internal, placed on their ability to realize their love on earth. They can only be united in death, since gender and class identities within their society stand in irresolvable conflict with their love for one another.[4] Neither they nor society can change quickly enough to remove the constraints on their actions.

The tragedy of Pauline's and Franz's death–they are shot down by the government troops Felchner has called upon to quell his workers' revolt–was meant to invoke indignation and agency in the reader. Only a negative ending makes possible such an appeal to action. Whereas Elisabeth's and Jaromir's relationship and its positive confirmation, their engagement at the end of the novel, serves as an example that *may* be followed, the impossibility of Pauline's and Franz's relationship exposes an injustice that Otto felt *must* be combatted. Thus, the deaths of these exemplary young people embody "a moment of protest" against the "connivances of a respectable community" (DuPlessis 16). It is up to the members of the community—the readers—to become "agents of cultural [*trans*]-formation" (Tompkins xvii).

Throughout *Schloß und Fabrik* Otto carefully constructs an ideal of love based on the mutual respect, intelligence, and financial independence that is central to both female and male gender roles. The articulation of this ideal involved testing its feasibility within the parameters of Otto's contemporary social setting. The constraints on this ideal point to the multifacetedness of the "woman question."

These constraints can be divided into two major categories, those that are self-imposed and those that are not. Bella represents the first category, for she realizes that the demands of her career are incompatible with those of marriage. Her conscious decision is articulated and her actions are represented as responsible. There is a hint, evident in the contrast with Elisabeth, that Bella is capable only of fleeting passion and not of sustained, nurturing love, and Otto implies that because of this, Bella will never fully know what it means to be a woman. Otto, however, does not belabor the point, and the reader is left with a positive impression of such women.

More important and problematic for Otto were the external constraints placed on women's abilities to attain Otto's feminine ideal. It was these factors—lack of education, financial dependency (Amalie), traditions (Elisabeth), and rigid gender and class norms (Pauline)—that had to be combatted. Elisabeth can overcome the barrier to her love, her parents' choice of another man, because it involves the least amount of risk in personal as well as in social terms. On the other hand, in order for

Amalie's or Pauline's love to be realized, major changes in social structures would have to occur—changes that would enable women to be fully active participants in society. Because Otto was depicting contemporary social reality in the 1840s, she was forced to code tenets of her ideal of womanhood in terms of the constraints placed on women striving for an ideal love relationship. This coupling of more radical notions of emancipation (education, financial independence, activism) with heterosexual love was an effective strategy because central to Otto's motivation for writing *Schloß und Fabrik* was the opportunity to reach a broad audience, an audience that was for the most part not yet politically educated. As the author herself wrote in regard to *Schloß und Fabrik,*

> Many endeavor, as do I, to interest those who first must be stimulated in order to engage themselves intellectually and excite them about the questions of the day, as well as to elucidate for them much about our current circumstances. Thousands welcome such stimulation when it *coincidentally* appears under the guise of fiction and fulfills the promise of entertainment and diversion ("Zur Antwort" 133).

In order to ensure that her audience understood her "smuggled" commentary on women's issues in contemporary society (Joeres, "Frauenfrage" 22), Otto employed an explicit "redundancy" of the motif of heterosexual love and partnership, which she assumed would lead to contrast or comparison on the part of the reader (Suleiman 55, 203-04). For the contrasts to be effective in elucidating her new ideal of womanhood, it was necessary for Otto to create female characters who, while sharing the biological category of gender, represented distinct segments of society and thus unique challenges to the realization of the ideal. The subversiveness of Otto's novel lies in her ability to exploit the accepted role of love and marriage in the lives of women and to invigorate this role with new meaning.

Otto linked the success or failure of heterosexual love and partnership directly to the social question, "the growing disproportionality in the social appropriation of knowledge, money and power" (Pankoke 15). Only in the case of Elisabeth and Jaromir, where all these variables were equal, could the relationship succeed. As important as this success story is for establishing new parameters for heterosexual love and partnership, it is the failures in the novel that highlight the cultural work still to be done. For Amalie and Pauline, imbalances between their shares of knowledge, money, and/or power and those of their male counterparts preclude the attainment of the ideal. Otto implied that only when these imbalances are addressed, that is to say, when women are allowed access on a broader scale to education and employment and are recognized as citizens with a voice, could her ideal of love and therefore of womanhood be realized.

Notes

All translations are my own. I would like to thank my anonymous readers and Glynis Carr for their suggestions in the reworking of this article.

[1] See Baym (ix–21).

[2] See, for example, the figure of Adeline in Ernst Dronke's novella, *Reich und Arm* (13–90). Of particular relevance is the chapter "Das Gastmahl der Rabenväter" (44–51).

[3] Otto underscores the fact that Elisabeth, in contrast to the social etiquette of the period, does not make a habit of "performing" for social gatherings in her parents' home. Otto is very explicit about her distaste for the musical dilettantism that has become fashionable among the upper classes. See also Otto's *Frauenleben* (221–28).

[4] See DuPlessis's discussion of the potentially subversive meaning of death, particularly for female characters in nineteenth-century novels (4, 14–16).

Works Cited

Adler, Hans. *Soziale Romane im Vormärz. Literatursemiotische Studie.* München: Fink, 1980.

Arnim, Bettina von. *Dies Buch gehört dem König.* 1843. Ed. Ilse Staff. Frankfurt a.M.: Insel, 1982.

Baym, Nina. *Woman's Fiction: A Guide to Novels by and about Women in America 1820-70.* 1978. Urbana: U of Illinois P, 1993.

Bogdal, Klaus-Michael. *Schaurige Bilder: Der Arbeiter im Blick des Bürgers am Beispiel des Naturalismus.* Frankfurt a.M.: Syndikat, 1978.

Dobson, Joanne. "The Hidden Hand: Subversion of Cultural Ideology in Three Mid-Nineteenth-Century Women's Novels." *American Quarterly* 38 (1983): 223–42.

Dronke, Ernst. *Aus dem Volk & Polizei-Geschichten.* 1846. Ed. Bodo Rollka. Köln: Leske, 1981.

DuPlessis, Rachel Blau. *Writing beyond the Ending: Narrative Strategies of Twentieth-Century Women Writers.* Bloomington: Indiana UP, 1985.

Harris, Susan K. *19th-Century American Women's Novels: Interpretive Strategies.* Cambridge: Cambridge UP, 1990.

Jantke, Carl, and Dietrich Hilger, eds. *Die Eigentumslosen: Der deutsche Pauperismus und die Emanzipationskrise in Darstellungen und Deutungen der zeitgenössischen Literatur.* Freiburg i.B.: Alber, 1965.

Joeres, Ruth-Ellen Boetcher. *Die Anfänge der deutschen Frauenbewegung: Louise Otto-Peters.* Frankfurt a.M.: Fischer, 1983.

———. "Frauenfrage und Belletristik: Zu Positionen deutscher sozialkritischer Schriftstellerinnen im 19. Jahrhundert." *Frauen sehen ihre Zeit: Katalog zur*

Literaturausstellung des Landesfrauenbeirates Rheinland-Pfalz. Mainz, 1984. 21-40.

―――. "An Introduction to the Life and Times of Louise Otto." *Woman as Mediatrix: Essays on Nineteenth-Century European Women Writers.* Ed. Avriel H. Goldberger. Westport, CT: Greenwood, 1987. 111-21.

―――. "Louise Otto-Peters." *Nineteenth-Century German Writers, 1841-1900. Dictionary of Literary Biography.* Ed. James Hardin and Siegfried Mews. Detroit: Gale Research, 1993. Vol. 129. 295-301.

Koepcke, Cordula. *Louise Otto-Peters: Die rote Demokratin.* Freiburg i.B.: Herder, 1981.

Kuczynski, Jürgen. *Geschichte des Alltags des deutschen Volkes.* Vol. 3. Berlin: Akademie Verlag, 1981.

Morris-Keitel, Helen G. *Identity in Transition: The Image of Working-Class Women in Social Prose of the Vormärz (1840-1848).* North American Studies in Nineteenth-Century German Literature 15. Ed. Jeffrey L. Sammons. New York: Lang, 1995.

Otto, Louise. "Frauenfrage und Belletristik: Eine offene Antwort." *Neue Bahnen.* 26.18 (1891): 137-39 as cited in Joeres. *Die Anfänge der deutschen Frauenbewegung.* 211-15.

―――. *Frauenleben im Deutschen Reich.* 1876. Quellen und Schriften zur Geschichte der Frauenbildung. Ed. Ruth Bleckwenn. Paderborn: Hüttemann, 1988.

―――. *Schloß und Fabrik.* 3 vols. Leipzig: Weinbrack, 1846.

―――. "Zur Antwort" as cited in Joeres. *Die Anfänge der deutschen Frauenbewegung.* 132-33.

Pankoke, Ernst. *Sociale Bewegung—Sociale Frage—Sociale Politik: Grundfragen der deutschen "Sozialwissenschaft" im 19. Jahrhundert.* Stuttgart: Klett, 1970.

Suleiman, Susan Rubin. *Authoritarian Fictions: The Ideological Novel as a Literary Genre.* New York: Columbia UP, 1983.

Tompkins, Jane. *Sensational Designs: The Cultural Work of American Fiction 1790-1860.* New York: Oxford UP, 1985.

Weerth, Georg. *Georg Weerth: Vergessene Texte.* 2 vols. Ed. Jürgen-W. Goette, Jost Hermand, and Rolf Schloesser. Köln: Leske, 1975.

Willkomm, Ernst. *Weisse Sclaven oder die Leiden des Volkes.* 5 vols. Leipzig: Kollman, 1845.

Otto Dix, "Metropolis," mixed media on wood, 1927–28, Galerie der Stadt, Stuttgart (reprinted with the permission of VG Bild-Kunst, Bonn)

Woman as Sexual Criminal: Weimar Constructions of the Criminal *Femme Fatale*

Barbara Hales

The construction of the sexual-criminal woman, evident in early twentieth-century medical and social discourses, is part of the cultural currency of Weimar Germany. The *femme fatale* as criminal monster occurs in mainstream journalism of the period as well as in Weimar scientific studies. In psychological and social treatises concerning the criminal woman, woman's innate vanity and excess of sexuality motivate criminal action. Weimar street films like Karl Grune's *The Street* and Joe May's *Asphalt* further demonstrate interest in the female criminal, as woman stands in for the evils of the city. Representations of the criminal woman reveal Weimar society's discomfort with modernity in general, including the fear of women's liberation, the new importance of the city, and the fledgling German republic. (BH)

The première of G.W. Pabst's film *Pandora's Box* in 1929 unleashed a flurry of responses in the Weimar press. The film's star Louise Brooks was the embodiment of dramatist Frank Wedekind's Lulu, "an instinct-driven woman, ruthless, egocentric, possessed by insatiable sexual desire, a flame that consumes everything, a whore by nature" (*"Büchse"*). Critics saw a sexual instinct in Lulu that they considered demonic and typically female.[1] The popular reception of Lulu's monstrous sexuality reveals a widespread trend in Weimar Germany to stamp the sexual woman as criminal. Present in early twentieth-century medical and social treatises, the idea of the sexual-criminal woman was manifest in Weimar psychological and sociological writings as well as in police reports of the time. In this paper, I explore the connection between female sexuality and criminality, as understood in the cultural currency of Weimar Germany. Contemporary scientific studies, police reports, and the mainstream journalism of the period portray a close relationship between the independent woman and manifestations of a perceived unnatural female sexuality resulting in criminal/psychotic behavior. Weimar street films such as *The Street* and *Asphalt* demonstrate a penchant for the female sexual criminal.

Implicit in these filmic images are the criminal woman's link to the city and her distance from the traditional bourgeois family.

In order to trace the notion of woman as sexual criminal, it is important to understand the early twentieth-century movement that branded her as a dangerous instinctual being. The years 1890–1910 marked a period of social, political, and economic upheaval in Europe, as women rallied for equal rights. This great debate sparked an interest in the true *nature* of woman. The scientific community felt compelled to explore perceived biological, psychological, and physiological traits that set women apart from men. German neurologist P.J. Möbius, for example, argued that women were "feebleminded" and unable to measure up intellectually to men (11–35).

In his 1907 treatise *Über den physiologischen Schwachsinn des Weibes* (Concerning the Physiological Feeblemindedness of the Female), Möbius begins by comparing the size of male and female brains. The female brain is, according to Möbius, less developed and thus less capable of functioning analytically. It is instinct, not analytical thinking, that drives the female being: "Instinct makes woman animalistic, dependent, naive and cheerful.... Like animals have behaved from times immemorial, so too would mankind remain in its primal condition, if there were only women. All progress originates from man" (18–19). Traits such as the inability to control oneself, jealousy, and vanity also allegedly stem from a life driven by instinct.

Möbius notes that the instinctual woman poses a threat to the very structures of society. Her feeblemindedness and her abnormal behavior, stemming from menstruation and pregnancy, make it more likely that she will break the law in times of change: "If woman were not physically and mentally weak, if she were not generally rendered harmless by various circumstances, she would be very dangerous. In times of political unrest one learns of woman's injustice and cruelty; likewise one learns of women who unfortunately have come to power" (20). For Möbius, it is the duty of the doctor to advise and warn the public about the threat of "feminism" and the modern woman.[2] Women operating in the public sphere, who fail to attend to motherhood, can only expect to be struck down with invalidism (26).[3]

Spearheading the movement to categorize the qualities of woman, Möbius argues that an instinct-driven woman lacks the ability to think independently. This sentiment is shared by his contemporary, Otto Weininger, who believed that woman, incapable of logical thought, also lacked an ego. For Weininger, woman's existence is based solely on the sexuality that is read into her: "Woman is nothing, and therefore and only therefore can she become everything" (394). Woman strives for recognition of her physical beauty, and derives her worth from the adoration that man bestows on her.[4] According to Weininger, "Since women have no respect in and of themselves, they strive to become the object of appreciation for others through desire and admiration" (260). While man is ineffable and indestructible, woman is an aggregate, "detachable" and "dissectable" (276).[5]

Weininger further maintains that woman provokes sex in order to get what she wants. Through coitus, woman can manipulate man into saying and doing things that are to her liking—even force him into criminal deeds on her behalf. Coitus, driven and motivated by woman, is finally a destructive mechanism: "Just as woman strives to self-destruct during coitus, her efforts generally aim at destruction" (309). Weininger ultimately portrays men as vulnerable victims, subject to women's control.

If woman uses eroticism as a weapon, she will be seen as a criminal in the eyes of society. When piety and want of passion are traded for self-assertion and individualism, then the criminal woman is born. Italian anthropologist Cesare Lombroso was the first member of the European medical community to attempt a full-scale systematic study of the criminal woman. *The Female Offender* (1899), written with Guglielmo Ferrero under the pretense of seeking fairness in penal law and administration, is a massive document tracing the alleged biological and psychological traits of the female criminal. While chapters entitled "The Skull of the Female Offender" and "The Brains of Female Criminals" address the physiological make-up of the unlawful woman, other sections discuss the psychological traits of the female recidivist. According to Lombroso and Ferrero, women have many traits in common with children, including vengefulness, jealousy, and cruelty. These traits can be neutralized by maternity and undeveloped intelligence, but if the childish qualities are released, a special type of evil rushes to the surface:

> [W]hen a morbid activity of the psychical centres intensifies the bad qualities of women, and induces them to seek relief in evil deeds; when piety and maternal sentiments are wanting, and in their place are strong passions and intensely erotic tendencies...it is clear that the innocuous semi-criminal present in the normal woman must be transformed into a born criminal more terrible than any man (151).

Here the authors find all women to be potential criminals, equipped with an inborn cruelty. The criminal woman is considered to be a "monster" (152).

For those turn-of-the-century scientists who chose to explore the nature of woman, notions of the instinctual, the sexual, and the non-maternal were seen as a threat to society and were directly linked to female criminality.[6] Much of their rhetoric pertaining to the criminal woman resurfaced again after World War I in the medical and social discourse of the Weimar Republic.

The Criminal Woman: Weimar Cultural Constructions

Möbius's declaration that injustice and cruelty at the hands of woman are immanent in times of political flux reads like a dark omen in predicting the resurgence of the trope of the criminal woman in the 1920s. War, revolution, industrialization, and the advent of the new working woman constituted major changes, which were not welcomed by a populace rocked by the ensuing political upheaval and inflation. Cultural critic Hans Ostwald documented these trends in *Sittengeschichte der Inflation* (The Moral History of Inflation, 1931). In the introduction, he asserts that the German woman who worked during World War I would not easily be pushed back into traditional family life. Ostwald blames the working woman for the breakdown of the family in Germany. In her desire to live life to the fullest, the Weimar woman produced an "erotic giddiness [that could send] the world into a tailspin."[7]

This notion of an erotically induced tailspin recurs in the work of many Weimar scientists and researchers. In the attempt to trace the etiology of female criminality, the connection was again made between the sexual and the criminal woman. In 1923 Erich Wulffen's mammoth project *Woman as a Sexual Criminal* traced first the "psychosexualis of woman," then analyzed various crimes attributed to females. The book explores not only the alleged physical characteristics of the criminal, but also her psychological motivation. Driven by a biological premise—that menstruation, pregnancy, and menopause unleash theft and cruelty in women—Wulffen posits that "female crime is rooted in sex" (49).

Wulffen begins his study by stating that sexual sensibility has a direct effect on criminal activity. Woman's sex instinct is weaker on the average than man's. It is this sexual passivity that is woman's "talisman against crime" (47). But woman also has the potential to develop an excess of sexuality. Her innate vanity urges her into acts of lustfulness as she plays with sex, often turning to prostitution, shoplifting, and murder, among other crimes. According to Wulffen, a woman's whole being is influenced by instinct and thus emotion. Because woman cannot grasp truth or justice, she is not able to observe laws and the authority of the police. Woman is also affected by her love-life, which fosters thoughts of jealousy, hate, and revenge that lead to criminal activity. In this state, she is not her lover's friend, but his enemy: "Erotic or sexual motives make her his adversary because she fears that she herself might be forgotten, or not sufficiently loved or cherished. Everything in the world she judges from an erotic or sexual point of view" (61–62). Finally, Wulffen believes that woman will always remain a sexual being, because she has a "primordial natural function." As long as woman has a connection to childbearing, she is in "bondage to sex" (62).

Like earlier critics Möbius, Lombroso, and Ferrero, Wulffen turns to instinct and sexuality in order to describe the criminal woman: "[A]s soon as the instinctive viciousness of woman is aroused it appears more primitive than man's, and under religious influences (woman-sexual sin) she could be regarded as evil itself" (69). Wulffen's frightening prescription is forced medical sterilization to prevent "degenerate progeny...to eliminate an excessive libido, nymphomania, homosexuality, incest; to prevent prostitution, illegitimacy, infanticide and other immoral offenses" (520).

Wulffen's psychological study of the criminal woman, while the most comprehensive of its kind in the 1920s, is not the only such treatise of its time. Criminal psychologist Hans Schneickert published an extended essay on woman as criminal that was part of a series of papers on female sexuality.[8] Schneickert's *Das Weib als Erpresserin und Anstifterin* (Woman as Blackmailer and Instigator, 1918-19) begins by stating that studies on the criminal woman belong in the area of sexual research. For Schneickert, sexually colored ideas lead the psychopathic woman to crime.[9] But woman is not only responsible for the crime that she directly commits, but also for the other crimes that she motivates. Schneickert believes that the idea of committing a crime may often be attributed to a woman, while the execution of the crime itself must be carried out by male accomplices who have greater bodily strength. There is also the possibility that a crime is perpetrated "because of or for a woman" (Schneickert 30).

Schneickert's study contains numerous examples of the woman criminal and woman's relationship to crime. One purported overriding motive for crime is the desire to dress nicely and look attractive. Schneickert tells the story of one woman who took part in the murder of a widow. When asked why she did it, the answer was "I needed nice hats" (36). Schneickert quotes Lombroso and Ferrero on the topic of woman and dress, as he notes: "A woman steals or kills in order to dress well, like a merchant makes questionable deals to look important" (36). Schneickert maintains that, compared to the turn of the century, crimes committed by women have increased. He echoes Ostwald's prognosis by positing that woman's "process of becoming independent" (*Verselbständigung*) is responsible for the criminality of the early Weimar Republic (39).[10]

While criminologists such as Wulffen and Schneickert produced book-length treatises on the criminal woman, Weimar journals of criminology also carried studies on women and criminality. The *Kriminalistische Monatshefte*, a journal concerned with criminal science and praxis, ran numerous articles on the difficulty of fighting prostitution. In an essay entitled "Prostitution und Kriminalität" (Prostitution and Criminality), Dr. Weinberger writes that prostitution must lie in the nature of a being, more specifically in the anatomy of woman whose degeneracy resembles that of the criminal man. Just as he will turn to theft and other criminal acts, she will play out her criminal tendencies in prostitution. The similarity here lies in each party's relationship to the "world of the anti-social"

(Weinberger 58). In a further *Monatshefte* article on prostitution, police commissioner [*Polizeipräsident*] Dr. Melcher defines female prostitution as an act of self-preservation. While man is affected by the drive to reproduce, moving him to aggressive and polygamous sexual activity, woman must simply meet this demand: "So we see prostitution in league with both of the primal urges [hunger and love]" (Melcher 97). The importance of biology in producing the female sexual criminal, already argued by Möbius and Wulffen, is underlined in the study of prostitution.

The discussion of the female sexual criminal in scholarly books and journals during the Weimar era represents one avenue of investigation running parallel to a wider public interest in crime. From articles in the mainstream press concerning the psychological make-up of the criminal to popular serialized fiction about crime and the rise of the detective novel, crime was a hit. While crime rates were declining in Germany after World War I, the undercurrent of political violence in the 1920s and early 1930s signaled instability at the very core of German democracy.[11] The high profile of crime in the mass media redirected anxiety about the fledgling republic onto a terrifying Other that could be understood and contained.[12] Psychological treatises on the criminal mind in the mass media gave the public "factual" information on the composition of the criminal, helping the average middle class German citizen to compartmentalize the evil Other in order to stabilize a sense of self.[13] Citizens could thus project their own insecurities (economic, political, social) onto a criminal psychosis that was not perceived as their own, unmasking and naming the criminal threat, thereby winning a sense of safety.

The mass media in Weimar Germany showed a penchant for describing crime, exposing the alleged psychological makings of the criminal. The criminal's disturbed state of mind separated her/him from the honest bourgeois individual. The criminal versus honest citizen paradigm was especially evident in coverage of the criminal woman. Just as the scientific community defined the female criminal as an instinctual monster, the mass media did much the same. Widely read newspapers such as the *Berliner Tageblatt* and the *Generalanzeiger für Dortmund* ran articles on the female criminal that sounded much like Wulffen's *Woman as a Sexual Criminal*. In a 1930 article woman is again pictured as instinctual and driven by feeling. She is more reserved by nature, but if the "dam breaks" (if her natural instincts are unloosened), she is a much worse criminal than her male counterpart: "If woman turns to crime, then we observe that all of the strong natural instincts like cruelty, revenge, hate, jealousy, anger, [and] rage break through more strongly in woman than in man" (Samuelsdorff 8).[14] Further, the author insisted, these traits are not immediately evident, as woman is a natural actor. When woman is beautiful and dressed elegantly, she has an easy time committing crimes against men.

The Weimar mainstream press was in agreement that the criminal woman showed a reluctance to perform her familial/reproductive duties.[15] The only way to curb crime then was to teach woman her ethical responsibilities (Samuelsdorff 8). Ethical accountability involved woman's place as protector of home and hearth. Any alternative behavior was labeled deviant.[15] The pairing of biology and criminality (menstruation, pregnancy, menopause = criminal activity) remained popular in the press. Woman's "corresponding stages of life" led to psychological problems, she being less able than man to reason and thus less able to answer for her criminal deeds.[17]

Female deviance and the link with criminality were often depicted in the mainstream press, as in the scientific community, in relation to prostitution. The lustful and lascivious woman criminal was a media obsession. Weimar critic Thomas Wehrling, in an article for *Das Tagebuch*, maintained that Berlin was becoming a whore. Borrowing from Otto Weininger's categories of mother and whore, Wehrling asserts that most women vacillate between the two categories. Given a chance (and access to "anti-impregnation devices"), woman will "learn to enjoy but she [will forget] how to have a destiny" (722). In the age of alleged postwar decadence, "short-skirted, silk-stockinged females" are no longer interested in bearing children, but instead walk the streets. Wehrling criticizes the good strong German men who mix and mingle with the "ghastly" street girls of Berlin. The whores of Berlin not only include those down-and-outs who walk the streets, but also bourgeois women, "[a] generation of females...that has nothing but the merchandising of their physical charms in mind" (721).[18] For Wehrling, a certain moral decay has descended on the middle class: woman has fallen prey to moral corruption. Berlin, as whoring capital of Germany, can only claim a type of Hellenism, "[a celebration of] its festivals in dark rooms adjoining every dance hall" (721).[19]

The German press too referred to Berlin as a whore (or the Whore of Babylon). Paul Gurk wrote about Berlin in 1923: "I am Berlin, the large city full of vice and desire! In me deceit goes around like a lap-dog on a blue leash, the lie like an adored flirt with her made-up mouth! Murder wears heroes' honors, and blessed unscrupulousness owns the earth!" (qtd. in Bergius 103). Berlin as sensual metropolis was a dangerous space where crime and death were associated with the prostitute. It was also a space in which money transactions, political struggles, industrial development, and perceived sexual perversions tore at the fabric of traditional bourgeois society. The prostitute's body represented this excess and chaos, and, like Otto Weininger's woman, the whore of the city was seen as a "dismembered, dead, phantasmagorical body" (Bergius 102). Expressionist artist Otto Dix's rendition of the city-as-whore, entitled *Metropolis*

(1927–28), is a look into fragmented city life involving the prostitute's relation to the metropolis in its various dismembered scenarios.[20]

Dix's *Metropolis* is a triptych painting in which a large scene at a jazz bar is flanked on the left by street walkers and on the right by androgynous beings dressed as women. Each aspect of the city—the cafe, the street, and the theater district, respectively—is portrayed. The women who inhabit these spaces are seductively dressed in silks, lace, jewels, and feathers. While the women in the center panel are most obviously wealthy, there is very little difference in the style of dress worn by any of them. These urban women dance, flirt, and otherwise parade themselves through the city space, claiming it as their own. It is clear that the street walkers in the left panel are prostitutes, but the elaborate costumes of all the women suggest a flirtatiousness and coquetry associated with women on the market.[21]

Read against the backdrop of the work of criminologist Wulffen, Dix's painting displays a city teeming with prostitutes. For while the common prostitute sells her body openly on the street, "the office girl merely changes her lovers every half year and only permits him to take her out, spend on her and give her presents" (Wulffen 496). Wulffen suggests that flirting, coquetry, and sexual relations outside marriage are refined forms of prostitution, which are in fact grounded in the "physiological makeup" of every woman and are "ineradicable" (496).[22]

Dix's women of the city are sexual and aggressive. Like the city, they offer themselves freely and generously.[23] In *Metropolis* they represent appendages to the wider being of the city, where a "good" time can be had by all. In Ursula von Zedlitz's rendition of a Berlin ball, it is evident that the objectified body of the prostitute is the city:

> The faces of women in the masses are untrue and uninteresting. They wilt surprisingly quickly with the spiritless rhythm, so that the individual layers of powder separate from one another and the lips become cracked under the rouge. They lose every sign of individuality and are only limbs of the thousand-headed beast (394).

For Otto Dix as well as for other critics who wrote about Berlin, the "thousand-headed beast" constitutes the city.[24] Just as Siegfried Kracauer's dancing Tiller Girls condense into ornamental figures in their stadium performances, their relation to the "locus of the erotic," their collective identity as "monstrous figure," is linked to the masses from the offices and factories of the city (Kracauer, "Ornament" 68–70). Thus, the sexual woman in her myriad forms is troped as city, collective, mass, and potential transgressor.

Weimar's Criminal *Femme Fatale* and the Street Film

The danger of the city and the draw of the prostitute are overriding themes in Karl Grune's 1923 film *The Street*. Grune's film projects the lure of the city, only to have the desirable metropolis manifested in the seductive prostitute, who wreaks havoc on her unsuspecting male victims. The film begins with an introductory text that foreshadows the threat of the city: "There comes a moment in the life of nearly every man, be he good or bad, when, appalled by the monotony and drabness of his daily life...he longs for the unknown, for the glamour and excitement of the other man, the man in the street." Before the first pictorial image appears on the screen, the threat of the unknown and the glamour of the "street" is established. When the initial text disappears, the establishing shot shows a man stretched out on a sofa in a dark room. The accoutrements of the room signal that he is a member of the petty bourgeoisie. His wife, busily preparing supper in the kitchen, also displays the stereotypical features of the lower middle class milieu: stout with a tight fitting shift and hair in a knot behind her head, she seems a dutiful if uninteresting housekeeper and cook. In the following sequence, it is not the wife's soup that stirs the man into motion, but the shadow play that is reflected onto the ceiling from the street outside. Light and dark combine to reveal silhouettes of people who meet and pass in the night. The shadow of a woman is greeted by the shadow of a man—the man follows the woman as she departs. The suggestion of a chance meeting or proposition intrigues the man on the couch who tries to touch the shadows, grasping at the moment. This brush with seduction draws him to the window where the evening activity of the street is turned into a montage of carnival images. Happy people, lighted advertisements, flaneurs, prostitutes, fireworks, and a roller coaster meld in and out of focus to create a frenzy of images representing his fantasy of city life. Moved by the perceived activity of the street, the man flees his wife and apartment, failing even to eat his evening meal.[25]

The beginning sequences of *The Street* promise a conflict between traditional petit bourgeois morality and the draw of night life. The place of seduction in this struggle is suggested in the shadow world, where men and women meet and mingle. The sexual draw of the city is further depicted in the next sequence where the male protagonist is peering into shop windows, inspecting advertisements depicting scantily-clad women in provocative poses. At this point the predatory woman makes her move. From the shadows of the street a woman emerges, claiming to have been robbed. Grune's prostitute figure is a trickster and an exhibitionist, whose pathetic appeal for help immediately calls her motives into question. Her black dress and black felt hat lend an ominous feeling of foreboding. Hemmed in by the dark streets and alley ways, the protagonist is locked in a dangerous scenario.

The street itself seems to play the role of prostitute, as the protagonist falls under its spell. A 1923 review of *The Street* likens it to a seductress (*Anlockerin*): "Her glittering flowing life, her flirting pairs and the places of modern excess have thrown an upright philistine off course" (*Vorwärts* 10). The classification of "street film" given retrospectively to Weimar films such as *The Street, Joyless Streets,* and *Asphalt* suggests a fascination with the street in all of its "dark corners and angles" (Rotha 206).[26] The street offers the seductive lure of the unknown and promises an escape from bourgeois sensibilities. It further holds the lure of cafes and nightclubs, where sexual pleasures abound, tempting its protagonist with "life in shimmering ballrooms" (*Deutsche Allgemeine Zeitung* 9). Here the threat of the street blends with the draw of the prostitute to threaten the everyman's existence.

The prostitute's hub is the nightclub. Here she tempts the protagonist who is already seduced by her beauty. Entering the club, he finds himself on a balcony with a view high above the crowd. In a moment of flushed vertigo, the scene spins out of control. Dancers are turned on their heads, and the protagonist envisions himself in the middle of this confusion. The overriding message that he is no longer in control of the situation is accentuated by the intoxicating opulence of the club. Beautiful women dressed in expensive silks, dapper men, and an abundance of champagne signal decadence, perversion, and chaos not unlike that of critic Wehrling's description of Hellenic rhapsody. In this atmosphere the prostitute seduces the protagonist as well as a wealthy man from the provinces, by partaking in a card game with two of her male accomplices who win the protagonist's money from him. The petty bourgeois hero is forced to give up a check that is not his in order to pay for his gambling debt.

At the card table, time and social convention seem to stand still. Feminist critic Mary Ann Doane's idea of a femininity that is outside of time ("the glance, the smile that signifies no lasting commitment") coincides with the game of chance that is not rooted in cause-and-effect logic (Doane 156–57). In this space the prostitute is best able to disrupt and displace. She comforts the protagonist, while his very bourgeois identity, symbolized by the wedding ring, is stripped from him. Like the *femme fatale* in G.W. Pabst's *Pandora's Box*, Grune's prostitute is a dangerous omen for the gambling man. Just as Lulu drives Alwa into exile and to the ship where he succumbs to his gambling urges, *The Street*'s prostitute coaxes the petty bourgeois adventurer into a card game that could potentially be his last.

Karl Grune's portrayal of the prostitute and her relation to the game of chance finds an echo in Weimar criminologists' assessment of prostitution. The prostitute has a strong connection to the "world of the antisocial," with little respect for traditional social conventions (Weinberger 58). The dance hall and the gambling table provide the prostitute with an environment apart from social restriction, a place where she can foster criminal action: "The practiced prostitute does not find it difficult to lead the aroused—and often also drunk—visitor to excessive spending. To cover the expenses, the first step away from the righteous path occurs, the removal of money from the entrusted cashbox, the embezzlement of others' money" (Aschaffenburg 108).[27] It is the prostitute who tempts *The Street*'s protagonist into gambling away a check that is not his own, reflecting Schneickert's notion that woman drives man to commit illegal deeds.

The chain of signification, prostitution—game of chance—criminality, is evident in both the film's narrative and in Weimar treatises on criminality. Ernst Engelbrecht and Leo Heller describe the relationship between prostitution and the criminal nature of the gambling hall in their 1926 essay *Figures of the City*:

> Just as dangerous are the wild gambling clubs.... Here, too, there are really always all kinds of scoundrels who become friendly with inexperienced guests and rob them and steal from them, not to mention that these wild gambling enterprises are greatly favored by sharps, among both the managers and the guests. In these wild gambling clubs, just as often as in the nightclubs, we find lots of "ladies" who have settled there for reasons of business, when they do not prefer strolling up and down the streets asking for love (724–26).

The above quote resonates with the narrative of *The Street* and reflects sentiments on criminality that were also evident in the Weimar press. For the street and the city, driven by the components of "asphalt, cars, people, street lights, the ballroom, the apartment house—wine, card-playing, murder" were to be taken in deadly earnest (*Montagspost* 9). A 1922 review of *The Street* underlines the notion that Grune's film was a sign of the times. In *The Street*, as well as in contemporary Weimar cultural constructions, the metropolis translated into danger and death: "The vision of the street...the caricature of an age that sacrifices its soul to the factory, and that deadens itself in crazy capers. The dance of death of an epoch that shouts itself down in order to drown out its own lamentation" (*Filmkurier* 13). The vision of the street illustrated in Grune's film anticipates Otto Dix's *Metropolis* and underlines the relationship between the city and the criminal woman.

In the last part of *The Street* the prostitute uncovers her true inclinations by seducing the film's protagonist in her rundown apartment. The next sequence of events—the prostitute's accomplices kill the man from the provinces and frame the protagonist for the murder—weaves a tangled scenario, from which the protagonist seemingly cannot escape.[28] The prostitute testifies against the protagonist in court, charging him with the murder of the man from the provinces. Only a small girl living in the apartment (the daughter of the prostitute and one of her accomplices) attests to the protagonist's innocence. At this point, her innocence is contrasted with the criminal inclinations of the prostitute. But as the prostitute wraps the girl in a large cloak, there is the suggestion that the daughter may in time follow the lead of her mother (and her criminal father). As criminologist Erich Wulffen stated: "[T]he prostitute lies dormant in every woman—physiologically and psychologically" (493), and "lowly birth or inferior education" could hasten a woman's already innate desire to practice the trade of prostitution (495). If one reads the film through Wulffen's text, the little girl is promised a bleak future. In a larger context, the germ of the criminal woman, found in the most unlikely places (and bodies) has the potential to strike at a moment's notice.

At the end of *The Street*, the protagonist is saved from his planned suicide and returns to his wife, who has waited up for him. Both wife and husband look out of the window at a street that is devoid of all activity in the pre-dawn hours. While the end of the film gives hope that solid bourgeois values will triumph over the dangers of the street, the continued importance of the street is a bad omen. Although the street is empty when the protagonist returns home, it will soon fill with the activity of daily life, only to be followed again by the rhythm of the night and the criminal activity that evening suggests. Read against the Weimar citizen's need to demonize the criminal as Other, the film's ending confirms the notion that the average burgher is not the criminal, but that the Other lurks just around the corner. Vigilance is needed to protect against the criminal, especially in recognizing and avoiding the prostitute whose "theatrical talents" can fool the unsuspecting male (Samuelsdorff 8).[29]

The theatrical talents of the criminal woman may also be seen in Joe May's classic street film, *Asphalt*. In a conflation of city life with criminality, May captures the motion and chaos of the street. *Asphalt* begins with a montage of fire, darkness, and men pounding the asphalt of the street. The intertitle in the opening sequence reads: "Asphalt pavement, noise and turmoil, feet and wheels constantly on the move: city life." The city's erratic movement, the presence of trams, cars, and people teeming in the streets, suggests the excess of city life. May's moving camera also gives the feeling of vertigo and helplessness, as the viewer is tossed about in the confines of tall buildings and structures. From scenes of the city, the film quickly cuts to a shot of a bird in a cage. The notion of being caged in or entrapped is underlined by the preceding montage of the city. *Asphalt*'s introduction thus establishes a conflict between the individual and the overwhelming forces of the street.[30]

The object of entrapment in *Asphalt* is again the petty bourgeoisie. The picture of the caged bird is followed by a representative view of a burgher's apartment: jars of fruit and vegetables are neatly displayed on a shelf, a clock is foregrounded, and an older couple appears drinking coffee and reading the newspaper at the kitchen table. The old woman's comment—"my goodness, nothing but sensational reports"—offers a juxtaposition of the safe but stagnant world of the small apartment to the world outside.

From the apartment of the bourgeois couple the film again cuts to scenes from the street. Street lights go on—evening approaches. People stream down the streets, some stopping to look at displays in the shop windows. The film focuses in on a purse being snatched amidst the turmoil of the throng. As passers-by stop to watch a woman in a shop window trying on a pair of silk stockings, criminals manage to steal the contents of an unsuspecting woman's purse. The viewer is invited to make a connection between female sexuality (the sensual act of brushing a silk stocking against the skin) and common criminality. The next scene confirms this linkage with the introduction of the criminal woman.

Asphalt's version of the criminal woman is a diamond thief. Petite and well-dressed, she appears quite harmless to the clerks in the jewelry store who are willing to display an assortment of loose diamonds for her. As the woman (Else) proceeds to flirt with the jewelry attendant, she skillfully knocks a diamond to the ground and picks it up with her umbrella point. Later, after being apprehended, she admits, "I didn't invent the trick—I read about it in a newspaper." Myriad associations concerning woman's relationship to the city and to the print medium immediately come to mind. Feminist critic Patrice Petro has noted that the illustrated press often assumes a gender-specific readership. Projects undertaken by the Ullstein press, among other publishing houses in Weimar Germany, addressed a female audience: "While media institutions clearly recognized the importance of female audiences, they also understood the need to channel and direct those audiences for commercial or political purposes" (Petro 90). The journalistic desire to cover women's issues and experiences, "bind[ing] them to pleasurable forms of consumption," is in line with the draw of big city department stores (90), inviting woman to become a modern consumer.

For those women who were seduced by the glitter of the city's goods, criminality was one way of obtaining desired items. Weimar criminal psychologist Aschaffenburg finds women drawn to the activity of stealing because they are naturally prone to dishonesty and also attracted to "others' property" (*fremd[es] Eigentum*). Especially appealing is the department store, which is filled with others' goods: "The offense of shoplifting is almost exclusively perpetuated by the female sex...women who are overwhelmed by the display of an abundance of goods want to acquire all kinds of things" (Aschaffenburg 181). Wulffen states that young women succumb to the "seductions of the colorful store displays, when a favorable opportunity is offered them.... 'There is so much of it lying about, that one thing wouldn't be missed,' these girls declare at the trial" (82-83). The space of the city as home for the burgeoning press and for the sparkle of fashions designed to appeal to female consumers supports a reading of *Asphalt*'s jewel thief as the archetypal urban criminal—one who is out to "gratify her vanity" (Wulffen 76). Also connecting the city to woman's desire to steal is the increased stimulation it offers them. Wulffen states: "It must be asserted generally that political unrest has increased—temporarily, perhaps—woman's motor urge, so that she is more easily tempted to crime and particularly to theft. Nor can there be any doubt that the social turmoil has excited and heightened her sexual energies" (84). The increased tempo of city life is linked here to sexual stimulation and female criminality.

It is clear that the jewel thief Else is not merely a criminal, but a sexual criminal. As the arresting officer at the jewelry store (Sergeant Holk) refuses to drop the charges against her, a sexual struggle ensues. When Holk agrees to go to Else's flat in order to retrieve her papers, she uses all the powers of her sex to win him over. Dressed in black lace pajamas, Else physically challenges Holk to disregard his duty as a policeman and succumb to her seduction. As she knocks off his hat in an act of passion, the suggestion that criminality has triumphed over the law is apparent. A shot of Holk's helmet lying on the floor represents the powerlessness of the law vis-à-vis the sexual woman as criminal.

Wulffen's thesis that criminal acts committed by woman are the ultimate release of sexual urges offers an interesting subtext for *Asphalt*. The jewel thief's intense sexuality, apparent in her relations with the jeweler, are underlined in her attempts to seduce the police officer and in her demeanor and lifestyle. Wulffen expands on the sexual woman as criminal in the specific category of the woman thief: "The human motor impulse in general and the criminal impulse in particular is nourished by the individual's sexual energy.... Women and girls of a stronger and more active sexuality are more disposed to it" (75). For Wulffen, the primitive grasping motion is heightened by sexual energy. If we follow Wulffen's line of reasoning that sexuality is the root of criminality, then an "excessive" female sexuality is the motor for the woman thief.

After the seduction scene, *Asphalt*'s narrative returns to the world of the petit bourgeoisie. Holk's father, at the kitchen table reading a copy of the *German Criminal Investigation Paper*, waits for his son to return home. The senior Holk, also a policeman, stands for stalwart traditional morals. Like the wife in *The Street*, the senior members of the Holk family represent old Wilhelminian values of order and virtue. In contrast, their son has been tainted. A victim of the modern woman, young officer Holk is a marker for changing times, the lure of the street and the dangerous criminal woman.[31] His inability to accept his father's cigar, a passing on of masculinity and authority, underscores the junior Holk's precarious position.

Else's appraisal of her lover Holk also symbolizes a Weimar in flux. As Else looks at a picture of Holk and compares it to one of her criminal lover, two ways of life are being contraposed. While one (law and order) seems to win out over the other when Sergeant Holk is forced to kill Else's criminal lover, the love scene between Holk and Else lends a feeling of foreboding with respect to the power of the female criminal. Else rejects Holk's suggestion of marriage, questioning the logic of pairing a policeman with a thief. She admits it is not necessity that has turned her into a thief. Displaying her collection of jewels, money, and clothes, Else notes: "Necessity, does this look like necessity?" Her compulsion to steal underscores woman's psychotic relationship to crime. Measured against Weimar criminologists' reports of the criminal woman, Else's irresistible desire to commit crime is an instinctual urge lying dormant in every woman, awakened by "unnatural" sexual drives and the desire to please men: "Vanity urges her to become the center of the world of men. Here jealousy, hate and falsehood lead her into crime, which again takes on a sexual coloring.... Her whole being, inward and outward...impels her to *lustfulness*" (Wulffen 53–54). Else's outbreak of laughter after admitting her criminal nature illustrates the psychosis of crime. The criminal woman's histrionic nature signifies fraud, narcissism, and ultimately death.[32]

In the final scene of *Asphalt* the criminal woman is put behind bars. Else is held at the police station for interrogation concerning the death of her criminal boyfriend. Her confession has allowed young Holk to be released. The Holk family is reunited and Else's criminal influence seems to have been eradicated from the law-abiding Holk clan. But Holk is still entranced by Else, and indicates that he will wait for her release. One reading of the film suggests that Else has changed her criminal ways, but the last filmic image gives evidence to the contrary.[33] As Else is led to her jail cell, Holk is separated from her by a metal grate, symbolizing the difference in their true natures. The criminal woman remains a criminal; the bourgeois man is different from and at the same time linked to the criminal woman in his desire for her.

Fear of the criminal woman and a dread of the street permeates Joe May's film *Asphalt*. The conflation of woman and city spells trouble for the unsuspecting man who is drawn in by "her" corruption. Woman as psychotic criminal, one who is forced by her urges to commit crime, is also foregrounded. Here criminal woman is a signifier, an overrepresented body that is used to create the notion of pure evil (Doane 2).[34]

In Weimar psychological and social discourse concerning the criminal woman, the attempt is made to foreground a certain difference vis-à-vis the middle-class bourgeois community. In the case of Helene Basedow for example, the trend of defiling and scapegoating woman as sinister and Other is apparent. Basedow, a young woman who committed a series of crimes in the late 1920s, becomes the embodiment of evil, the "small blonde satan," dangerous in her eroticism: "This small girl is such a pronounced vampire-type, that even the juvenile court judges, used to so much misery, cross themselves.... [T]he absolute lack of shame in word, gesture, and deed clearly shows the extent of her spiritual inferiority" (Hyan 101).

Basedow, like the criminal woman in *The Street* and *Asphalt*, is emblematic of Weimar society's discomfort with modernity in general, and the development of the New Woman in particular. The obsession with criminality in the Weimar press and in criminal journals of the time does not correspond to an actual rise in criminality. Rather it portrays a fear of change and the threat of urban lifestyle and industrialization that characterized the 1920s and early 1930s in Germany. The construction of the criminal woman became a signifier for the fear of women's liberation, the new importance of the city, and for the fledgling nature of the German republic. To identify the criminal, specifically the female criminal, was to differentiate good from bad, and thus extract evil from the community.

Notes

Unless otherwise noted, all translations are my own.

[1] Weimar critics commented extensively on Pabst's Lulu character. In his short sketch of Lulu, Ritter reiterates the notion of feminine sexual instinct: "[D]er Sexualtrieb, den [Lulu] verkörpert, ist dämonisch. Sie ist die Urgestalt des Weibes. Selbst triebhaft, entzünden sich die Triebe aller an ihr. Alle begehren sie und gehen an ihr elend zugrunde." Pabst's film is based on Frank Wedekind's 1902 drama of the same title.

[2] Möbius states: "Viel wichtiger scheint mir das zu sein, dass die Aerzte sich eine klare Vorstellung von dem weiblichen Gehirn- oder Geisteszustande verschaffen, dass sie die Bedeutung und den Werth des weiblichen Schwachsinnes begreifen, und dass sie alles thun, was in ihren Kräften steht, um im Interesse des menschlichen Geschlechtes die widernatürlichen Bestrebungen der 'Feministen' zu bekämpfen. Es handelt sich hier um die Gesundheit des Volkes, die durch die Verkehrtheit der 'modernen Frauen' gefährdet wird" (26).

[3] Möbius makes the claim: "Versagt das Weib den Dienst der Gattung, will es sich als Individuum 'ausleben,' so wird es mit Siechthum geschlagen" (26).

[4] Woman does not exist, but for the thoughts of others: "Die weibliche Eitelkeit ist also stete Rücksicht auf andere, die Frauen leben nur im Gedanken an die anderen" (Weininger 260).

[5] Weininger continues the above line of reasoning: "Der Mann ist unendlich rätselhafter, unvergleichlich komplizierter. Man braucht nur auf die Gasse zu

gehen: es gibt kaum ein Frauengesicht, dessen Ausdruck einem da nicht bald klar würde. Das Register des Weibes an Gefühlen, an Stimmungen ist so unendlich arm!" (277).

[6] For further information regarding the *femme fatale* of the early twentieth century, see Heller and von Braun.

[7] Ostwald saw a Germany in flux with respect to the position of woman: "Ein erotischer Taumel wirbelte die Welt durcheinander. Viele Dinge, die sonst im stillen sich abgespielt...traten in die grelle Öffentlichkeit. Vor allem stellten sich die Frauen auch auf anderen Gebieten gänzlich um. Sie traten mit ihren Forderungen, besonders auch ihren sexuellen Forderungen, viel deutlicher hervor" (introduction).

[8] Together with Schneickert's paper, other papers in this series include *Die Prostitution bei den gelben Völkern, Der Frauenüberschuß nach Konfessionen, Beiträge zum "Zahlenverhältnisse der Geschlechter,"* and *Die Scham*. Another publication appearing around 1920 was *Die sexuelle Untreue der Frau*, a two-part study by Dr. Heinrich Kisch exploring "die Ehebrecherin" and "das feile Weib."

[9] Typical crimes of this nature include blackmail and forgery. Schneickert states: "Das Weib neigt seiner ganzen Veranlagung und Erziehung nach erfahrungsgemäß mehr zu hinterlistigen Erpressungen...ganz entsprechend seiner Vorliebe für anonyme Beleidigungen und Verleumdungen, oder für Gift bei Mord [sic]" (8).

[10] Schneickert's use of the German word *"Verselbständigung"* appears in a negative context, implying that something is getting out of hand.

[11] Political assassinations in the early 1920s were followed by communist/national socialist antagonisms in the late 1920s and early 1930s. For a more detailed look at political crime, see Blasius. For a comparison of criminal statistics (specifically statistics involving the female criminal) from 1911 to 1927, note *Kriminalistische Monatshefte* 3/6 (June 1929) (136-37), and von Koppenfels (16-33).

[12] Leslie Pahl, in her dissertation on crime in the Weimar Republic, offers an excellent discussion of Weimar crime and perceptions of the criminal Other (1-16). I am indebted to Pahl for my argument.

[13] The economic plight of the German middle class during the inflation period of the Weimar Republic on into the late 1920s and early 1930s is a much-discussed phenomenon. For a Weimar viewpoint of this cultural occurrence, note "White-Collar Workers" (181-94).

[14] The study of the criminal woman could signal a heightened sense of self for the Weimar citizen looking to establish a strict delineation between good and bad, healthy and sick. This thesis is complicated by the fact that the construction of the criminal woman, in psychological treatises as well as in the general press, claimed that the criminal woman was a normal woman out of control. Thus, every "normal" woman was a potential criminal.

[15] For further information, see "Verstimmte Frauen: Seelische Abweichungen durch Generationsvorgänge."

[16] Ostwald describes the atmosphere in the lesbian clubs of Weimar, identifying lesbianism with criminality and drugs. Ostwald thus produces an alleged example of supposedly deviant sexual behavior related to criminality (123-25).

[17] The phrasing referring to woman's "corresponding stages of life" is interesting: "Jedenfalls wirken die Generationsvorgänge der Frau in den einzelnen entsprechenden Lebensabschnitten steigernd auf seelische Störungen" ("Verstimmte Frauen").

[18] Here the demarcation between good woman/bad woman is disturbed by Wehrling's pronouncement that bourgeois women are also self-serving prostitutes. Wehrling's social criticism and his direct challenge to the bourgeoisie was atypical of the rhetoric concerning the criminal woman. The sexual woman as criminal, while attributed to every woman, was in fact not advertised as such. Wulffen's monstrous prostitute and Schneickert's woman who kills in order to obtain new hats are very different beings from the petty bourgeois woman, who is interested in hand cream or weight loss.

[19] Note that Wehrling's article first appeared in 1920 (Thomas Wehrling, "Die Verhurung Berlins," *Das Tage-Buch* I [6 November 1920]: 181-83). The road to whoredom, or the trade of sex for money, was associated with both pathology and criminality. Emil Raimann in his article "Sumpfpflanzen der Großstadt" sees the largest group of morally corrupt (*verwahrlost*) young women as psychotic. Characteristics such as "Unbeständigkeit, Schaukelhaftigkeit der Stimmung, Unausgeglichenheit von Willensneigungen" could lead a young woman to a destructive criminal nature. This tendency often led to prostitution. Also contributing to prostitution was a trend towards laziness evident in all women, "das normale weibliche Bedürfnis, sich versorgt und erhalten zu fühlen, entartet zu Faulheit und Willensschwäche und findet in dem haltlosen Bummelleben der Straßendirne Genüge" (Raimann 48-49).

[20] Otto Dix, *Metropolis*, mixed media on wood, 1927-28; Stuttgart, Galerie der Stadt. See Fritz Lang's Weimar film, *Metropolis* (1926), for a sexualized view of the city. The evil robot Maria, who incites a workers' rebellion, is the heart and soul of the industrialized metropolis. A technological marvel (like the city itself), the sexualized robot Maria traverses various markers of the city (nightclub, boardroom, factory), as she fills/represents the space of the modern metropolis.

[21] For an in-depth discussion of Dix's *Metropolis* triptych, see McCall. My discussion of the Dix triptych profits from her excellent interpretation.

[22] Again, the virgin-whore motif is disrupted by suggesting that every woman is in fact a prostitute. Dix's painting, however, does not depict the everywoman of the bourgeoisie, but caricatured bodies. Dix's women are degenerate, sensual, and slightly monstrous.

[23] Maria Tatar in her work *Lustmord* explores representations of sexual murder in Weimar Germany. She examines paintings by Otto Dix and George

Grosz, in which sexual predatory women are mutliated by the male artist who depicts murder as normal "male" rage against women. In creating fragmented and mutilated female bodies, the male artist rejuvenates his masculinity, which had been called into question by World War I.

[24] For an excellent work that discusses woman as the city, see Petro.

[25] Grune's use of light and dark (chiaroscuro lighting) gives the film a feeling of expressionist frenzy or loosening of emotions. Shadow figures seem ghostly, while particular objects (the optician's glasses on the street) take on a life of their own. For a discussion of *The Street* and Expressionism, see Eisner (252–56). Also see Murray (33–41).

[26] For a discussion of the street film, see Kracauer (157–60).

[27] Also see Aschaffenburg for a discussion on gambling and criminality: "Wenn sich auch für die durch Spielleidenschaft und Spielverluste mittelbar veranlaßten Diebstähle und Unterschlagungen keine Zahlen angeben lassen, so ist doch ein enger Zusammenhang kaum zu bezweifeln" (108).

[28] The prostitute first brings the man from the provinces back to her apartment and then leaves him in one part of the flat while entertaining the film's protagonist in another room. This arrangement seems to be the "set-up" for the crime, as the two male accomplices charge the house and rob/kill the provincial man. Both the accomplices and the prostitute flee the house, leaving the protagonist alone (together with a blind man and a child) to answer for the crime.

[29] Samuelsdorff goes on to state: "Wenn nun auch die Frau zwar in einigen berühmt gewordenen Fällen der neueren und neuesten Zeit...den Mann auf dem Gebiet des Betrugs überboten hat, so steht doch fest, daß eine Frau als Betrügerin und Hochstaplerin zwar eine zeitlang, nie aber so lange anhaltend wie ein Mann Erfolg hat" (8).

[30] A 1929 review of *Asphalt* states: "*Asphalt* ist der Film der Großstadt, der Großstadtstraße.... Aus ihren grellen Lichtern, aus ihren tiefen Schatten hebt sich das Schicksal, dem der Held dieses Films, der junge Wachtmeister Holk, unterliegt." *Die Filmwoche* 27 March 1929.

[31] Sergeant Holk is a pointsman for a busy intersection in the city. In this capacity, he lives in the pulse of the city. It is no surprise then that he is finally overcome/seduced by the city-woman.

[32] In *Pandora's Box*, Lulu's laugh also has frightening consequences. Lulu's outbreak of laughter on her wedding night is followed by the death of Dr. Schön.

[33] A Weimar critique of May's film states: "Waren Wahl und Bearbeitung des Manuskriptes von dem Schupomann, der in Gewissenskonflikte gerät, weil er eine Diebin liebt, die sich dann, ohne daß man das ohne weiters für glaubhaft hält, für ihn opfert, auch nicht ganz glücklich" ("Asphalt" 12). This interpretation posits that Else retains her criminal nature at the end of the film.

[34] Doane sees the *femme fatale* as an overrepresented body: the body is given agency independent of consciousness. For a general discussion of the *femme fatale*, see Doane (1–17).

Works Cited

Aschaffenburg, Gustav. *Das Verbrechen und seine Bekämpfung*. Heidelberg: Carl Winters Universitätsbuchhandlung, 1923.
Asphalt, dir. Joe May, with Gustav Fröhlich and Betty Amann, Ufa, 1929.
"Asphalt." *Reichsfilmblatt* 16 March 1929: 12.
Bergius, Hanne. "Berlin als Hure Babylon." *Die Metropole: Industriekultur in Berlin im 20. Jahrhundert*. Ed. Jochen Boberg, Tilman Fichter, and Eckhart Gillen. München: Beck, 1986. 102–19.
Blasius, Dirk. *Geschichte der politischen Kriminalität in Deutschland. 1800–1980*. Frankfurt a.M.: Suhrkamp, 1983.
Braun, Christina von. "Die Erotik des Kunstkörpers." *Lulu, Lilith, Mona Lisa...Frauenbilder der Jahrhundertwende*. Ed. Irmgard Roebling. Pfaffenweiler: Centaurus-Verlagsgesellschaft, 1989. 1–17.
"Die Büchse der Pandora." *Welt am Abend* 2 November 1929.
Deutsche Allgemeine Zeitung. Pressestimmen—Die Strasse. Berlin: Hansa Film Verleih, 1923: 9.
Doane, Mary Ann. *Femmes Fatales: Feminism, Film Theory, Psychoanalysis*. New York: Routledge, 1991.
Eisner, Lotte H. *The Haunted Screen: Expressionism in the German Cinema and the Influence of Max Reinhardt*. Trans. Roger Greaves. Berkeley: U of California P, 1973.
Engelbrecht, Ernst, and Leo Heller. "Night Figures of the City." *The Weimar Republic Sourcebook*. 724–26.
Filmkurier: Pressestimmen—Die Strasse. Berlin: Hansa Film Verleih, 1923: 13.
Heller, Reinhold. *The Earthly Chimera and the Femme Fatale: Fear of Woman in Nineteenth-Century Art*. Chicago: David and Alfred Smart Gallery, 1981.
Hyan, Hans. "In Sachen Basedow und Genossen." *Berliner Illustrirte Zeitung* 20 January 1929: 101–02, 112.
Koppenfels, Sebastian von. *Die Kriminalität der Frau im Kriege*. Kriminalistische Abhandlungen II. Leipzig: Ernst Wiegandt Verlagsbuchhandlung, 1926.
Kracauer, Siegfried. *From Caligari to Hitler: A Psychological History of the German Film*. Princeton: Princeton UP, 1947.
_____. "The Mass Ornament." *New German Critique* 5 (Spring 1975): 67–76.
Lombroso, Cesare, and Guglielmo Ferrero. *The Female Offender*. New York: Appleton, 1899.
McCall, Janet Lee. "Otto Dix's *Metropolis*: Gender and German Identity in the Weimar Republic." MA thesis. U of Pittsburgh, 1993.
Melcher, Dr. "Stellung der Polizei gegenüber der Prostitution nach dem Geschlechtskrankengesetz." *Monatshefte* 4.5 (May 1930): 97–101.
Möbius, P.J. *Über den physiologischen Schwachsinn des Weibes*. Halle: Marhold, 1907.
Montagspost: Pressestimmen—Die Strasse. Berlin: Hansa Film Verleih, 1923: 9.

Murray, Bruce. "The Role of the Vamp in Weimar Cinema: An Analysis of Karl Grune's *The Street*." *Gender and German Cinema: Feminist Interventions*. Ed. Sandra Frieden, Richard W. McCormick, Vibeke R. Petersen, Laurie Melissa Vogelsang. Providence, RI: Berg, 1993. Vol. 1. 33–41.

Ostwald, Hans. *Sittengeschichte der Inflation: Ein Kulturdokument aus den Jahren des Marksturzes*. Berlin: Neufeld & Henius, 1931.

Pahl, Leslie Ann. *Margins of Modernity: The Citizen and the Criminal in the Weimar Republic*. Diss. University of California at Berkeley, 1991. Ann Arbor: UMI, 1993.9203675.

Petro, Patrice. *Joyless Streets: Women and Melodramatic Representation in Weimar Germany*. Princeton: Princeton UP, 1989.

Raimann, Emil. "Sumpfpflanzen der Großstadt." *Kriminal und Abenteuer* 10 July 1929: 48–49.

Ritter, Karl. "Lulu und ihr 'großes Gefolge.'" *Textbeilage zum Illustrierten Filmkurier—Die Büchse der Pandora*. Berlin, 1929.

Rotha, Paul. *The Film till Now*. London: Cape, 1930.

Samuelsdorff, Anny. "Die Kriminalität der Frau." *Generalanzeiger für Dortmund* 14 September 1930: 8.

Schneickert, Hans. *Das Weib als Erpresserin und Anstifterin*. Abhandlungen aus dem Gebiete der Sexualforschung Band I/Heft 6. Bonn: Marcus & Webers, 1918–19.

The Street, dir. Karl Grune, with Eugen Klöpfer and Lucie Höflich, Stern-Film, 1923.

Tatar, Maria. *Lustmord: Sexual Murder in Weimar Germany*. Princeton: Princeton UP, 1995.

"Verstimmte Frauen: Seelische Abweichungen durch Generationsvorgänge." *Berliner Tageblatt* 23 September 1930: 1. Beiblatt.

Vorwärts. Pressestimmen—Die Strasse. Berlin: Hansa Film Verleih, 1923. 10.

Wehrling, Thomas. "Berlin Is Becoming a Whore." *The Weimar Republic Sourcebook*. 721–23.

The Weimar Republic Sourcebook. Ed. Anton Kaes, et al. Berkeley: U of California P, 1994.

Weinberger, Hofrat Dr. "Prostitution und Kriminalität." *Kriminalistische Monatshefte: Zeitschrift für die gesamte kriminalistische Wissenschaft und Praxis* 2.3 (March 1928): 57–59.

Weininger, Otto. *Geschlecht und Charakter*. Wien: Braumüller, 1903.

"White-Collar Workers: *Mittelstand* or Middle Class?" *The Weimar Republic Sourcebook*. 181–94.

Wulffen, Erich. *Woman as a Sexual Criminal*. (Germany 1923) Trans. David Berger. New York: American Ethnological Press, 1934.

Zedlitz, Ursula von. "Berliner Bälle." *Der Querschnitt* 5 (1926): 394–97.

Searching for the (M)Other: The Rhetoric of Longing in Post-Holocaust Poems by Nelly Sachs and Rose Ausländer

Kathrin Bower

The post-Holocaust poems of Nelly Sachs and Rose Ausländer demonstrate shifts toward experimentation in form and message, particularly in relation to religious belief and the expressive potential of poetic language. The experience of the Holocaust forced both authors to confront the interconnections between their Jewishness, their relationship to the German language, and their displacements as homeless exiles. They turned to poetry as a means of mediating the past in the present, and their post-Holocaust writings represent acts of both remembrance and reproduction. As victims and witnesses to suffering, devastation, and loss, Sachs and Ausländer appealed to images of the maternal in an effort to recreate the intimacy and security of the irretrievably lost past, adapting the multivalence of the Mother for their own purposes in the pursuit of a new language of faith. (KB)

Every God, even including the God of the Word, relies on a mother Goddess. —Julia Kristeva ("Stabat Mater" 176)

The biographies of German-Jewish poets Nelly Sachs (1891–1970) and Rose Ausländer (1901–88) are conjoined by the common experiences of growing up in culturally cosmopolitan environments conducive to assimilation and the subsequent violent rupture of this peaceful world by the rise of Nazism. For Nelly Sachs, this was pre-war Berlin; for Ausländer, the city of Czernowitz in the Bukovina. Their writings diverge, however, in the responses to and representations of the past, the trauma of exile, and the shock of the Holocaust. In the aftermath of the Holocaust, Sachs and Ausländer confronted their feelings of trauma and loss, displacement and homelessness through the medium of the poetic word. Their poetic transformations of these experiences demonstrate both parallels—in theme and message—and differences—in form as well as in attitude towards language's capacity to express and represent the tensions between mourning and hope.

Nelly Sachs was born in Berlin as the only child of an assimilated German-Jewish couple. Her father, a manufacturer and inventor, placed high value on German cultural traditions. A sensitive, introverted child, she was drawn to music, dance, poetry, and German Romanticism. She did not identify herself as a Jew and it was not until the enforced implementation of Nazi racial ideology that she confronted her Jewish heritage. Sachs reacted to this coerced categorization by immersing herself in learning the teachings and traditions of Judaism, and was most intrigued by the Kabbalah and Jewish mysticism as these were described and transmitted in the works of Gershom Scholem and Martin Buber. Her readings and reflections on Jewish mysticism further developed her synthetic approach to religion and belief, and resulted in a melding of elements from Christian and Jewish traditions, both in her spiritual conceptions and in her poetry. After fleeing to Sweden together with her aging mother in 1940, Sachs settled in Stockholm and eked out a modest existence by translating and writing poetry. In 1952, she became a Swedish citizen, but although she was welcomed there and had no desire to return to Germany, she never truly felt at home either in Sweden or in the Swedish language and remained loyal to her mother tongue as her language of poetic creation.

Ausländer was born Rosalie Scherzer in German-speaking Czernowitz, the capital of the Bukovina (then part of the Austro-Hungarian empire) in 1901. She was raised in a consciously Jewish household familiar with both the traditions and languages of Judaism. The culturally rich environment and the atmosphere of tolerance in Czernowitz left lasting impressions on her, and her poetry reflects a certain nostalgia for a lost and irretrievable childhood past. Unlike Sachs, who did not make her exodus from her home city until 1940, Ausländer was forced into a life of wandering and exile already in 1921. As a young woman, she emigrated to the United States and eventually settled in New York. She returned to Czernowitz at regular intervals, however, to care for her ill mother. During one of these care missions to Czernowitz in 1939, the outbreak of war made it impossible for her to leave again. She and her mother survived the German occupation in the Czernowitz ghetto, escaping deportation and the fate of tens of thousands of Romanian Jews in the camps of Transnistria by going into hiding.

After the war, Ausländer returned once again to the United States, hoping to earn enough so that her mother could join her in New York. Her mother's death in 1947 before this reunion could take place triggered a nervous collapse that left Ausländer unable to work or write for almost a year. When she began writing again, she wrote only in English. The return to her native German in 1956 took place as inexplicably as her retreat from it, and her use of German as a medium of poetic creation brought with it dramatic differences. Gone was the conventional, rhymed verse that had characterized her pre-war poetry. Her lyric became terse and spare, yet in a form that underscored the multivalence inherent in the word. Her poems after 1956 are alive with neologisms, metaphors, and wordplay, but most characteristic is an unmitigated longing for words to give voice to the past and shape to the future.

As survivors of the Holocaust, Sachs and Ausländer shared a commitment to preserving the memories of that catastrophe and the suffering that accompanied it. Faced with events that defied understanding, both looked to new means of figuring the disjunctive relationship between faith and history, for metaphors and articulations reflective of the conflicts between experience and belief. In different ways, their writings demonstrate a distancing from conventional structures and the security of a mellifluous rhyme, moving instead into a realm of equivocation, fragmentation, and condensation that characterizes much post-Holocaust poetry. Sachs reveals the destabilization of form and familiarity by breaking off lines abruptly and by synthesizing images that seem to aspire to the mystical realm while still trailing roots in the reality of human suffering. Ausländer's lyric becomes increasingly spare and condensed, yet the paucity of words and the brevity of the lines heighten rather than diminish the multiplicity and elasticity of meaning.

For both, the Holocaust catalyzed a crisis of belief and raised questions about the nature of God as well as the capacity to keep the faith in the face of extremity. In their responses to this crisis, they came to question the supremacy of a monotheistic God whose apparent indifference to the fate of his people was shattering and inexplicable if one had accepted the conception of a benevolent and omnipotent divinity. Their questions and explorations led them in search of alternative spiritual images capable of expressing the simultaneity of good and evil, a search that resurrected older configurations of the life cycle as an alternation of destruction and regeneration: the cycle of existence as portrayed in Hasidic mysticism and traditional Jewish theology and as embodied in the even more archaic figure of the Cosmic Mother, the maternal goddess conjoining life and death, creation and destruction.[1]

Both Sachs and Ausländer lost their fathers long before the onset of World War II. Sachs's father died in 1930. The death of Ausländer's father in 1920 catalyzed the first major rupture in her life, forcing her to leave both mother and motherland and venture forth on her own. The poetic depictions of paternal deities in Sachs's and Ausländer's works after the Holocaust indicate a kind of delayed response to their fathers' early deaths, offering a contradictory combination of reverence and disappointment: a nostalgic reverence for the deceased, biological father and a disappointment mixed with lingering expectations in the Divine

Father (Dinesen 30 ff.).[2] The loss of the father effectively intensified and enhanced the maternal bond, which in Sachs's case had been especially close even before her father's death. Once they had settled in Stockholm, Sachs's bond to her mother grew even stronger. Margarethe Sachs was all that she had left of the home and family she had known, and Sachs looked to her mother as an anchoring force, the connection to the reality and home that had been, treating her as patient and muse, confidante and child (Fritsch-Vivié 94).

Ausländer's relationship to her mother was also strong and complex, and many of her poems reflect her attempts to come to terms with her conflicting desires for a reunion with the maternal force even as she remained aware of its destructive potential. Common to the poetry of both Sachs and Ausländer was the turn to the maternal image as a means of negotiating a destabilized relationship to reality.

In the discussion to follow, I examine contrasting figurations of the paternal and the maternal in poems after the Holocaust and explore how myth, archetype, and Jewish and Christian theology intersect in these representations. The cosmic figurations of Father and Mother stand in contrast to more terrestrial and domestic images of the mother in poems thematizing the mother/daughter relationship. To date there has been no systematic reading of the maternal in the poetry of either writer. Claudia Beil's recent comparative study addresses aspects of the maternal, but her primary concern is with the mystical and Romantic resonances in Sachs's and Ausländer's writings and how their poetry exemplifies what she regards as a successful synthesis of German and Jewish traditions. While not denying the significance of mysticism in Sachs's and Ausländer's works, I see the maternal as a provocative point of departure for a rereading of their lyric that takes into account the destabilization of faith and identity engendered by the trauma of the Holocaust.

In Sachs's 1947 collection *In den Wohnungen des Todes* (In the Residences of Death), God is an abstraction, a name spoken with reverence but whose divine presence is absent from the events of the world. This God is an entity apart, hidden, and inexplicable, an essence mediated only in and through dreams. The image of the mother, in contrast, appears repeatedly in many manifestations, both positive and negative: as a nurturing force that ensures peace and love, as the vessel and guardian of memory and suffering, as maternal animal and protectress, and as a barrier to the child's painful acquisition of autonomy. Yet at moments the lyric persona feels bereft of all hope and faith and identifies with a collective of orphans, poignantly articulated by the voice of the "we" in the poem "Chor der Waisen" ("Chorus of Orphans") from the 1946 cycle "Chöre nach der Mitternacht" ("Choruses after Midnight," *Fahrt* 54–55):

WIR WAISEN
Wir klagen der Welt:
Herabgehauen hat man unseren Ast
Und ins Feuer geworfen—
Brennholz hat man aus unseren Beschützern gemacht—
Wir Waisen liegen auf den Feldern der Einsamkeit.
....
Wir Waisen
Wir klagen der Welt:
Steine sind unser Spielzeug geworden,
Steine haben Gesichter, Vater- und Muttergesichter
Sie verwelken nicht wie Blumen, sie beißen nicht wie Tiere—
Und sie brennen nicht wie Dürrholz, wenn man sie in den Ofen wirft—
Wir Waisen wir klagen der Welt:
Welt warum hast du uns die weichen Mütter genommen
Und die Väter, die sagen: Mein Kind du gleichst mir!
Wir Waisen gleichen niemand mehr auf der Welt!
O Welt
Wir klagen dich an![3]

This poem uses the form of a lament together with images of severance and destruction to convey the injustice that was done while the "world" stood by and did nothing. Yet the accusation is directed at a disturbingly anonymous object: "one" has done these things and the world stands accused, but who exactly is to be blamed? The depersonalization of the perpetrator in effect heightens the sense of frustration and loneliness expressed by the orphans. Bereft of mother and father (although not of their memories), and of the opportunity to exact retribution from their oppressors, the orphans can only impotently cry out their denunciations to the world. Their only solace is in the durability of stone, the stone that now holds the memories and legacies of the annihilated parents and the lost past.

The tone of lament and denunciation in Sachs's "Chor der Waisen" underscores the sense of bereavement and betrayal felt by the survivors, but addresses the accusation to the world. In Ausländer's "Vater unser" (Our Father, 6: 274), the accusation is levelled directly at the Divine Father, who is held responsible for the abandonment of his children. The divine claim both to paternity and omnipotence is derisively refuted. In the aftermath of catastrophe and horror, language and the possibility of prayer are called into question and by extension also the validity of the divine word. The credibility of the Father, the power of his word, and the legitimacy of his name are the subject of Ausländer's critique in "Vater unser," a conscious parody of the Christian prayer that provokes reflection on the degree to which Judaism and Christianity, as well as the crisis of belief and the crisis of expression, are interrelated.

Vater unser
nimm zurück deinen Namen
wir wagen nicht
Kinder zu sein

Wie
mit erstickter Stimme
Vater unser sagen

Zitronenstern
an die Stirn genagelt

Lachte irr der Mond
Trabant unserer Träume
lachte der tote Clown
der uns einen Salto versprach

Vater unser
wir geben dir zurück
deinen Namen
Spiel weiter den Vater
im kinderlosen
luftleeren Himmel[4]

By virtue of his exaltedness and his distance from his followers, God as the heavenly Father has sacrificed both credibility and loyalty. Ausländer characterizes the "we" of the once faithful as anxious children, abandoned by the father they had trusted in to protect them. The demand that this false Father take back his name reflects both disappointment and bitterness at the Father's failings, reactions among the "we" that have a stifling effect in the second stanza. The demand that the name be taken back is made after the fact, however, and is preceded by an inability to pray. In the third stanza, the synthesis of Christian and Jewish traditions becomes obvious in the use of the yellow star image. As the symbol of Jewish oppression, not only during the Holocaust but also much earlier in the long history of anti-Semitism, the yellow star here becomes a hybrid of the Nazi-assigned stigma, the mark of Cain, and the crown of thorns in Christ's martyrdom. The Jews are the chosen people, but this chosenness carries with it a stigma, the association of difference and privilege that inspires maltreatment and hate from the other peoples of the world. In the denunciation of the name of the Father there is a mixing of Jewish and Christian conceptions of deity, of the God of the covenant and the merciful Father of the New Testament, but neither one has proven deserving of unquestioning devotion or childlike faith.

Bitterness and disappointment toward an absent God and the lack of divine intervention do not, however, lead to rejection of the Jewish religious world view *per se,* but rather to a selective appropriation of those elements, especially those drawn from Hasidic mysticism that seem to address the poet's specific situation. Thus the figure of the Shekhinah, the female-gendered emanation of God-in-the-World and the tenth and lowest *sefirah* in the hierarchy of divine emanations outlined in the Kabbalah,[5] becomes a figure of identification. The Shekhinah as divine presence is simultaneously part of and apart from God and serves as the mediator between divine and human realms. As the representation of exile, as divine presence in an atmosphere of divine absence, the Shekhinah embodies the diaspora, shame, mourning, and remembrance, wandering the earth in dark garments (Scholem, *Idea* 74). Despite her apparent benevolence, however, the Shekhinah, like the ancient mother that serves as her model, is a conglomeration of both good and terrible aspects: she is both "the merciful mother of Israel" and the "Tree of Death" (Scholem, *Kabbalah* 107). Her attribution as the mother of Israel (Scholem, *Trends* 230) associates her with the condition of exile, defining the historical situation of the Jews, and the fundamental ambivalence that informs the portrayal of the Shekhinah reflects this connection to the Diaspora. The moon and the ocean also represent the Shekhinah and illustrate by their very nature the cyclical condition of redemption and exile, implying that this alternation is as regular and natural as the waxing and waning of the moon or the ebb and flow of the tide (Scholem, *Kabbalah* 151 f.; *Trends* 220).

The Shekhinah, undecidable, hopeful, subject to the vicissitudes of the people's faith and symbolic of their redemption as well as their guilt (Scholem, *Kabbalah* 108), serves for Ausländer as a dualistic mediator between human and divine, imaged in alternating and overlapping figurations of mother and other, and invested with the potential for both good and evil, presence and absence. The Kabbalistic conception of the Shekhinah explicitly indicates that her relative distance to and from the chosen people is determined by their faith and actions. If they doubt and commit evil acts, she retreats further into a state of exile. Conversely, she is drawn closer if the people adhere to the principles of their faith and commit themselves to good works and the study of Scripture (Unterman 181). The figure of the Shekhinah as a construct that contains opposition and conflict without reconciling them offers Ausländer a possibility of negotiating a religious understanding after the Holocaust, one grounded neither in divine omnipotence and exclusionary monotheism nor in an acceptance of the ultimate triumph of evil.

In Sachs's "Immer hinter den Rändern der Welt" (Forever beyond the limits of the world, *Fahrt* 194–95), the poetic subject allies herself with a series of archetypal female representations of marginalization: the sixth-century Christian saint Genoveva, unjustly banished with her newborn child; the Shekhinah, who also represents the state of Israel in exile; and finally the mythical figure of Melusine,[6] the embodiment of otherness as half-woman/half-animal. By linking herself to these diverse representations of excluded otherness, the lyric persona conjoins the Jewish mystical tradition with Christian legend and folk mythology.

> IMMER HINTER den Rändern der Welt
> die ausgesetzte Seele Genoveva wartet
> mit dem Kinde Schmerzensreich
> im Heimwehgestrahl.
>
> Auch *Schechina* kannst du sagen,
> die Staubgekrönte,
> die durch Israel Schluchzende
>
> Und die heilige Tierfrau
> mit den sehenden Wunden im Kopf,
> die heilen nicht
> aus Gotteserinnerung.
>
> In ihren Regenbogenpupillen
> alle Jäger haben
> die gelben Scheiterhaufen der Angst entzündet.
>
> Auch mein Fuß
> hier auf der Straße
> stößt an den Aschenhorizont—
> ein Granatsplitter,
> nachtbehaustes Fragezeichen,
> liegt in der Fahrtrichtung.
>
> Aus der Kriegerpyramide,
> blitzverkleidet,
> erschießt wehrlose Sehnsucht
> die Liebe
> im letzten Schwanenschrei—[7]

The banished maternal figure of Genoveva pining away with homesickness at the edges of the world parallels the image of the Shekhinah, the feminization of Israel. In fact, the two figures are presented as equivalents: "Auch *Schechina* kannst du sagen" (Shekhinah you can also say). True to Buber's depiction of the Shekhinah in *Die Legende des Baalschem* (The Legend of Baalshem, 27) with which Sachs was familiar, she is portrayed here in the second stanza as the suffering woman who weeps and wanders.

With the addition of the figure of the *Tierfrau* with her prescient wounds, the maternal figural chain becomes associated with memory, a connection significant for the poet's own perceived duty as the guardian and vessel of the historical, collective, and individual memories of her people. This animal-woman holds the pain, suffering, and fear of the victims in her eyes, which reflect the fires set by the perpetrators. The heterogeneity of the victims and their experiences is expressed in the fourth stanza in the spectrum of colors refracted in these human/animal eyes, a colorful multiplicity that is contrasted by the monochromatic and single-minded destructiveness of the oppressors. The yellow of the bonfires recalls the stigmatic yellow star used to identify the Jews in Nazi Germany and, like fire, it has an almost elemental, mythic quality, with a history traceable back to before the thirteenth century as the color of choice for designating the Jewish Other.

In the fifth stanza the lyric persona joins the succession of archetypal female figures of exile, suffering, and memory, thereby connecting the mythic past with the literal present. Her figurative foot stubs against the horizon of ashes left by the bonfires that had been burned into the eyes of the *Tierfrau*. Her path leads through a wasteland, a war-ravaged landscape represented *pars pro toto* by a piece of shrapnel: "ein Granatsplitter, / nachtbehaustes Fragezeichen, / liegt in der Fahrtrichtung" (a grenade splinter, / night-housed question mark, / lies in the forward direction). The grenade splinter is not only a synecdoche for the destruction wrought by the war, but in its physical shape as a question mark lying in the path also symbolizes the questioning and doubt that causes the lyric subject to deliberate about how and where to continue her wandering journey. The entrance of the lyric persona in this stanza signals her participation in the process of mourning and memory. Yet the mission to carry on the legacy passed down to her is one fraught with longing and despair and the final lines of the poem leave the outcome open. The dangers to the continuity of memory thematized semantically in the text are formally reinforced by the brutal dash at the end of the last line, where both form and content emphasize the tone of dramatic undecidability. The ambiguity of the poem's end is deepened by the apparent contradiction between the hope for a better world implied in the appearance of love and the portrayal of this appearance as a swan song, a last outcry, which is cut off or interrupted by the final dash and thus left open and undecided.

In the first poem in the 1966 cycle "Die Suchende" ("The Seeker"), Sachs transforms the mythological figure of the Shekhinah into a trope for sorrow, loss, and the lyrical search for home (*Suche* 100):

Sie sucht sie sucht
brennt die Luft mit Schmerz an
die Wände der Wüste wissen von Liebe
die jung in den Abend steigt
diese Vorfeier auf den Tod—

Sie sucht den Geliebten
findet ihn nicht

muß die Welt neu herstellen
ruft den Engel
eine Rippe aus ihrem Körper zu schneiden
bläst sie mit göttlichem Atem an
weißes Palmenblatt im Schlaf
und die Adam träumend gezogen
Die Suchende in ihrer Armut
nimmt zum Abschied die Krume Erde in den Mund
aufersteht weiter—[8]

The female seeker in this poem is in mourning, but her mourning is neither passive nor accepting. On the contrary, she assumes the role traditionally associated with Adam, establishing an alternative tradition of female precedence and transformation by fashioning an object out of her own rib to compensate for her love and pain. She has a privileged relationship to divinity and creation. The reference to godly breath is a further allusion to Genesis (2:7) with its portrayal of the (re)generative power of divine exhalation: "And the Lord God formed man of the dust of the ground and breathed into his nostrils the breath of life; and man became a living soul." The seeker's aspirations to imitate the divine creation of man remain unrealized, however, fixed at the level of a dream, and in her disappointment she ingests the clod of earth that she had sought to imbue with life. The clod of earth that was to become her self-created other becomes instead a part of her, incorporated as substitute gratification for both her desire and her loss.

In the sixth poem in this cycle, the seeker represents not only the condition of exile but also an embodiment of a line of demarcation, a border between the familiar, terrestrial realm and the *horror vacui*[9] of the unknown (*Suche* 102):

Wo sie steht
ist das Ende der Welt
das Unbekannte zieht ein wo eine Wunde ist
aber Träume und Visionen
Wahnsinn und Schrift der Blitze
diese Flüchtlinge von anderswo her
warten bis Sterben ist geboren
dann reden sie—[10]

The seeker as the poetic figuration of the Shekhinah here is missing something that would provide her with a sense of wholeness and harmony, a masculinized other whose loss she mourns. In Kabbalistic mysticism, the Shekhinah is portrayed as joining with God in his male aspect in an act of erotic mystical union, the *hieros gamos*, which was viewed as the symbolic marriage of God and Israel and a celebration of the covenant (Scholem, *Kabbalah* 138). In Sachs's cycle, the female seeker is described as the source of longing in the world, the embodiment of a plea for reunion, incomplete without her Other, figured in the closing poem as a strange hybrid of maternal and paternal qualities:

Was für eine Himmelsrichtung hast du eingenommen
gen Norden ist der Grabstein grün
wächst da die Zukunft
dein Leib ist eine Bitte im Weltall: komm
die Quelle sucht ihr feuchtes Vaterland

Gebogen ohne Richtung ist das Opfer—[11]

This image is paradoxical in its associative conflation of moistness and paternity. The adjective *feucht* (humid) inspires associations with swamps, oceans, and fecundity, which are more often connected with the maternal than with either paternity or fatherland. This play on the concept of wetness and its liquid, oceanic associations in anticipation of a return to origins occurs frequently in Sachs's poetry, where elemental images of water and air recur as multivalent metaphors for maternity, memory, mystical union, and female creative and destructive power. The final line, broken off like an open question, recalls both the form and meaning of the question mark-shaped piece of shrapnel in "Immer hinter den Rändern der Welt" (Forever beyond the limits of the world, *Fahrt* 194–95). Here, however, the victim has become the physical manifestation of that unanswered question, bent with the weight of inquiry and uncertainty that seemingly has neither direction nor resolution.

The ambiguity surrounding the figurations of the cosmic maternal demonstrate that neither Ausländer nor Sachs is engaged in simple substitution, rejecting untenable faith in an omnipotent Father in favor of unequivocal belief in a maternal power. The absence of the father does not result in an unwavering belief in the mother as a protective force and eternal presence. The figuration of the mother is fraught with conflict and contradiction, compounded by fear of loss, desire for power, and longing for peace. The maternal metaphor that best demonstrates the ambivalent interconnections of desire and resistance, the longing for dissolution and autonomy, is the recurring association of the mother with the sea that permeates the poetry of both. The oceanic maternal metaphor represents the fluctuation of opposing forces as well as the oscillation between fear and desire that characterizes the lyrical mother/daughter relationship. The use of oceanic imagery ranges from allusions to the sea, as a simultaneously creative and destructive originary force, to anthropomorphic representations of the ocean, as a wild and passionate female entity.

The desire for union with the maternal ocean is simultaneously escapist, emancipatory, and erotic, a combination of attraction and repulsion that marks the daughter poet's relationship to her mother muse. In the poems "Pupillen" (Pupils, 2: 89) and "Meer II" (Ocean II, 2: 306–07),

Ausländer plays with the multivalence of the sea as a trope, combining its various associations as a primal originary source and as the fluid commotion of life and death, passion and submersion. "Pupillen" opens with a question that already presumes an affirmative answer, a question intended to provoke the reader into reflecting on the commonality of all origin represented by the maternal sea:

> War nicht das Meer das wellengestufte unsere Mutter
> mit Brüsten voll salziger Milch
> War nicht der Fisch der silbergezackte unser Bruder
> brüderlich herzlich im Schweigen
> Wohnten wir nicht Äonen im kühlen Brand der Wogen
> Waren die strahlenden Sterne uns nicht gewogen
>
> Sie leugnen es nicht sie schweigen beredt
> Nachkommen sind wir nicht erste nicht letzte
> Urrunde Muscheln sind wir wo die Mutter noch träumt
> noch seufzt noch das Wiegenlied singt
> noch die Perlen weint ihre Tränen
>
> Sieh die Pupille die Perle im Glanz unsres Blicks
> Perlmutterrund ist die Welt in ihr die sternende Erde
> grün ist der Grund des Meers wie das Eden der Erde
> wie der erstaunte Wald im See der Pupille[12]

The opening question appears to the poetic voice more rhetorical than real since she seems already convinced of the answer. In "Pupillen" the sea is figured as maternal infinitude, forever bringing forth new life and reabsorbing the lost and the mourned. But despite its encompassing capacity for both life and death, the sea in the opening stanza represents a utopian potential, albeit a remembered and not a present one, for harmonious co-existence. This utopian condition is not denied in the shift from the past to the present tense in the second strophe, but it is represented as a lost condition, or at best the residue of dreams. Yet, afloat in the expansive generosity of the ocean, the eye of the poetic persona reflects on the implications such a condition has for the world. The reflection of the originary ocean in the eye of every beholder implied in the poem's last lines is both a signal and a reminder of those common origins that should encourage harmonious coexistence. With the comparison of the elemental ocean to the fluid lake of the human eye, the poetic voice connects the self with infinity, collapsing the boundaries between the self and the world as well as between the terrestrial and the celestial, the mortal and the eternal. This parallel between the eye (as synecdoche for the poetic "I") and the sea is an empowering and hopeful gesture strengthened by the references to paradise and the implied desire to celebrate the positive potential for life in this world.

This all-encompassing, oceanic, self-regenerating environment is not taken for granted but is rather noted with some perplexity in Ausländer's "Meer II" (2: 306)—a perplexity that is accompanied by the shift from the collective "we" of "Pupillen" to the solitary "I" in relation to the sea.

Ich weiß nicht wie es kam
daß alles was ich sehe und höre
zu Meer wird
der Fremde der Nachbar der Freund
Wellen
die Stadt
      brüllende Brandung
Worte
      Bewegung Schimmer und Schaum

Ich
eine ungenaue Gestalt aus Tropfen
deine authentische Tochter
      Meer
zusammengeballt
und wieder in deine
Wasserschaft gesogen
flüssiger Staub

Wir atmen dich ein
du atmest uns aus
mich und meine Quecksilberschwestern
die Fische
unser Wald aus
Korallen Seemoos Sirenen
hat viele Funktionen
den Tauchern vertraut[13]

Here the poetic persona speaks directly in the first person singular, admitting her filial relationship to the ocean that formed her and addressing it as her mother. This admission of daughterhood, however, does not give the poetic voice a privileged relationship to the life force. She is aware that her appearance in the cycle is momentary, that she too will be reabsorbed in the flow of appearance and disappearance that is echoed in the visual structure of the poem, especially in the weaving and undulating lines of the opening stanzas. The daughter-persona feels a sense of community and solidarity in this amniotic atmosphere, where the symbiosis between mother ocean and her "children" is as natural and regular as breathing. But the oceanic mother also embodies a vast wildness and a violent playfulness that the lyrical persona envies, suffers, and desires:

> Den Delphin auf dem Rücken
> reitest du nachts
> durch Sternsteppen
> dein saftiges Fleisch
> von Haien und Walen massiert
> der heilige Monster Leviathan
> wacht über deine Seele
>
> Dich begleiten darf ich nicht
> nur meine Nerven folgen dir
> aber auch das ist ein Übergriff
> und ich leide die Strafe der
> Steine Scherben gemarterten Muscheln
> Ich trink mich satt an Salz
> Schlamm und den Schickanen der Wetter[14]

She recognizes that a joining with this maternal element is taboo, that even her desire to imagine such a union is subject to punishment, yet she persists in her fantasy of incestuous fulfillment with the maternal substance that both identifies and excludes her. This fantasy escalates from an enjoyment of being tossed about by the waves to the wish to be impregnated by the phallic oceanic mother, who in her infinitude displays both male and female characteristics:

> Auf einer Schäre
> unter Ravello
> möchte ich deinen letzten Anprall erfahren
> deinen kühlen Kuß ohne Kontur
> Eine Perle wächst mir ins Fleisch
> eine harte Träne
> du wächst in mir Meer
> du wächst in mir
> flüssig und hart[15]

The choice of the pearl image here remarkably parallels that in Sachs's poem "Verzeiht ihr meine Schwestern" (Forgive me my sisters) from the *Glühende Rätsel* (Glowing Enigmas) cycle (*Suche* 27):

> Verzeiht ihr meine Schwestern
> ich habe euer Schweigen in mein Herz genommen
> Dort wohnt es und leidet die Perlen eures Leides
> ....
> Es reitet eine Löwin auf den Wogen Oceanas
> eine Löwin der Schmerzen
> die ihre Tränen längst dem Meer gab[16]

In contrast to the bold eroticism of Ausländer's imagery, however, Sachs here uses the oceanic trope as a representation of suffering. The sisterly identification with the silent oppressed is internalized like a pearl, an impregnation with sorrow that does not climax in a dissolution of a sensual, celebratory *jouissance*, but rather reflects the hardened pain of the tormented that can only join with but not be washed away by the salt waters of the sea.

In Ausländer's "Meer II," the daughter's narcissistic desire to join with the watery mirror that reflects her own image is a wish to be reunited with her origins, to combat the fragmentation resulting from separation from the maternal by dissolving into an ocean that is at once the other and the self. She finds herself both reflected and inscribed by the sea of her desire. As a reflection she is outside and separated, but as a mussel-like body etched with markings of her origins, she is physically (re)marked as an insider. The surface of the sea becomes the permeable boundary between the self and/as other and the desire for dissolution is concurrently a desire to disrupt this state of suspension in favor of an erotic union that is paradoxically both expansive and explosive. Through her longing for the oceanic mother the poetic daughter is able to represent her self, utilizing the ocean as a maternal mirror in which she engages in an act of reflection that is at once narcissistic and escapist (Kristeva, *Tales* 42). This self, however, is diffuse, pluralistic, unbounded like the sea it seeks to emulate and converge with in an act of desire that can be read as both destructive (in that the boundaries of the self as a separate entity are dissolved) and emancipatory (in that the self has become open and expansive).

The depiction of the ocean as a kind of mirror for a plurality of selves occurs elsewhere in Ausländer's work. In the poem "Treue I" (Allegiance I, 8: 139), the sea is portrayed as the loyal servant to the lyric persona who, in contrast to the poetic daughter in "Meer II," here seems to be in control of oceanic power. In "Treue I," the otherwise omnipotent ocean is figured as merely a lady-in-waiting, attending the narcissistic musings of the poetic subject with multiple mirrors. The infinitude of the ocean has here become a quality claimed by and embodied in the now unabashedly multiple poetic self.

> Mein Meer
> bewahrt mir die Treue
> in seinen Spiegeln
> find ich mich wieder
> vielfältig
>
> Es singt mich
> zur Ruh zur Unruh
> aufgelöst
> in endlose Rhythmen
> singt es

meinen wässrigen Leib
in den Sand[17]

The multiplicity nurtured in the maternal mirror and the spectoral affirmation of the first stanza is offset by the tonal shifts in the concluding stanza. The ocean's aspect has undergone a sea change from visual to aural and the replication of the image that had affirmed the self becomes equivocal in its tonal variation. The melody brings both harmony and discord, a sense of peace but also disquiet accompanying the fear that the submission to the oceanic maternal lullaby will ultimately lead to the dissolution of the self.

The oceanic imaging of the mother in these poems represents the dualism inherent in the maternal trope and the poet's attitude towards it. The ocean as mother offers the possibility of a return to an originary state of communion with nature and the world as well as the danger of dissolution and engulfment. Thus it inspires oppositional fears in the daughter-poet: the fear of separation as well as the fear of destruction. This oceanic maternal metaphor serves as a point at which the figurations of the Great Mother of myth and the Terrible Mother of ego psychology converge. The poetic attitude of simultaneous longing for union and fear of dissolution evidenced in both Sachs's and Ausländer's oceanic images connects with the ambivalent figuration of the preoedipal mother in ego psychology: "all-giving and all-punishing, an all-powerful being who contains within her the means of satisfying every desire" (Waugh 65). This mother is simultaneously terrible and benevolent and inspires conflicting feelings in the child: fear of destruction and fear of separation. The tension within this polarity is parallel to the tensions that define and inform the mother/daughter relationship and its suspension of an ambivalent oscillation between longing and resentment, mourning and bitterness, desire and language.

Sachs's "Rufst du nun den einen Namen verzweifelt" ("If now you desperately call the one name," *Suche* 18), demonstrates the intersection of desire, disappointment, and dissolution in the sea image.

Rufst du nun den einen Namen verzweifelt
aus dem Dunkel—

Warte einen Augenblick noch—
und du wandelst auf dem Meer
Das Element durchdringt schon deine Poren
du wirst mit ihm gesenkt und gehoben
und bald im Sand wiedergefunden
und bei den Sternen anfliegender erwarteter Gast
und im Feuer des Wiedersehens verzehrt
    still—still—[18]

The poem begins with a desperate call to the One, the incantation of the Name that should bring forth life and light. But the use of the word "desperate" (*verzweifelt*) already predisposes a sense of doubt about the outcome, a doubt reinforced by the abrupt break at the end of the second line that leaves both a visual and a semantic space in which the cry of the lyric persona echoes. The poem is structured to reflect a contiguity and continuity of form and message: the gap between the first and second stanzas concretizes the sense of emptiness and anxiety in the act of waiting for a response. The first line of the second stanza underscores this anticipatory attitude and the hopefulness that inspires the lyric persona to wait just a bit longer in a state of expectancy signalled by a dash into nothingness. The moment of anticipation passes and the "du," designating both the Other and the lyric persona in monologic dialogue, returns to an elemental state of union with the sea.

The absence of the Father is evidenced in the lack of response to the Name, without which the lyric persona cannot become an agent of language. At the end of the poem the lyric voice leaves the realm of language and is engulfed by the stillness of the cosmos. The final dash can be read as symbolic of the plunge into a reunion with inexpressible, maternal silence (Kristeva, *Tales* 311) or of a cathartic absolution preceding potential rebirth. This silence is the infinitude of the void, the threat of engulfment by the Cosmic Mother as well as the anticipation of union with nothingness. By confronting this danger, however, the lyric persona opens herself up to unknown possibilities. What here could be read as a silence on the verge of a rebirth of language, as Gisela Dischner understands the meaning of silence in Sachs's poetry (330), can also be seen as the threshold to a new, self-aware stage of being.[19]

The complexity and ambivalence inherent in the daughter-poet's relationship to maternal infinitude, caught between the desire for identification and the fear of dissolution, give rise to poems that seek to elude the power of the metaphysical, cosmic maternal force and appeal instead to more terrestrial and mortal maternal incarnations: the mother tongue and the mother land. Language for Ausländer became both a reminder of her perpetual exile and of her unstilled longing for the motherland. After the war and the destruction of the fatherland, the word was the only home left to her (5: 98):

Mein Vaterland ist tot
sie haben es begraben
im Feuer

Ich lebe
in meinem Mutterland
Wort[20]

The love of the (lost) homeland is related or connected to the love of a (mother) tongue. In her comparative study of Ausländer and Sachs, Beil argues rather pragmatically that for the poet in exile, the mother language assumes a compensatory function, substituting for the home the poet has lost: the love of country is displaced onto a love of the language associated with that country (62). This substitution principle, however, is not as simple as Beil makes it appear, and becomes especially blurred and confused in Ausländer's peripatetic biography culminating in her return to Germany. Ausländer's decision to settle in Germany in 1965 has been touted as a literal return to the German language.[21] It is important to distinguish, however, that language in this instance is no longer an abstract surrogate homeland, but has become conflated with a geographical place, and that by this act of re-location, the poet hopes to overcome the disjunction of language and home. The displacement moves between the literary and the literal, where the physical context takes on a level of meaning for the poet that cannot be isolated into the realm of the referent (and the word). Therefore Ausländer's retreat into language, although apparent, cannot be viewed as absolute. The discursive space was not enough: she required a locus, a place of association that reinforced her sense of being in the wor(l)d.

In contrast to Ausländer's increasing retreat into language as the last refuge of hope and outlet for subjective if sublimated agency, Sachs's relationship to language was characterized by repeated ruptures, questions, and fundamental doubts about its expressive possibilities. This was especially true of her poetological self-understanding in the years immediately following the Nazi genocide and the traumatizing knowledge that accompanied it. In a 1947 letter to Hugo Bergmann, she despaired that language, worn thin and meaningless with use, abuse, and time, could ever be adequate to the task of representing experience: "Es reicht ja doch kein Wort zu nichts mehr hin, von gestern zu morgen ist eine Kluft wie eine Wunde, die noch nicht heilen darf" (No word suffices for anything anymore; between yesterday and tomorrow there is a chasm that is like a wound, which still cannot heal, *Briefe* 85). For Sachs, the wound, the suffering, was inseparable from its articulation, an intertwining of experience and representation that she expressed vividly in reference to the physicality of her own relationship to poetic language: her metaphors, she stated, were her wounds (Fritsch-Vivié 99). Not only were representation and suffering indistinguishable for Sachs, but both connected back to the religious associations called forth by the Word. This mystical word, the Divine Word made flesh, as the articulation of the heterogeneous multiplicity of human experience and suffering could, however, only be approximated in the language available to the poet. For Sachs, language served both as a tool for probing and fathoming that "other" realm she sensed beyond language and as a means of communicating her deepest fears, desires, hopes, and beliefs.

The loss of faith in a Divine Father and the ambivalent relationship to the maternal confound and disturb the sense of being in the world and in language. To bridge this gap between uncertainty and the desire for stability, for belief, images of the maternal presence counter and offset paternal absence. In Ausländer's poem "Der Dom" (The Cathedral, 2: 214), the cathedral serves as a metaphor for the paternal religious tradition that has lost credibility.

> Ich habe einen Dom geerbt
> Ich kann nicht beten
> Ich stammle Blume Waldruh Wolkenstern
> ich stammle Mutter Meermund du und du
>
> Meine Gebete sind mir nicht geglückt[22]

The poetic "I" has inherited a tradition to which she ultimately lacks access because she does not have the language necessary to participate in it. The image of the cathedral itself represents a barrier between the self and the world, and the poetic subject feels cut off from nature, communication, and language. Her stammered "prayers" are not recognized by the divinity whose house of worship has ironically become her property. She bitterly notes the gap between her words and an absent God who does not or will not hear them. The self-contradictory nature of this admission, however, in which she claims on the one hand to be unable to pray and on the other insists that her prayers were unsuccessful, indicates the absorbing ambivalence of her relationship to God. It is a relationship shadowed with doubts and disappointments, yet one that the poetic "I" can never fully reject or abandon.[23] Significantly, her presence in the cathedral reflects her exploration of her paternal legacy in the house of God, but she has no connection to his language and instead can only speak in maternalistic associative fragments. In the Father's house she speaks the (M)Other's name, an Other with whom she shares a bond that is beyond or outside the language sanctioned by paternal law ("ich stammle Mutter Meermund du und du" [I stammer Mother ocean-mouth you and you]). This stuttering disruption of speech can be read as a conflict between symbolic (linguistic, conscious) and semiotic (prelinguistic, unconscious) processes, representing the poet's oscillation between paternal and maternal allegiance at the level of language.[24]

For Sachs, the striving to articulate the multiplicity and contradictions of experience in the anomie of the post-Holocaust world cannot be separated from her mystical self-understanding and her belief that the capacity to achieve such representation was somehow a demonstration of divine grace: "Wer leidet und wer liebt, muß sich überlassen können bis zum letzten Atemzug, den Staub zu durchseelen ist eine Mission—das

Wort zu finden—Gnade" (Whoever suffers and whoever loves must be able to abandon him/herself until the last breath, to inspire the dust is a mission—to find the word—grace, *Briefe* 173). This connection of suffering and grace, aspiration and language, is what Alvin Rosenfeld referred to as Sachs's unique yet ultimately poetic construct of language as a surrogate home in an atmosphere of absence (364). Language for Sachs was inextricable from suffering, at once pierced with pain, implicated in violence, and steeped in faith it was never merely a medium of literary expression, but rather her spiritual connection to lived existence and future hopes.

Mysticism and doubt, belief and rejection, maternal metaphors and paternal images coexist in both Sachs's and Ausländer's struggles to mediate history, tradition, and experience. The maternal imago in Sachs's and Ausländer's writings serves as the stage upon which religion, history, and biography meet and enact the conflicts informing the struggle for identity and self-realization. In the constructed world of the poem, the lyrical self's perceptions are mediated by the relationship to the maternal as divinity, cosmos, logos, homeland, mother, and originary other. As the German language came to represent the one remaining maternal connection for both poets, their acts of literary creation not only symbolized confrontations with their identity vis-à-vis the past, but also attempts to wrest some control over the configuration of that history through their own re-productions of memory. The play with figurations of the maternal as an approach to history and theology is not unproblematic[25] and could be read as a mere substitution of one reductive trope with one less reductive. A careful reading of Sachs's and Ausländer's figurations of the maternal, however, reveals their revisionary impetus as well as an underlying impulse to reconcile ethics with reality, memory with continuity, and subjective autonomy with community.[26] The daughter-as-poet appropriates the mother as figure and ground, absorbing the maternal qualities she both fears and admires in an embracing gesture of inclusion, seeking through poetry to discover and inhabit the space between self and other, subject and object, secular and spiritual.

Notes

All translations are my own, except where otherwise attributed.

[1] The point has often been made, especially in feminist criticism and theory, that the cult of mother goddess as earth goddess predates worship of a paternal god. See Kahn: "Female earth goddesses antedate male gods...and were associated with the organic cycle of life" (24) and Du Plessis (119).

² Ausländer's respect and awe for her father, who died in 1920, was also attested to by Helmut Braun, editor of Ausländer's collected works and a close friend to the poet during the last twelve years of her life, in a personal communication in August 1993.

³ "We orphans / We lament to the world: / Our branch has been cut down / And thrown in the fire— / Kindling was made of our protectors— / We orphans lie stretched out on the fields of loneliness. / ... / We orphans / We lament to the world: / Stones have become our playthings, / Stones have faces, father and mother faces / They wilt not like flowers, nor bite like beasts— / And burn not like tinder when tossed into the oven— / We orphans we lament the world: / World, why have you taken our soft mothers from us / And the fathers who say: My child, you are like me! / We orphans are like no one in this world any more! / O world / We accuse you!" (*Chimneys* 29–31).

⁴ "Our Father / take back your Name / we do not dare / to be children // How to say Our Father / with a choked voice // Lemonstar / nailed to one's forehead // The moon laughed maniacally / satellite of our dreams / the dead clown laughed / who promised us a leap // Our Father / we give you back / your Name / continue to play the Father / in childless / airless Heaven"

⁵ See Gershom Scholem's excellent and concise discussion of Talmudic treatments of the Shekhinah in *On the Kabbalah* (104 f.). Scholem further explains that the feminine quality of the Shekhinah is interpreted as akin to that of mother, wife, and daughter simultaneously (105).

⁶ Gisela Brinker-Gabler, in accordance with Kersten (178), makes this associative connection in her article on Sachs's poem "Bin in der Fremde" (37). This interpretation is contested in Anke Bennholdt-Thomsen and Alfredo Guzzoni (160), which Brinker-Gabler does not refer to in her analysis. Claudia Beil associates the figure of Melusine with Romanticism and argues that the use of this image in Sachs's poem is evidence of the degree to which Sachs was influenced by the Romantic tradition (226).

⁷ "Forever beyond the limits of the world / the banished soul Genoveva waits / with her child pain-realm / in the homesick-beam. // *Shekinah* you can also say, / the dust-crowned, / the one who weeps through Israel // and the holy animal-woman / with the seeing wounds in her head, / that do not heal / because of God-memory // In her rainbow-pupils / have all hunters lit / the yellow pyres of fear // My foot also / here on the street / stubs against the ash-horizon— / a grenade splinter, / night-housed question mark, / lies in the forward direction. // Out of the warrior-pyramid, / lightning-robed, / shoots defenseless longing / Love / in the last swansong—"

⁸ "She searches she searches / ignites the air with pain / the walls of the desert know of love / which climbs new into the evening / the pre-celebration of death— // She seeks her beloved / does not find him / must re-create the world / calls on the angel / to cut a rib from her body / blows on it with divine breath / white palm leaf in sleep / and the veins drawn dreaming / The seeker in her

poverty / takes the crumb of earth in her mouth as farewell / her resurrection continues—" (*Seeker* 3–5).

[9] Bloom uses this term to designate fear of a godless world, a condition of spiritual anxiety inspired by the anchorless state of exile (83).

[10] "Where she stands / is the end of the world / the unknown enters where a wound is / but dreams and visions / madness and the script of lightnings / these fugitives from somewhere else / wait until dying is born / then they speak—" (*Seeker* 9).

[11] "What quarter of the sky have you taken up / to the north the gravestone is green / does the future grow there / your body is a plea in outer space: come / the source seeks its humid fatherland // bent without direction is the victim—" (*Seeker* 9).

[12] "Was not the ocean the wave-terraced our Mother / with breasts full of salty milk / Was not the fish the silver-serrated our Brother / fraternally sympathetic in silence / Did we not live eons in the cool fire of the waves / Were not the beaming stars inclined to us // They do not deny it, their silence speaks / we are not the first not the last progeny / we are ancient-round mussels in which the Mother still dreams /still sighs still sings the lullaby /still weeps the pearls her tears // See the pupils the pearls in the sparkle of our glance / the world is mother o' pearl-round in it the starry earth / green is the fundament of the ocean like the Eden of Earth / like the astonished forest in the lake of the eye"

[13] "I do not know how it came to pass / that everything that I see and hear / is transformed into ocean / the stranger the neighbor the friend / waves / the city / howling surf / words / movement glitter and foam // I / an inexact form made of drops / your authentic daughter /ocean / compressed / and then drawn back / into your watery realm / fluid dust // We breathe you in / you breathe us out / me and my quicksilver-sisters / the fishes / our forest of / coral sea-moss sirens / has many functions / known to divers"

[14] "On the back of the dolphin /you ride at night / through star-steppes / your succulent flesh / massaged by sharks and whales / the holy monster Leviathan / guards over your soul // I am not allowed to accompany you / only my nerves follow you / but that also is a transgression / and I suffer the punishment / of stones shards martyred mussels / I slake my thirst with salt / slime and the vicissitudes of the weather"

[15] "On a reef / beneath Ravello / I would like to experience your last impact / your cool kiss without contour / a pearl grows in my flesh / a hard tear / you grow in me ocean / you grow in me / fluid and hard"

[16] "Forgive me my sisters / I have taken your silence into my heart / There it resides and suffers the pearls of your suffering / ... / A lioness rides on Oceana's waves / a lioness of agonies / who long ago bequeathed her tears to the sea—"

[17] "My ocean / remains true to me / in its mirrors / I find myself again / multiplied // It sings me / to restfulness to restlessness / dissolved / in endless rhythms / it sings / my watery body / into the sand"

[18] "If now you desperately call the one name / out of the darkness— // Wait a moment longer— / and you walk upon the sea / Already the element transfuses your pores / you are lowered with it and lifted / and found again soon in the sand / and on the stars an awaited guest arriving by air / and consumed in the fire of reunion / be still—be still—"(*Chimneys* 249-51).

[19] Cf. Karen Elias-Button: "By confronting the Terrible Mother in order to move beyond the entanglements of the mother/daughter relationship, and by claiming her as metaphor for the sources of our own creative powers, women are creating new self-configurations in which the mother is no longer the necessary comfort but the seed of a new being..." (205).

[20] "My Fatherland is dead / they have buried it / in fire // I live / in my Motherland / word"

[21] This is the view presented by Helmut Braun and one found in several secondary studies, cf. Kessner and Beil.

[22] "I have inherited a cathedral / I cannot pray / I stammer blossom forest-peace cloud-star / I stammer Mother ocean-mouth you and you // My prayers were not successful"

[23] Judith Butler discusses the temporary rebellion inherent in poetic language, a resistance to paternal law that ultimately submits to it: "poetic language and the pleasures of maternity constitute local displacements of the paternal law, temporary subversions which finally submit to that against which they initially rebel" (88).

[24] I am taking the terms symbolic and semiotic here in all their associative plurality from Julia Kristeva's distinctive brand of psychoanalytic semiotics in *Revolution of Poetic Language* and *Desire in Language*. In *Desire in Language*, Kristeva contrasts the situation of the subject within symbolic language, who has repressed the desire for the maternal semiotic with the more unsettled and dangerous situation of the "questionable subject of poetic language" who "maintains itself at the cost of reactivating this repressed, maternal element" (136).

[25] The images of the maternal in the poems discussed here can also be read as efforts to take back the mother from the ideological iconography of Nazism, which appropriated the maternal as a means of manipulating and realizing an ideal of racial hegemony. For a thorough discussion of the cultification of motherhood under Nazism, see Weyrather.

[26] Alicia Ostriker offers the thesis that women poets' revisionist approaches to religious belief fall into three categories that all share a common goal of comprehension: a hermeneutics of suspicion, a hermeneutics of desire, and a hermeneutics of undecidability (57 ff., 66). These levels are also relevant to the shifting revisionary processes that I see at work in Sachs's and Ausländer's poetic explorations of the intersections of faith, doubt, and desire.

Works Cited

Ausländer, Rose. *Gesammelte Werke in acht Bänden.* Ed. Helmut Braun. Frankfurt a.M.: Fischer, 1984-90.

Beil, Claudia. *Sprache als Heimat: Jüdische Tradition und Exilerfahrung in der Lyrik von Nelly Sachs und Rose Ausländer.* München: tuduv, 1991.

Bennholdt-Thomsen, Anke, and Alfredo Guzzoni. "Melusine: Herkunft und Bedeutung bei Nelly Sachs." *Euphorion* 81.2 (1987): 156-70.

Bloom, Harold. *Kabbalah and Criticism.* New York: Seabury Press, 1975.

Braun, Helmut, ed. *Rose Ausländer: Materialien zu Leben und Werk.* Frankfurt a.M.: Fischer, 1991.

Briefe der Nelly Sachs. Ed. Ruth Dinesen and Helmut Müssener. Frankfurt a.M.: Suhrkamp, 1985.

Brinker-Gabler, Gisela. "Mit wechselndem Schlüssel: Annäherungen an Nelly Sachs' Gedicht 'Bin in der Fremde.'" *German Quarterly* 65.1 (1992): 35-41.

Buber, Martin. *Die Legende des Baalschem.* Zürich: Manesse, 1955.

Butler, Judith. *Gender Trouble: Feminism and the Subversion of Identity.* New York: Routledge, 1990.

Dinesen, Ruth. *Nelly Sachs: Eine Biographie.* Trans. Gabriele Gerecke. Frankfurt a.M.: Suhrkamp, 1992.

Dischner, Gisela. "Zu den Gedichten von Nelly Sachs." *Das Buch der Nelly Sachs.* Ed. Bengt Holmqvist. 1968. Frankfurt a.M.: Suhrkamp, 1977. 309-54.

Du Plessis, Rachel Blau. *Writing Beyond the Ending.* Bloomington: Indiana UP, 1985.

Elias-Button, Karen. "The Muse as Medusa." *The Lost Tradition: Mothers and Daughters in Literature.* Ed. Cathy Davidson and E.M. Broner. New York: Ungar, 1980. 193-206.

Fritsch-Vivié, Gabriele. *Nelly Sachs.* Reinbek bei Hamburg: Rowohlt, 1993.

Kahn, Robbie Pfeufer. "Women and Time in Childbirth and During Lactation." *Taking Our Time: Feminist Perspectives on Temporality.* Ed. Frieda Forman and Caoran Sowton. Oxford: Pergamon Press, 1989. 20-36.

Kersten, Paul. *Die Metaphorik in der Lyrik von Nelly Sachs.* Hamburg: Lüdke, 1970.

Kessner, Michaela. "Die Lyrik Rose Ausländers." MA thesis. Ludwig-Maximilian-Universität München, 1990.

Kristeva, Julia. *Desire in Language.* Trans. Thomas Gora, Alice Jardine, and Leon S. Roudiez. New York: Columbia UP, 1980.

———. *Revolution of Poetic Language.* Trans. Leon S. Roudiez. New York: Columbia UP, 1984.

———. "Stabat Mater." Trans. Leon S. Roudiez. *The Kristeva Reader.* Ed. Toril Moi. New York: Columbia UP, 1986. 160-86.

———. *Tales of Love.* Trans. Leon Roudiez. New York: Columbia UP, 1987.

Ostriker, Alice. *Feminist Revision and the Bible*. Cambridge, MA: Blackwell, 1993.

Rosenfeld, Alvin."The Poetry of Nelly Sachs." *Judaism* 20.3 (1971): 356-64.

Sachs, Nelly. *Fahrt ins Staublose*. Frankfurt a.M.: Suhrkamp, 1961.

———. *O the Chimneys*. Trans. Michael Hamburger, et al. New York: Farrar, Straus and Giroux, 1967.

———. *The Seeker and Other Poems*. Trans. Ruth and Matthew Mead and Michael Hamburger. New York: Farrar, Straus and Giroux, 1970.

———. *Suche nach Lebenden*. Frankfurt a.M.: Suhrkamp, 1971.

Scholem, Gershom. *Major Trends in Jewish Mysticism*. New York: Schocken, 1954.

———. *The Messianic Idea in Judaism*. New York: Schocken, 1971.

———. *On the Kabbalah and Its Symbolism*. Trans. Ralph Manheim. 1965. New York: Schocken, 1969.

Unterman, Alan. *Dictionary of Jewish Lore and Legend*. London: Thames & Hudson, 1991.

Waugh, Patricia. *Feminine Fictions: Revisiting the Postmodern*. London: Routledge, 1989.

Weyrather, Irmgard. *Muttertag und Mutterkreuz: Der Kult um die 'deutsche' Mutter im Nationalsozialismus*. Frankfurt a.M.: Fischer, 1993.

Renderings of *Alice in Wonderland* in Postwar German Literature

Charlotte Melin

This article examines reworkings of *Alice in Wonderland* in works by postwar authors writing in German. While writers of both genders use Lewis Carroll's fictional character to question the expressive capacities of language, Rose Ausländer, Sarah Kirsch, Elisabeth Plessen, and Angelika Mechtel optimistically interpret her protean character as essential to poetic creativity and psychological autonomy. H.C. Artmann and Jürg Federspiel, by contrast, associate Alice with a postmodern loss of coherence in identity and narrative form. (CM)

Alice in Wonderland's status as a figure preoccupied with language and logic has made her uniquely available to postwar German writers for articulating the unstable relationship between words and what they represent. Her reconstruction by these authors, however, follows two distinct modes. Rose Ausländer ("Alice in Wonderland," 1985), Sarah Kirsch ("Death Valley," 1982), Elisabeth Plessen ("Grenzüberschreitungen," 1981), and Angelika Mechtel (*Gott und die Liedermacherin*, 1983) chart new Alice adventures that are ultimately rewarding transitions to physical, psychological, and semantic autonomy. H.C. Artmann (*Frankenstein in Sussex*, 1969) and Jürg Federspiel (*Die Ballade von der Typhoid Mary*, 1982), on the other hand, appropriate Alice in ways that suggest her manipulation and victimization by topsy-turvy circumstances, i.e., as a cipher for a progressive loss of speech. These relatively optimistic or pessimistic readings of Alice confirm in general the gendered pattern of response to the literary canon discerned by Ellen G. Friedman. The lack of nostalgia for the past that Friedman associates with modern and postmodern texts by women—and hence a penchant for fragmentation, nomadic characters, and the displacement of authority figures—distinguishes the works by Ausländer, Kirsch, Plessen, and Mechtel. But German authors of both genders further extend the model of reception Friedman proposes by using Alice figures to examine the expressive capacities of language.

Lewis Carroll has provided ample inspiration to postwar German writers who have experimented with language and scrutinized rhetoric with the overt intent of critiquing society. Elisabeth Lenk makes the point in her far-ranging study *Die unbewußte Gesellschaft* (The Unconscious Society) that dreams appropriated in modern art (for which Carroll serves as a salient example) possess the capacity to disclose the self-contradictory realities that society suppresses (260). In this spirit, Arno Schmidt invoked Carroll in his massive novel *Zettels Traum* (Zettel's Dream, 1970) and Friederike Mayröcker playfully rewrote the March Hare's refrain in her montage poem "Text 'bei mozambique'" (Text 'near mozambique') as "'keine-zeit-keine-zeit-no-time-no-time!" (126).[1] Likewise, Michael Ende in *Die Jagd nach dem Schlarg* embedded a translation of Carroll's "The Hunting of the Snark" within an amalgam of texts that simultaneously parodies book conventions and the Romantic schism between Philistines and artists. In another instance, Hans Magnus Enzensberger employed Alice's exchange with Humpty Dumpty to illustrate the entangled story of the Flick financial scandal in the 1980s. Doubtless conscious of the fact that he was writing for *Der Spiegel,* where the article originally appeared, Enzensberger advised his readers, tongue-in-cheek, to consult an unusual reference work to make sense of politicians' evasive answers, namely his brother's translation of *Through the Looking Glass.*[2] As a quite literally protean individual who experiences interrelated spatial and linguistic dislocations, Alice has furthermore often become attached to portrayals of the former division between East and West Germany and accounts of travels by Europeans to the United States in which geographical boundaries prompt speculations on personal and aesthetic sovereignty.

Carroll cast the original Alice as a fantastic and somewhat private heroine—half fictional and half real (Madden), a questionably androgynous little girl who navigated a perilous course to discover the limits of rationality and the "nice grand words" (Carroll, *Annotated Alice* 27) that had been drummed into her head in school. In the hands of Ausländer, Kirsch, Plessen, and Mechtel, Alice appears as an uncannily genuine person, closely identified with her respective authors. Their characters earnestly seek an elusive self, a self that has become foreign because the external realities of social codes or pragmatic circumstances have oppressively defined and estranged Alice from her innate sense of identity. These Alices revel in the expansive synesthesia of their adventures. When they eventually return to the world as mature writers, they do so having won a coherence distinct from external social structures. Federspiel and Artmann, by contrast, use a fictionally constructed character to enact the progressive isolation and control of an immature, female element that, quite tellingly in Federspiel's text, constitutes a disruption to patriarchal society.

The Alice experiences described by Ausländer, Kirsch, Plessen, and Mechtel accordingly reflect a process by which individuals establish their identity through what the art historian Lucy R. Lippard terms "naming."[3] Language, Lippard observes in a discussion of artists of color, defines persons and groups, hence, "Labeling is the social mire from which individuals and groups must extricate themselves in the process of self-naming" (36). The converse of this process is a questionable imposition of language: labeling. As Lippard notes, "Some names are acceptable within a community but entirely unacceptable when used by an outsider" (36). The name Alice apparently stands at such an interface, for when Ausländer, Kirsch, Plessen, and Mechtel write Alice into their texts, the focus becomes the creation of an identity from within and by the named character. An external application of the name to an other occurs in the examples by Artmann and Federspiel.

The literary allusions to Alice signal a disconcerting collapse of conventional assumptions about the world, which for some authors implies a change or disruption in their ability to write. In Rose Ausländer's poem "Alice in Wonderland," altered poetic ability is, nonetheless, welcomed, for it emanates from nature. Ausländer's highly original Alice-adventure recounts an immersion in a wooded landscape and the subsequent discovery of new forms of speech. After grass magically rouses the poem's sleeping first-person speaker, Ausländer abruptly identifies her protagonist as "Alice" and leads her into a pine woods inhabited by stags and hares. Amidst these fairy tale-like surroundings, Alice drinks mushroom milk and shrinks, remaining unalarmed because her transformation gains her the capacity to listen to nature: "Clear ripples the conversation of bees of birds / my mother tongues" ("Deutlich rieselt Bienengespräch Vogelgespräch / meine Muttersprachen" [101]). Finally, she eats from a mushroom again and grows until her new perspective affords her a nearly omniscient view of a rainbow that "colors sevenfold the secret of the circle" ("färbt siebenfach das Geheimnis des Kreises" [101]).

Like the original Alice in Wonderland, Ausländer's heroine thus enters her adventure through the liberating threshold of sleep, although in this instance her physical transformations give her comforting access to nature's mysteries. The delicate stroking of grass on her forehead and the biting of the mushroom (with its allusions to the Biblical Eve's eating from the Tree of Knowledge) suggest Alice's ease with her sensual nature. Her attentive recognition of creaturely mother tongues, moreover, implies both her preexisting competence in these languages and her receptivity to alternative, pre-poetic idioms—the bee's whisper, the bird's musical chatter, and, later, advice from a friendly deer. It consequently appears that the ingredient this figure has lacked to become a poet is not language itself, but rather an unmediated openness to nature that prompts her language and perspective on the world.

She meets these needs by sinking to the level of the forest creatures and then rising skyward, a development reminiscent of Iris's descent and ascent via the rainbow to release Dido's soul from her body after she has been abandoned by Aeneas (Hall 103). The allusion to the rainbow further establishes a link to Ausländer's creative work as a whole, for it is an image that frequently appears in her first volume of poetry *Der Regenbogen* (The Rainbow, 1939), a text lost by the author during the war and only partially reclaimed in the complete collected edition of her work.[4] Alice—the constructed poetic identity in this text—gains the power of lyrical capacities once thought lost, since in the closing lines Ausländer rhetorically asks "when are you song / ALICE" ("wann bist du Lied / ALICE"). The initial strangeness of the transformation now leads to poetic competence that incorporates rootedness to a place (the tree), transcendence (a bird's flight), and language (the song).

Sarah Kirsch's poetry sequence "Death Valley" from *Erdreich* (Earth, 1982) similarly expresses longing for unity with nature, yet here the adventurer finds herself repulsed by a stark landscape.[5] The third of twelve poems in the collection describing the United States, and the only one that explicitly names its protagonist Alice, "Death Valley" and its companion pieces describe a journey during which the main character, like Alice in Wonderland, repeatedly crosses borders and seeks paths, even as she experiences chronic sensory confusion.[6] The borders she encounters are geographical, seasonal, psychological, and ultimately political in nature. Indeed Kirsch, by filling these poems with mirroring experiences, disorientation, and boundaries, enacts a decidedly female aesthetic, very much in the terms Elisabeth Lenk describes:

> In woman's new relationship with herself she is Many, or rather she occasionally melts for moments into pure movement. In these moments femininity is as distanced from her as masculinity and the world of stereotyped sex characteristics. It is this movement, which for so long was a dream-like movement, which expands wherever it wakes into consciousness; an external action which becomes internal and thus a mirror-image action, an action which reverses sides as a mirror does. It is aesthetic action ("Woman" 53).

In *Erdreich,* the eclectic, exotic, and disorienting impressions of the New World provide an index of the freedom given the poet's imagination by her travels and, hence, of her new aesthetic self-realization.

Kirsch's insistence on tangible elements invests the poems' vast catalogue of descriptive details with elusive, symbolic import. Her protagonist traverses the Tioga Pass, then moves from winter to spring as she descends from the mountains. In "Death Valley," Alice very purposefully sets foot over the threshold of what Kirsch terms a "geological museum," a place later called a Hades (10) and a vale of tears (13), separated from her homeland by the Atlantic Ocean (14). Elsewhere travel turns into free-form journeys—the dogged search for the name of a particular tree that takes the poet to a vast library in "Bäume" (Trees), or the transformation of the woman and her companion into birds that soar over the city of New York in "Das Aussichtsplateau" (The Observation Plateau).

The physical and psychological confusion of the New World confounds the orderliness the central character ostensibly seeks, much in the way the illogical rules of Wonderland bedeviled the fictional character Alice. Emotional and climatic extremes predominate, while perceptions of uncontrollability intensify toward the end of the journey. The poet faints on the street and watches the scenery sway before her dimming sight in "Die Verwandlung" (The Metamorphosis 25). Finally in "Die Entfernung" (The Distance), she likens her experience to a violent process of disembodiment: "Three weeks in a centrifuge and have / Not arrived here yet" ("Drei Wochen in einer Zentrifuge und bin / Hier noch nicht angekommen" [27]). The unpleasant travel experiences enhance the conflation of the United States with Carroll's fantastic realms, because they occur side by side with an extensive catalogue of exotic imagery that includes Chinatown (San Francisco), African-Americans, and twirling figure skaters at Rockefeller Center. As ambiguous for the European traveler as the original Wonderland itself, this America overloads the senses with new impressions, triggering sensations of vertigo, fainting, nausea, and writerly self-doubt.[7]

The extended pattern of imagery related to Alice becomes more strongly attached to the United States (the democratic West) once Kirsch juxtaposes this "Wonderland" against the equally fantastic, but politically repressive East, to which she applies fairy tale motifs in the remainder of *Erdreich*. Kirsch, of course, left the GDR in 1977 in the wake of the Biermann affair.[8] In this volume of poetry she sets the atmosphere of control and stifled dissent (which the black-and-white definitions of behavior supplied by fairy tales underscore) in contrast to the sense of freedom and exhilarating chaos evoked by the allusions to Alice in Wonderland.

Kirsch frames the pivotal "Death Valley" cycle with allusions to Carroll, mentioning Alice as the descent begins into the desert and again as she completes her adventure. The text's first five sections unfold an uncanny tale of sensory disorientation through kinesthesia and synthesia. The sixth and final section, by contrast, situates the poet once again in familiar and predictable circumstances, at her writing desk. Unlike Ausländer's serene protagonist, Kirsch's Alice abruptly senses her own mortality as she sinks into the wilderness.[9] Her elation over her unmediated encounter with nature nonetheless persists, enhanced by an elusive longing manifested in her efforts toward adventure, sexual freedom, and political autonomy.[10] This kind of longing corresponds to Friedman's notion of a "liberating image" (244) and to Lippard's description of "landing," whereby

> The landing process is not always a matter of geographical turf, nor of coming to rest; it can be equally a process of change, of being sent away or of "taking off" on a quest for home that may never be satisfied. For those in internal or external exile, landing can become a psychic image, even a vision (105).

The landing set in motion in "Death Valley" encompasses a drive toward sexual and individual freedom that the text repeatedly understates. Alice plays a foregrounded Beatrice to a receding Dante in this poetic sequence—the poet who initiates the journey, she observes a male companion who accompanies her. Only later she discovers flirting couples painted on the panels of a fresco in a ghost town theater who seem to confirm her own physical *joie de vivre*. Further, the protagonist of the poem seems to become anonymous in the mid-sections of the cycle, where the poet evidently has no need for a named identity while in the midst of her experience. Once she prepares to leave Death Valley, she reassumes the persona of Alice.[11]

Kirsch decisively returns to questions of language and naming when Alice appears in the fifth section, this time leafing through a Baedeker travel guide as she furtively attempts to make sense of a strange opera house she has visited. Her agitated effort to verify her observations confirms a precarious relation between experience and language, for she finds no satisfying answers to her questions in the book.[12] Alice seems caught in what Foucault calls "the inextricable tangle of words and images and...the absence of a common ground to sustain them" (38-39). The dry prose of Baedeker is no match for the bewildering realities she witnesses. Kirsch then initiates the transition of her protagonist from the strange environment back to home and writing via two bookish gestures: Alice thumbs through guide pages and receives car papers from the opera's coat check.

Returned to Germany, Alice finds herself able to master her daunting "look behind the mirrors," as Kirsch terms it (14). Life in Germany seems "nice" (*hübsch*) and sexually conventional, since she once again assumes her role as a mother. The poet purposefully resumes her daily tasks, much like Kirsch, who herself acknowledged in a 1991 interview that her visit to the United States was a turning point that posed two alternatives—living in New York or moving to the German countryside—the latter of which she chose (Graves 275-76).

A comparison of the poems by Kirsch and Ausländer establishes the intriguing fact that both authors refer to Alice in Wonderland to construct descriptions of mature writers. Ausländer's poem appeared in *Die Sichel mäht die Zeit zu Heu* (The Scythe Mows Time into Hay), a volume of poems spanning the years 1957–1965. Kirsch, on the other hand, published *Erdreich* in 1982, ten years after her third volume of verse, *Zaubersprüche* (Magic Charms, 1972 GDR/1973 FRG), had firmly secured her reputation as a poet. Both authors represent Alice as possessing the uninitiated naiveté of an innocent and undertaking a quest. The composition dates of the poems, by contrast, position her attributes and adventures at a relatively advanced moment in the careers of Ausländer and Kirsch. Thus, Alice's disorientation and constant redefinition of herself culminate in an enabling epiphany for these poets who have already mastered their craft. Assuming an identity as Alice in these texts signals creative initiative and, quite crucially, that masquerade for both Ausländer and Kirsch precedes the synthesizing act of writing.

In Elisabeth Plessen's short story "Grenzüberschreitungen" (Border Crossings) and Angelika Mechtel's novel *Gott und die Liedermacherin* (God and the Song Writer), established women writers again evoke the figure of Alice, this time in prose. Plessen's three-page narrative recounts a border crossing from West to East Berlin that begins with the writer's inward confession that as a creative mind she poses a threat to the tightly controlled country she wishes to visit: "I am an author, I have an elephant lying in the back of my car. Be careful" (105).[13] During a moment of awkwardness when an East German customs official perfunctorily searches her car, she thinks of Alice and lapses into a narrative rhapsody. Remembering Carroll's tale, she observes how the official mimics her behavior: "Just because I laughed, he laughed. Just because I started to tell him some sort of half-witted nonsense—once upon a time there was a girl who was named Alice behind the looking glass, once upon a time there was a German-Germanism that was anachronism, etc." (105).[14]

This banter amuses the official. Neither he nor the narrator takes the customs formalities seriously, yet the border between East and West strictly inhibits their interactions. Laughing, these two Germans briefly respond to their mutual discomfort as if they were mirror images; then the inspection proceeds as usual. The narrator shows him her copy of *Der Spiegel* (a further pun on Carroll's work), which the guard would have otherwise overlooked for lack of genuine interest in finding materials to confiscate. After the search Plessen's narrator wonders without reaching any conclusions what prompted her reaction. Clearly, Lenk's observations on dreams as social critique find application here, for the allusion to Alice echoes the strangeness of having a politically divided Germany.

Political, and also gender, questions cause an unsettling of the psyche for Angelika Mechtel, the author who offers the most radical version of Alice and whose protagonist experiences her adventures as a form of schizophrenia or amnesia. Mechtel's novel *Gott und die Liedermacherin* (1983) describes a journey to the United States undertaken by Julia Ritter, a recently divorced singer on concert tour. An outspoken feminist, Julia begins telling stories that her American audiences find offensively radical. She brazenly recasts traditional characters (Adam and Eve, Romeo and Juliet, Scheherezade, Red Riding Hood, Cassandra, and others) in narratives that place the women in conspicuously dominant positions, much in the way Aristophanes reversed gender roles in *Lysistrata,* a work to which Mechtel refers.[15] At the end of her tour, Julia refuses to return to Germany and disappears for ten days, during which time she assumes the identity of "Alice."

Mechtel relates these events on the pretext of reconstructing a court case subsequently brought against Julia by her offended American sponsors. To determine whether Julia is liable for her actions, the court is asked to decide whether she suffered from real or feigned amnesia during the ten days when she became Alice, in short to pass judgment over the significance of her "Wonderland" experience. The novel overtly toys with stereotypic European views of the United States under Ronald Reagan's presidency, cataloguing "American" preoccupations with religion, power, and the sexual subjugation of women. Julia's willful attempt to reverse male-female roles, nonetheless, results in shattered illusions for her.

Late in the book, Julia chooses the identity of "Alice," though Mechtel presages the transformation early in the text. When Julia first arrives in the United States, she listens to a patron's wife, Carolyn Copper, recount a dream about a garden kept inaccessible by doors, a kind of *hortus conclusus.* This prompts Julia to remember a similar dream she had during her recent divorce. The shared dream recalls Alice's harrowing attempts to follow the White Rabbit into the beautiful Wonderland garden. When Mechtel introduces the name Alice at the novel's close, the reader belatedly learns that Copper, like Julia, has left her husband. The pseudonym Alice seems initially to be a coincidental choice—a name agreeable to both the hitchhiking Julia and the truckers who picked her up (211). But as Alice Forster (the surname alludes to the travel accounts of Georg Forster), Julia Ritter escapes prescribed behaviors and the tour schedule that had precipitated a progressive sense of disorientation. She subsequently discovers through her metamorphosis that some of her most fundamental suppositions are untenable.

Her split personality experience culminates when she lies down in a seedy San Francisco hotel bed that she has dramatically surrounded with candles. Prone as if on a bier, Julia senses that she is a doubled person, at once Shakespeare's vulnerable, tragically fated Juliet and the quixotic Alice (213). Her odyssey, which Mechtel hints might have resulted from amnesia caused by a bump on the head and an unhealthy mixture of alcohol and sedatives, calls into question the power of social influences on an individual's conception of the world. Julia ostensibly comes to the

United States prompted by a lofty search for God, yet she discovers the precariousness of her visions when she measures them against reality:

> The only possibility was to admit the reality. She was not Alice. She had never been Alice. Wonderlands exist only in her head and in the minds of others. They can exist in every mind. Alice is then always the other, the one who enters from outside and takes part in the world inside our heads (212).[16]

While dispensing with her search for God frees Julia from the burden of immediately reforming a patriarchal system, her subsequent loss of faith in Alice and utopian Wonderlands poses a dilemma.

This conversion nudges Julia toward a postmodern outlook to the extent that "...the postmodern's initial concern is to de-naturalize some of the dominant features of our way of life; to point out that those entities that we unthinkingly experience as 'natural' (they might even include capitalism, patriarchy, liberal humanism) are in fact 'cultural'; made by us, not given to us" (Hutcheon 2). The schizophrenia that divides her personality into Alice and Julia—a symptom of the difficulty women face in reconciling contradictory, prescribed roles—develops into an attenuated and schizophrenic relationship to language, such as Fredric Jameson has suggested corresponds to the textual features of postmodernism, since " as temporal continuities break down, the experience of the present becomes powerfully, overwhelmingly vivid and 'material': the world comes before the schizophrenic with heightened intensity..." (120).

Mechtel's novel, though, lifts itself out of the conundrum of postmodernism's infinite undermining of givens and political efficacy. First, the trial that concludes the book focuses on the issue of free speech, underscoring the importance for Mechtel of semantic authority. When Julia wins an acquittal with the assistance of an eloquent female defense attorney, she discovers that her prerogatives for self-expression are quite circumscribed. The singer then decides to return to Germany, prompted by homesickness for her native country, which now seems so distant to her that the tourist brochures she stumbles across in an airport show her mere "Wonderland pictures" of it (222). In her homeland, she should be more able to wield language effectively.

Secondly, like the feminist artists Linda Hutcheon describes who "...use postmodern strategies of parodic inscription and subversion in order to initiate the deconstructive first step..." (168) and then remain politicized, Mechtel constructs a book that stylistically maintains its own resolute skepticism about language. The novel appears to be an intentional exercise in bad taste, which, as Lippard emphasizes, can constitute a form of resistance to the dominant aesthetic (202). The text contains virtually no dialogue and its subject matter at times turns blatantly crass. Poetic interludes taken from the canon of German literature from the Baroque to

Biedermeier periods contrast sharply with Mechtel's prose. Placed throughout *Gott und die Liedermacherin,* these lyrical intrusions undermine the privileged status often accorded narrative prose, for they confirm the essential value of individual, subjective experience and poetic texts as a means of conceiving and reshaping the world.

A particularly feminine approach to gaining semantic authority thus emerges from the texts by Ausländer, Kirsch, Plessen, and Mechtel as the authors explore how language can be reconnected to intimate observations and immediate experiences. For H.C. Artmann and Jürg Federspiel, by contrast, Alice represents the limits of narrative capabilities because she becomes associated with a general collapse of textual coherence. In their works, the more detail occurs, the more fictional turmoil and destabilization of language prevail.

In Artmann's "Frankenstein in Sussex," a prose piece that reflects a widespread fascination with nonsense literature by Carroll among German authors, Alice's appearance signals the author's abiding mistrust of literature. Launched into what at first seems merely an entertaining account of madcap adventures, Alice plummets down a chimney to a massive, subterranean residence and encounters the monster Frankenstein from Mary Shelley's work. Frankenstein tries to claim Alice as his bride while a proper English gentleman melodramatically struggles to her rescue. The tale evinces deep skepticism about the unstable balance between fiction and reality and the text rapidly crosses over into the realm of metafiction. Artmann interrupts the central plot by shifting to a description of two women, Mary Wollstonecraft Shelley and Frau Holle (a German fairy tale character), who argue over tea about how the tale's events should proceed. Mary wants to liberate the monster; Frau Holle favors saving Alice, the damsel in distress. Finally they intervene directly by moving from the subplot into the main action. Frau Holle rescues Alice, and Mary becomes Frankenstein's mate.

This cleverly designed "happy ending" nevertheless leaves the reader adrift, for it suggests that authors, like Mary Shelley, or indeed Artmann, have lost their privileged position as omniscient outsiders to the works they create. Under these circumstances fiction threatens to engulf the mundane world in chaos, while fictional characters like Alice become mere pawns in a narrative randomly peppered with an admixture of literary figures and real-life luminaries. Traditional distinctions between high and low culture blur as Artmann inserts into his text protagonists from literary classics (Alice and Frankenstein) next to clones of real persons (like Wilbur von Frankenstein, who resembles pop star Frank Zappa). Whereas Carroll carefully mediated transitions into and out of his tales by employing narrative frames, Artmann drops this literary pretense. His characters are reduced to manipulable items, as if to suggest to authors have become mere scribes and no longer hold the semantic authority to create and direct a narrative. As a consequence, the author (Mary Shelley) even devolves into a victim of her own fictional character (Frankenstein).

In a final example appropriating Alice, Jürg Federspiel shows a preoccupation with the interplay between fact and fiction commensurate to Artmann's, while employing references to Carroll's work that corroborate the aptness of Kirsch's and Mechtel's equation of Wonderland adventures with journeys through the United States. His novel *Die Ballade von der Typhoid Mary* (The Ballad of Typhoid Mary, 1982) mentions Lewis Carroll casually in the fifth chapter. By this point, the reader has learned of Mary's arrival in late nineteenth-century New York and has witnessed how a port physician, Dr. Dorfheimer, has surreptitiously taken the orphan girl into his care, thereby circumventing the examinations that might have identified her as a typhoid carrier. While his housekeeper reluctantly bathes Mary and puts her to bed, Dorfheimer retires to his rooms to read Carroll's book, which has recently become popular in England and the United States. Federspiel comments, "Dorfheimer was particularly fascinated by the fact that this book had been written by a mathematics instructor: 'Alice in Wonderland'" (22).[17]

The curt interjection of the title at the chapter's end belies its actual importance to the narrative. Dorfheimer, as it turns out, molests young girls. Mary is not the first he has brought home with him, but she becomes the last, since he contracts typhoid from her and dies. Mary herself resembles John Tenniel's well-known illustrations of Alice. Like Alice, whose head seems her most prominent feature, Federspiel's Mary is fine-boned, strong, blond, and has a long Botticelli-like neck (27–28). The resemblance between the two heroines hinges further on the notion of Wonderland and the corruption of its utopian potential. America proves a horror land for Mary. The ship's cook, Dorfheimer, and others she encounters sexually exploit her. Devoted to the culinary arts, Mary learns in the course of her life that her profession is fatal to others since she carries a lethal disease. She initially preserves her remarkable innocence by fleeing jobs the instant illness descends and, as a result, she remains long ignorant of her destructive powers.

For Federspiel, the oblique equation of Mary with Alice opens a wealth of provocative considerations about the relationship between reality and literature.[18] Rumors about Carroll's sexual proclivities become manifest in Dorfheimer's inappropriate actions. The book *Alice in Wonderland* stands as an unheeded warning to its reader, Dorfheimer, about the biological chaos that will engulf him once he contracts typhoid. Federspiel subsequently describes how America, the fabled Wonderland, in reality operates according to a skewed logic grounded in power and wealth, rather than by its espoused, egalitarian principles. In addition he plays with the tension between fact and fiction as the fictive narrator, Dr.

Howard Rageet, confesses his sense of identification with his protagonist, noting, "It becomes more and more difficult for me not to view Mary Mallon as my own daughter. Am I using her as an instrument for revenge?" (124).[19] By articulating this intuited kinship, Federspiel problematizes a patriarchal categorization of women as evil or the agents for undoing order and proposes instead men's complicity in the creation of chaos.

Federspiel thus calls into question the ontological status of art and life. What, after all, should be viewed as real, if Dorfheimer, a fiction, seems as perversely eccentric as Carroll, a person writing under a pseudonym, if literary fictions like *Alice in Wonderland* address a fictive audience (Dorfheimer), or if an imagined Wonderland resembles a real America? And what becomes of the text if Federspiel's created narrator, Rageet, merges his identity with that of his own fictional subject, who herself resembles Alice? Mary, the novel consistently asserts, was a real person, but she also became an infamous, mythical figure of death. Hence, she herself has turned ambiguous, a textual sister to Alice, the fictional character, who was also the sweet little girl Alice Liddell, who once simply wanted to hear an engaging tale. Federspiel underscores the shock of the geographical passage Mary makes to the United States by referring to Alice, yet more broadly he signals the metafictional ironies of his narrative with the allusion.

Like Artmann in 1969, Federspiel in 1982 ultimately deprives Mary (or Alice) of her capacity to speak, and hence, of semantic competence. Typhoid Mary ends her life in virtual solitary confinement, an infected person permanently quarantined, an outcast whose tale others tell. Furthermore, those others are male doctors of privileged social status and scientific training who assert their rationalizing authority over her feminine, lower-class, untutored, and forcibly muted voice. Artmann and Federspiel may not necessarily wish to imprison Alice, or women—their texts explore the narrative capacities of an ostensibly universal writer—but the silenced Alice joins the ancient tradition that associates femininity with passivity. Moreover, her crucial presence in these works adumbrates a general silencing of narrative, especially of dissident voices.

Ausländer around 1960, then Kirsch, Plessen, and Mechtel in the early 1980s, by contrast, show their heroines adopting an identity as Alice during a moment of transition toward a position of semantic competence. The degree of materialism exhibited in their texts (the open emphasis on sexuality, sensory perceptions, and disparate imagery) is, to be sure, more familiar in the visual arts than in literature and suggests a recrafting of the written media. The Alices of these authors learn by experiencing flux that identity, language, and society are interdependent. They, like the ideal poet described in Richard Rorty's extension of Nietzschean philosophy, find that, "The process of coming to know oneself, confronting one's contingency, tracking one's causes home, is identical with the process of inventing a new language—that is, of thinking up some new metaphors" (*Contingency* 27). But while Rorty optimistically contends that persons outside the center can gain semantic authority and escape archaic epistemologies ("Feminism" 10), feminist critics have debated whether women as already marginal individuals can, in the terms of Gisela Brinker-Gabler, afford the luxury of deconstructing their identity if such a deconstruction implies relinquishing utopian, political aims (239, cf. also Miller, Modleski).

A remarkably enduring protagonist, Alice in her recent incarnations encompasses the vexing predicaments posed by contemporary, social change. Karl Krolow in his poem "Einzelfälle" (Individual Cases) cites Alice Liddell as one of those exceptional instances in which a humble individual is transformed into the artist's muse (69).[20] As a literary figure with arguably postmodern features, Alice in Wonderland, too, has proved highly malleable. The roles constructed for her by Artmann and Federspiel do imply that yielding to a flexible identity impinges on and irrevocably compromises an artist or individual. Ausländer, Kirsch, Plessen, and Mechtel, on the other hand, seem to view the momentary chaos associated with the private act of writing as a transitional condition, which is admittedly stabilized when their texts are later made public to the reading audience in published form.[21] For their adventuresome Alice, dismantling and reconstructing one's identity is in the end a form of self-invention and of renewing language, and the creativity won in the process is well worth the hazards involved.

Notes

All translations are my own unless otherwise noted.

[1] Mayröcker grew up reading *Alice in Wonderland,* according to Jürgen Serke's biographical account (116).

[2] Carroll's tales are currently available to German audiences in over a dozen editions, most notably *Alice im Wunderland* (1970) and *Alice hinter den Spiegeln* (1974), translated by English literature scholar Christian Enzensberger. For further information on earlier translations, see Weaver.

[3] I would like to acknowledge my husband, Matthew Rohn, an art historian, for bringing to my attention parallels in the contemporary visual arts to what occurs in literary texts about Alice in Wonderland.

[4] The problematic relation of the poet to language and the rainbow motif of this poem suggest tantalizing links to Ausländer's biography as well, for Ausländer, a Jew, survived persecution and avoided deportation from Czernowitz during World War II, then emigrated to the United States in 1946 and returned

to Europe to take up residence in Düsseldorf in 1965, thus experiencing multiple estrangements from her cultural roots (Braun 11-34).

[5] For a detailed analysis of the political aspects of Kirsch's poetry, see Barbara Mabee and, in addition, Christine Cosentino's discussion of the mirror metaphor.

[6] My interpretation of Kirsch's texts is indebted to Karla Lydia Schultz's thesis that the Alice persona extends to other poems about the United States in which Kirsch does not mention the literary heroine by name.

[7] Interestingly, Hans Christoph Buch recounts a comparable episode of travel sickness and exhaustion in *Aus der Neuen Welt: Nachrichten und Geschichten* (From the New World: Reports and Stories).

[8] After poet-singer Wolf Biermann's citizenship was revoked by the East German government on 17 November 1976, writers including Sarah Kirsch drafted an open letter on his behalf that was published in the West. The GDR, which responded with arrests and tighter controls, began to encourage or force other dissident intellectuals to leave the country. This exodus of writers to the West continued unabated through the 1980s (Emmerich 185-87).

[9] As a point of comparison it should be noted that artist Markus Lüpertz similarly viewed Alice's descent as a journey leading to an underworld in his series of forty-eight paintings, "Alice in Wonderland" (Kuspit). Karl Krolow, as well, evokes Alice as a figure associated with mortality in his poem "Einzelfälle."

[10] The isolation of the female in a garden-like setting has echoes of the medieval convention of depicting Mary inside a rose bower, the *hortus conclusus* or enclosed garden, a rendering of her virginal qualities based on the *Song of Songs* 4:12 (Hall 329). For Ausländer and Kirsch, however, the individual set apart does not relinquish her sensual nature.

[11] Carl G. Jung's descriptions of the dreams of a ten-year-old girl, which incorporate descents, ascents, and travel to America, offer an intriguing parallel to the events Kirsch describes in "Death Valley" (69-72).

[12] For a fuller discussion of this poem see my discussion of Kirsch's conception of landscape and writing.

[13] "Ich bin Schriftstellerin, ich habe hinten im Wagen einen Elefanten liegen. Seien Sie vorsichtig." The convention of representing the writer as a conspirator or criminal, of course, derives from the Romantic tradition, continued in this century especially in the works of Thomas Mann.

[14] "Bloß weil ich lächelte, lächelte er. Bloß weil ich angefangen hatte, ihm irgendwelchen Schwachsinn aufzubinden—es war einmal ein Mädchen, das hieß Alice hinter den Spiegeln, es war einmal ein deutsch-deutscher-ismus, der hieß Anachronismus etc."

[15] Cf. also Friedman on the longing of the main character to replace God in *Two Serious Ladies* by Jane Bowles (246 ff.).

[16] "Es gab keine andere Möglichkeit, als die Realität anzuerkennen. Sie ist nicht Alice gewesen. Sie ist niemals Alice gewesen. Wunderländer existieren nur

in ihrem Kopf und in anderen Köpfen. In jedem Kopf können sie existieren. Alice ist dann immer die andere, die von außen hereinkommt und teilnimmt an der Welt in unseren Köpfen."

[17] "Was Dorfheimer besonders faszinierte, war die Tatsache, daß dieses Buch von einem Mathematiklehrer geschrieben worden war: 'Alice im Wunderland.'"

[18] Federspiel's novel, like Artmann's briefer "Frankstein in Sussex," clearly fits Patricia Waugh's definition of metafiction by virtue of its elaborate construction. One American reviewer, in fact, termed the narrative post-modern for its fragmented quality (Batchelor 11).

[19] "Es fällt mir immer schwerer, Mary Mallon nicht als meine eigene Tochter zu sehen. Ob ich sie als Instrument der Rache benütze?"

[20] The universality of her figure seems further confirmed by Elizabeth Kamarck Minnich's choice of the name Alice to designate the female equivalent of the male, presumed universal in *Transforming Knowledge* (39).

[21] The term private here refers to the sphere of the individual as marked in these texts by her physical isolation; public refers to her interactions in social and political settings. Dorothy Rosenberg acknowledges the difficulty of defining the boundaries of the private and public spheres in GDR literature and distinguishes between a vision of the private as a "Zufluchtsort" (23) distinct from public areas of life controlled by the government and society, which in East Germany extended to the family. Jürgen Habermas, on the other hand, underscores the connections of economics and ethics between the two spheres and the hazards of dividing them (323–26).

Works Cited

Artmann, H.C. *Frankenstein in Sussex: Fleiß und Industrie.* Frankfurt a.M.: Suhrkamp, 1969.

Ausländer, Rose. "Alice in Wonderland." *Die Sichel mäht die Zeit zu Heu: Gedichte 1957–1965.* Frankfurt a.M.: Fischer, 1985. 101.

Batchelor, John Calvin. "Death Dogged Her Footsteps." *The New York Times Book Review* 12 February 1984: 11.

Braun, Helmut, ed. *Rose Ausländer: Materialien zu Leben und Werk.* Frankfurt a.M.: Fischer, 1991.

Brinker-Gabler, Gisela. "Alterity—Marginality—Difference: On Inventing Places for Women." *Women in German Yearbook 8.* Ed. Jeanette Clausen and Sara Friedrichsmeyer. Lincoln: U of Nebraska P, 1993. 235–45.

Buch, Hans Christoph. *Aus der neuen Welt: Nachrichten und Geschichten.* Berlin: Wagenbach, 1975.

Carroll, Lewis. *Alice hinter den Spiegeln.* Trans. Christian Enzensberger. Frankfurt a.M.: Insel, 1974.

——— . *Alice im Wunderland*. Trans. Christian Enzensberger. Frankfurt a.M.: Insel, 1970.

——— . *The Annotated Alice*. Ed. Martin Cardner. New York: Potter, 1960.

Cosentino, Christine. *"Ein Spiegel mit mir darin": Sarah Kirschs Lyrik*. Tübingen: Francke, 1990.

Emmerich, Wolfgang. *Kleine Literaturgeschichte der DDR*. Darmstadt: Luchterhand, 1981.

Ende, Michael. *Die Jagd nach dem Schlarg: Variationen zu Lewis Carrolls gleichnamigem Nonsensgedicht*. Stuttgart: Weitbrecht, 1988.

Enzensberger, Hans Magnus. "Kassensturz: Ein Bonner Memorandum." *Mittelmaß und Wahn*. Frankfurt a.M.: Suhrkamp, 1988.

Federspiel, Jürg. *Die Ballade von der Typhoid Mary*. Frankfurt a.M.: Suhrkamp, 1982.

Foucault, Michel. *This Is Not a Pipe*. Trans. and ed. James Harkness. Berkeley: U of California P, 1983.

Friedman, Ellen G. "Where Are the Missing Contents? (Post)Modernism, Gender, and the Canon." *PMLA* 103.2 (1993): 240-52.

Graves, Peter. "Sarah Kirsch: Some Comments and a Conversation." *German Life and Letters* 44.3 (1991): 271-80.

Habermas, Jürgen. *The Theory of Communicative Action*. Vol. 2. Trans. Thomas McCarthy. Boston: Beacon, 1987.

Hall, James. *Dictionary of Subjects and Symbols in Art*. New York: Harper & Row, 1974.

Hutcheon, Linda. *The Politics of Postmodernism*. London: Routledge, 1989.

Jameson, Fredric. "Postmodernism and Consumer Society." *The Anti-Aesthetic: Essays on Post-Modern Culture*. Ed. Hal Foster. Port Townsend: Bay, 1983. 111-25.

Jung, Carl G. *Man and His Symbols*. New York: Doubleday, 1964.

Kirsch, Sarah. *Erdreich*. Stuttgart: Deutsche Verlags-Anstalt, 1982.

——— . *Zaubersprüche*. Ebenhausen: Langewiesche-Brandt, 1974.

Krolow, Karl. "Einzelfälle." *Luchterhand Jahrbuch der Lyrik*. Darmstadt: Luchterhand, 1984. 69-70.

Kuspit, Donald. "Acts of Aggression: German Painting Today, Part II." *Art in America* 71 (1983): 90-101, 131-35.

Lenk, Elisabeth. "The Self-Reflecting Woman." *Feminist Aesthetics*. Ed. Gisela Ecker. Boston: Beacon, 1985. 51-58.

——— . *Die unbewußte Gesellschaft*. München: Matthew & Seitz, 1983.

Lippard, Lucy. *Mixed Blessings*. New York: Pantheon, 1990.

Mabee, Barbara. *Die Poetik von Sarah Kirsch*. Amsterdam: Rodopi, 1989.

Madden, William A. "Framing the Alices." *PMLA* 101 (1986): 362-73.

Mayröcker, Friederike. *Ausgewählte Gedichte 1944-1978*. Frankfurt a.M.: Suhrkamp, 1979.

Mechtel, Angelika. *Gott und die Liedermacherin*. München: List, 1983.

Melin, Charlotte. "Landscape As Writing and Revelation in Sarah Kirsch's 'Death Valley.'" *The Germanic Review* 62 (1987): 199–204.

Miller, Nancy. "Changing the Subject: Authorship, Writing, and the Reader." *Feminist Studies/Critical Studies*. Ed. Teresa de Lauretis. Bloomington: Indiana UP, 1986. 102–20.

Minnich, Elizabeth Karmack. *Transforming Knowledge*. Philadelphia: Temple UP, 1990.

Modleski, Tania. "Feminism and the Power of Interpretation: Some Critical Readings." *Feminist Studies/Critical Studies*. Ed. Teresa de Lauretis. Bloomington: Indiana UP, 1986. 121–38.

Plessen, Elisabeth. "Grenzüberschreitungen." *Zu machen, daß ein gebratener Huhn aus der Schussel läuft*. Zürich: Benziger, 1981. 104–06.

Rorty, Richard. *Contingency, Irony, and Solidarity*. Cambridge: Cambridge UP, 1989.

―――. "Feminism and Pragmatism." *Radical Philosophy* 59 (Autumn 1991): 3–24.

Rosenberg, Dorothy. "Neudefinierung des Öffentlichen und des Privaten: Schriftstellerinnen in der DDR." *Zwischen gestern und morgen: Schriftstellerinnen der DDR aus amerikanischer Sicht*. Ed. Ute Brandes. Berlin: Lang, 1992. 17–41.

Schmidt, Arno. *Zettels Traum 1963–1969*. Stuttgart: Stahlberg, 1970.

Schultz, Karla Lydia. "'Here is not Disneyland': On Sarah Kirsch's America Poems." German Studies Association Annual Meeting. Milwaukee, 6 October 1989.

Serke, Jürgen. "Friederike Mayröcker: 'Von kommenden Dingen kehren die Schiffe zurück.'" *Frauen schreiben*. Hamburg: Stern-Magazin im Verlag, 1979. 102–21.

Waugh, Patricia. *Metafiction*. London: Routledge, 1984.

Weaver, Warren. *Alice in Many Tongues*. Madison: U of Wisconsin P, 1964.

"Society Is the Biggest Murder Scene of All": On the Private and Public Spheres in Ingeborg Bachmann's Prose

Helgard Mahrdt

In her prose Ingeborg Bachmann took up the Frankfurt School's cultural criticism and extended it by adding the dimension of gender. Violence and oppression are thus shown to be *structural moments* of the public and the private spheres. Against a sketch of the background and cognitive implications of my use of the concepts private and public, I describe Bachmann's critique of the politics of a public sphere that requires the splitting off of feelings. After demonstrating that feelings, sensuality, and trust have no "place" in the private sphere either, and that this sphere can be deadly for "woman," I explore how Bachmann goes beyond the Frankfurt School's critique by portraying the return of "woman" to the public sphere and asking how she can survive there. (HM)

In the interplay of the impossible and the possible we expand our possibilities.—Bachmann IV: 276

On the Public Sphere

My point of departure is the conceptual pair "public" and "private," specifically as they relate to Jürgen Habermas's elaboration of the bourgeois public sphere.[1] While feminists have made use of Habermas's now classic text,[2] German feminist debates in the 1990s have also questioned the usefulness and clarity of this conceptual pair, establishing that "pioneering studies" like those of Habermas or Lucian Hölscher were valid only for the public sphere. Women scholars are therefore advised to use a suitable measure of critical reflection with respect to these concepts.[3] Differentiation of the private and public spheres for reasons of analysis does not signify that they are separate. Rather, even in social theory, the spheres are understood as mediated by one other.[4] In connection with feminist criticism and interest in a "feminist counter-public sphere," Ruth-Ellen B. Joeres also proposed in a recent article that "another sort of social sphere" was created on the basis of friendship between women authors of the late eighteenth and early nineteenth centuries (39).

Before I can employ the concept of the public and the private spheres as a heuristic principle for a gender-specific reading of Bachmann, it is necessary to provide a brief explanation of the concept's historicity and its basic characteristics. There is general agreement that the public and the private spheres exist in a delicate balance and that their borders are continually being redrawn. At a time when the public sphere is in danger of being reduced to a media public, Bachmann's prose can be read both as a site of self-understanding and a site of memory of Enlightenment ideals that were originally connected to the bourgeois public sphere; that is, the bourgeois public sphere also contains a potential specifically for women.

Inasmuch as "feminist public sphere" is a utopian concept—still on the horizon, so to speak—I must, in the interest of criticism, derive my model from the existing concept of the bourgeois public sphere as used by social scientists. I begin not with dialogue as the basic form of the public sphere but, like Habermas in *The Structural Transformation of the Public Sphere,* with Kant's understanding of the bourgeois public sphere as a formal relation (*Formzusammenhang*). My reading of Bachmann's prose, then, focuses not on the formation of new "communities" (*Gemeinschaften*), but on the individual and social conditions that are necessary for women to be able to operate as independent subjects in public space.

Certainly social relations have changed since Kant's time, and the crisis of Enlightenment postulates cannot be solved by a "back to Kant movement." However, a return to Kant's concept of the bourgeois public sphere might, under altered conditions, be of some importance precisely for a feminist interest in justice and morality (cf. Brandt 120). These ideas can only be presented in abbreviated form here. Most importantly, we must bear in mind that despite its contradictory character, the bourgeois public sphere is more than a mere fiction. The Kantian concept of the public sphere attempts to organize communal life according to rules of reason and universally valid laws. This claim involves the hypothesis that law, politics, and morality should be in harmony, or, to put it another way, only when public action can be reconciled with moral principles is it not a pure exercise of power (Kant, *Perpetual Peace* Appendix II; Saage 129 ff.).

Among the central points of this model were general accessibility, freedom of the press and freedom from censorship, the security (*Verläßlichkeit*) that results from generally binding laws, and rationality in opinion-formation and truth-finding. The ideal model was constituted by the discourse of all educated and interested participants. The bourgeois coffeehouse could still claim the public-sphere function in that all differences were suspended and everyone could take part in the conversation.

Proceeding from Kant to the nineteenth century, we find that the public sphere is further divided into a *political* sphere, which relates to the public citizen, and one that concerns the social world or, in modern terms, the professional world.[5] Both political and social intercourse are separated from the private sphere, which consists primarily of the family. The public sphere at this time also entailed a communicative model based primarily on direct communication among citizens, their public consideration of general, i.e., generalizable concerns.

At the beginning of the twentieth century, sociohistorical developments in the direction of mass society led to the linking of the public sphere with foreignness. The sociologist Ferdinand Tönnies wrote: "All intimate, private, and exclusive living together...is understood as life in Gemeinschaft (community). Gesellschaft (society) is public life—it is the world itself.... One goes into Gesellschaft as one goes into a strange country" (33-34). For the private citizen, however, "intimate" living together had its "site" in the family. As we now know, this separation into private and public is not gender-neutral.

The Regulars' Table (*Männerstammtisch*) as Semi-Public Sphere

Already in 1961, Ingeborg Bachmann's story "Among Murderers and Madmen" shows the splitting of society into a public and a private sphere, the assignment of the sexes to these spheres, the gender-specific access to both spheres, and the damage to individuals caused by this split. In addition, the story addresses a problem that only becomes obvious in the twentieth century and is still relevant for questions of political practice thirty years later: the lack of social homogeneity.

The story was written before the *Todesarten* (Death Styles) cycle, but its title suggests an important thematic connecting line: "Among Murderers and Madmen" exposes not only the murderous law of war, but that of the postwar period as well. The table reserved for regulars (*Stammtisch*) around which the story takes place can be read as a kind of semi-public sphere that is male-defined and to which only men have access; the women are home alone:

> Barefoot or in slippers, with tied-up hair and tired faces, the women wandered round at home, turned off the gas and looked fearfully under the bed and in the cupboard, soothed the children with absent-minded words or sat dejectedly by the radio and then went to bed after all with thoughts of vengeance in the lonely house (84).

The women's access to the public sphere is a mediated one. It turns them, via the radio, into listeners who are isolated in their homes. The place where the men meet to drink is a wine cellar "in Vienna, more than ten years after the war" (83). This date is not unimportant, for it points to a cultural connection familiar to us as the "Restoration," which refers to the failed hopes of a new political beginning after 1945.

In the daily life of contemporary bourgeois society, at least in Germany and Austria, the wine cellar represents a kind of cultural form for the middle layer of society. If we interpret it, with certain class-specific limitations, as analogous to the tavern, the meeting place of workers, both can easily be deciphered as places where men go to recuperate not just from work, but also from home. Bachmann writes:

> Men are on the way to themselves when they get together in the evening, drink and talk and express opinions.... and [when] their opinions rise with the smoke from pipes, cigarettes and cigars and when the world turns to smoke and madness in the village inns, in the private rooms, the back rooms of the big restaurants and in the wine cellars of the big cities (83).

The participants in the *Stammtisch* discussion are described in terms of their public, social positions. Among those seated at this table are four persons with an authoritarian character who have reestablished themselves in society after having been guiltily enmeshed in the National Socialist past. They are Bertoni from the press, Haderer from the radio station, Ranitzky from the university, and Hutter from the ministry of culture. In them we have the moving forces of public cultural opinion-shaping, and these forces are male. In their conversations they remain fixated on the past and glorify the war. Also at the table are Friedl, Mahler, and the first-person narrator. The narrator hopes "that the conversation would come round to the next elections or to the vacant post of theater director, which had provided us with a topic for three Fridays already," i.e., to acceptable discussion topics that do not touch the lives of individuals. However, the others "wouldn't stop talking about the war" (93).

We may recall the public-sphere function of the bourgeois coffeehouse, which was basically that everyone could take part in the conversation without regard for differences. Bachmann's narrator insists, however, that no such equality of common humanity exists and that a generalizing discourse is thus not possible. Mahler draws a clear line separating himself, Friedl, and the narrator from the four *Stammtisch* regulars with latently fascist character when he says: "There are only three of us Jews here this evening" (85). On the one hand, this statement makes clear that the dividing line refers to recent history and emphatically separates perpetrators from victims. On the other, it also means that being "on the way to themselves" signifies different things for the various participants. Probably the narrator is a Jew, but Mahler's separation of the three of them, including himself and Friedl, from the other regulars without an objective justification shows that "Jew" is being used metonymically for "victim." In this way, Bachmann signals that the aggressivity of the authoritarian characters seated around the table is inhibited at the time of the story (1955), but that under other political conditions the "latent aggressivity in the behavioral patterns of post-war citizens can change back into open aggression at any time" (Bartsch 444).

Agreement is impossible not only because of past history, but because the group of men is not homogenous. The narrator says, in reply to Friedl's anguished exclamation that "everyone is in league with everyone":

> We're not in league, there is no league. It's much worse. I think we all have to live together and can't live together. In every brain there is a world and a demand that excludes every other world, every other demand. But we all need one another, if anything is ever to become good and whole (98).

On the basis of only isolated autonomous individuals, consensus is no longer *a priori* thinkable—as it still could be in the nineteenth century for the political self-understanding of the middle class and also of the proletariat. Instead, the question of common interests or even of a binding morality must be reformulated. The text demonstrates that Bachmann had thought through this problem early on:

> I told Friedl I understood everything and he was wrong not to understand anything. But then all at once I didn't understand anything any more either, and now I thought to myself that I couldn't even live with him, and of course still less with the others. One couldn't possibly live in one world with a man like Friedl, with whom one was in agreement but for whom a family was an argument, or with Steckel for whom art was an argument. There were times when I couldn't even live in one world with Mahler, whom I liked best of all. Did I know whether, at my next decision, he would come to the same one? "Looking back" we were in agreement, but what about the future? (102)

Let us return briefly to the memories of war. In their reminiscences the men are human beings who have feelings, are brave, or are afraid and become powerless. In connection with the war they describe themselves not in terms of their public functions but as individual, emotional subjects. In their professions and politics, however, they are separated from this side of themselves, for the only allowable subjects of discourse are interests that are split off from private life. Bachmann summarizes this with the statement: "So all of them operated in two worlds and were different in the two worlds, divided and never united egos which were never allowed to meet" (95). The lack of emotionality that men are so often accused of would be, according to Bachmann, readable as a *structural* lack, because the organization of public life produces it and men reproduce it.

172   On the Private and Public Spheres in Ingeborg Bachmann's Prose

By 1961, then, Bachmann had developed a critique of the public sphere that was to some extent gender-specific. In the *Todesarten* cycle the gender-specific critique is more closely worked out.

The Private Sphere: A Loss of Female Solidarity

In the self-understanding of the middle class, the need for emotion, warmth, and closeness was supposedly met in the private sphere, in the family; this was regulated not by law but by "love" and "trust." Until the very recent past, this task was assigned to women. For example, the introduction to the equal rights statute in contemporary German law states: "One of the husband's basic functions is to be the breadwinner and provider for the family, while the wife must regard it as her most noble duty to be the heart of the family" (Ramm). The dark side of this "noble" duty for women is described by Bachmann; that is, she introduces a very early gender-based critique of ideology. Her critical gaze is more easily recognizable if we recall that the public sphere was certainly populated by women as well as men at the beginning of the modern era.

In view of the fact that general access to public life was determined in part by *spatial* aspects, social history shows that public meeting places were still available to women in the eighteenth century but that they disappeared in the course of industrialization, on the one hand, and the spread of Rousseau's image of women, on the other. We also see that a class-specific analysis is appropriate. Though they cannot be generalized, individual examples of a female presence in public space have been uncovered by social historians. Public laundry sites, for example, which existed into the nineteenth century, were more than just a functional site for "women of the people (*Volk*)": They were a "meeting place at which tips of all kinds were exchanged and an open community of mutual assistance was constituted"; retrospectively, they can be seen as "scenes of feminism in practice" (Perrot 87).

It is important to recall that until the middle of the last century, the "interior," the home as a "site" for women, was not established for all social classes. Thus, women from the urban underclass (*Unterschicht*) came together several times a week to do laundry, even forming organizations like the 1848 Cooperative of Parisian Washerwomen, which—by the way—accepted prostitutes as well. Moreover, cooking was not yet private and isolated. Women from the urban underclass cooked for many people and gave shelter to wandering journeymen. These women also had a mastery of the spoken word. That a woman's tongue was feared can be seen in proverbs: "An angry woman has a whip in her mouth to flog men with," or "A woman's tongue is a scissors, first cutting, then stabbing, ready for battle" (Althans 47). Analyses of women workers' songs reveal still another aspect, one that has been disciplined in the course of so-called civilization: the women's conversations directly connect work and sexual desire: "When I wash the young man's pants / I swing the laundry-stick / high above my head and think: / Oh if I only had the stick / that's usually in these pants" (Althans 47).

The communication that took place at such meetings was devalued as gossip by men. Gossip is considered to be the negative form, so to speak, of "rational discourse," an attitude that has persisted into our day, visible, for example, in the slightly pejorative term "Kaffeeklatsch," which never refers to a men's gathering. Middle-class women's meetings were also regarded with amusement by male society as a caricature of the coffeehouse. Thus we see that what was still possible until the middle of the nineteenth century later gets lost, leading first to the devaluation of "women" and then to their exclusion from the public sphere.

Looking back at history not only reveals the social class differences between women and their significance for women's freedom of movement but also clarifies the degree of isolation of middle-class women in the 1950s and 1960s. Separate homes rob women of their erstwhile solidarity and mutual help, for a secure private space in the city can certainly be understood in a double sense: as protection but also as isolation. And this precisely is Bachmann's theme. In *Der Fall Franza* (The Franza Case), which remained a fragment of her *Todesarten* cycle, she uncovers the social pathology located in the very homes that guarantee anonymity and seclusion:

> For in this city [Vienna] it took an interminably long time before anyone realized what wretched rental apartments a person lived in, next door to how many illnesses and macabre family relationships—the same person who would confidently push open the door of Demel's during the day or had tickets to a premier performance in the evening—or before one understood what tasteless new high-rise apartments someone was working and vegetating in (III: 364).

These seemingly separate spheres allow a pretense, a difference between a person's appearance in public life and his/her actual life circumstances. In addition, it is part of so-called good manners not to look at this realm. Indeed, Bachmann continues, "respect for this [privacy] is a matter of honor," one would note "only the other person's telephone number," and "even if one could not get through to someone in the city, one didn't go to their house, but sent a telegram" (III: 364).

The Private Sphere: A Danger of Terror

The private sphere also represents for "woman" a danger zone of physical and psychic terror. Bachmann assumes a radically critical position toward marriage, not only throughout her works, but biographically as well. Indeed, that which is defended as inviolable in the self-understanding of the patriarchal state and the history of civil rights is represented by Bachmann from a female perspective as a lawless sphere, as a "jungle" in which "woman" is unarmed and in danger of going under. In the entire *Todesarten* cycle, Bachmann depicts the history of the destruction of women, and in the *Franza* fragment in particular she depicts the danger in the private sphere, the menace for a woman who trustingly enters the institution of marriage. The very title, "The Franza Case," can be "understood in the sense of crime fiction" (Höller 229); the criminal moves about everywhere "within the customary and the permissible" (Bachmann III: 342). Contemporary history becomes visible along the path of criminal investigation; that is, the *Todesarten* cycle unveils "crimes of murder against women represented by individual cases that are symptomatic for our time" (Höller 231),[6] "crimes that require thought, that touch our minds more than our senses, that touch us in our deepest places—where no blood flows.... But the crimes have not decreased, they only require greater refinement, a different degree of intelligence, and they are horrible" (Bachmann III: 342). Because Bachmann undertakes criminal investigation in order to "provide proof that even today many people do not die but are murdered" (III: 342), her literature is far ahead of a politics that has only in the 1990s begun to understand that this so-called "idyll" must be penetrated by legal protections against intimate crimes. In *Der Fall Franza,* she shows how Franza is observed and defined by her psychiatrist husband, turned into a "case," robbed of her possessions, her name, and her language. This is a subtle way of killing, for a woman who is robbed of language, even in the private sphere that is postulated by patriarchy as protected, cannot make herself heard in public.

An incident in the text demonstrates this phenomenon. Franza tells her husband about her first kisses, which she received at the end of the Second World War at age fifteen from an English captain upon his departure from her Galician village. There were "perhaps ten kisses that might have meant 'thank you' or 'please'" (III: 383), and Franza, who knows that these kisses "were not really kisses," calls them "English kisses." Jordan, who is interested only in a Franza who can be studied, shows *one* of the subtle ways of killing by his reaction as the story continues:

> Jordan, who never let a sentence go by without interpretation, interrupted her, that's very interesting, what you just said, English kisses, that's a slip, you must have meant angelic, and she said vehemently no, not at all, and he said don't always interrupt me, and he studied the little problem and analyzed her kisses from the linguistic side and then from the experiential side... (III: 383).

This story sheds light on the asymmetrical division of power between the sexes in this communicative situation. Franza is robbed, dispossessed, reduced to having to listen to her own story, which her husband not only analyzes and evaluates; he also has the power to reinterpret it.[7]

The forms of robbery[8] are escalated, for example when Franza, who was a co-investigator on Jordan's research project before their marriage—ironically, the project focused on eliminationist programs of the Third Reich—sees that her name is missing when their joint research is published: "The bubble had burst...my name was missing" (III: 419). Jordan also has control over her body; it is he and not she who decides she will have an abortion.

Even in its narrative technique, this fragment is an attempt to make a "female" voice audible over the dominant discourse. Bachmann takes the outcome of Franza's own experience, turns against the journalistic style of writing and asserts the evidential character of individual experience as opposed to general. She insists on Franza's experience of Jordan as her murderer vis-à-vis a society, a public sphere, that not only has no concept of this, but is complicit:

> ...the gaze of an uncomprehending environment, a public.... What could I have said? My husband...is murdering me. I'm being murdered, help me. That's what I should have said, but just think, in this society, when someone comes and says: I'm being murdered. Please tell us how and by whom and why. Facts please. Proof (III: 406).[9]

Bachmann's critique can be seen as resembling Max Horkheimer's and Theodor W. Adorno's critique of civilization. Already in the *Dialectic of Enlightenment,* they point out that in Christian civilization, woman's defenselessness represents the legal grounding for her oppression.

> Woman...is marked out by her weakness; her weakness puts her in the minority, even where women are numerically superior to men. As with the oppressed aboriginal inhabitants in early national states, or the colonial natives whose organization and weapons are primitive compared with those of their conquerors, or the Jews among the "Aryans," women's defenselessness is the legal title of their oppression (110).

Violence is the basis of social hierarchy, and Bachmann understood her writing as directed against violence. In an interview she said: "I had the feeling that I was writing against something, against an ongoing terror. One dies...not really from illnesses. One dies from what is done to one" (*Gespräche* 110).

Seen from today's perspective, two things become visible: For one, the way Bachmann's prose is time-bound, and for another, the pioneering quality of her work—the latter with respect to her having extracted a case like Franza's from the privacy in which it was threatening to disappear. Since then, certain things have improved, thanks to the women's movement. Violence and abuse in marriage no longer have to be dealt with as a private matter, internal to the parties' relationship, so to speak; rather, battered women *can* raise their voices in public. The time-bound element and the challenge it simultaneously presents also become clear when we consider that Bachmann finds in the private sphere, in relations between the sexes, the origins of a concept that we customarily apply to the public, political sphere: the concept of fascism. "You call it fascism, that's strange, I've never heard that used for private behavior, no, forgive me, it makes me laugh, no I'm certainly not crying. But that's good, it has to start somewhere, of course, why talk about it only when dealing with opinions and public actions" (III: 403).[10] Here, Bachmann picks up on the scientific discourse of the 1960s, in which the focus was not on the economy or politics as causes for fascism, but on what kind of human being it was that had tortured and murdered. When Franza says that Jordan oppresses her by modern means, which she calls "torture instruments of intelligence" (III: 404), and when she adds that "sadists are not only found in psychiatric wards and courts of law...but they are among us, with snowy white shirts and professorial titles" (III: 404), Bachmann emphasizes that this type did not disappear with the end of World War II. Here, she takes up Adorno's concept of "character structure." Adorno and his coauthors emphasized in *The Authoritarian Personality* that character structure means something relatively permanent: "[it] is above all a potential, the readiness for a response rather than the response itself." The actual behavior will "always depend on the objective situation" (9).

Not only is Bachmann's protagonist Professor Jordan an authoritarian personality, but his judgments are invested with power by virtue of his social position, indicated by his professorial title. In this, Bachmann formulates an early connection that sociologists later made explicit: the connection between a title as status symbol and masculine gender (Bourdieu 25, and note 10).

I would like to emphasize, however, that Bachmann does not claim that men *are* fascists. Rather, her concern is that a public, social structure reaches into the most personal realms, so that not only the men themselves suffer from being split in two, but women also are left with only an alienated ability to love. This can be seen in a text passage that on the surface appears to be saying that men are not good lovers, but at a deeper level shows that men too suffer under these splits and separations, they are "sick," as she says. In *Malina* she describes this separation of feelings and one's own corporeality in relation to a question posed by Malina, the narrator's male *Doppelgänger,* as to whether there are any good lovers. The answer is:

> That is a legend which has to be destroyed someday, at most there are men with whom it is completely hopeless and a few with whom it's not

quite so hopeless. Although no one has looked for it, that is where the reason is to be found why only women always have their heads full of feelings and stories about their man or men. Such thoughts really do consume the greatest part of every woman's time. But she has to think about it, she needs to evoke feeling, to provoke feeling—and she can do this without harming herself—otherwise she could literally never bear being with a man, since every man is really sick and hardly takes any notice of her. It's easy for him to think so little about women, because his diseased system is infallible, he repeats, he has repeated, he will repeat (*Malina* 178).

Our reading thus far could also show that the splitting off of emotional life is not rescinded even in the private sphere, which is reserved for feelings, because the coldness required by society does not promote trust and love, but represents a potential for destruction.

"Society is the biggest murder scene of all"

The often-quoted sentence "Society is the biggest murder scene of all" is from the novel *Malina*. One might assume that, at the time of the novel's publication in 1971, this provocation was widely accepted, given the cultural climate of the time, which was highly politicized in the wake of the events of 1968. But that was not the case for women readers in the women's movement. For this reason, Regula Venske and Sigrid Weigel speak of a certain "non-synchronicity" between the "politically active times" at the beginning of the 1970s, the political discourse of the women's movement with its "campaigns against the abortion statute (Paragraph 218)," and "women's literature" (245). The most widely read literature was not Bachmann's writing, but autobiographical accounts of female experience, such as Verena Stefan's *Häutungen* (*Shedding*).[11] Today, however, Bachmann's novel has become something of a "cult book" among feminists.

When *Malina* appeared, reviewers agreed with few exceptions that Bachmann's first novel had nothing at all do to with historical reality (cf. Atzler). Yet this novel's saturation with criticism of the public sphere can be seen not least by pursuing my question of what sort of society the novel's female "I" actually lives and works in. The main character is a nameless female "I," a writer by profession; the title figure Malina is her male double. The focus of the first chapter is the love of "I" for Ivan, and in the second chapter she experiences her destruction in a series of nightmares. At the end, after overcoming her fear with Malina's help, the "I" formulates the insight she has gained as follows:

Malina: So you'll never again say: War and Peace.
Me: Never again.
It's always war.
Here there is always violence.
Here there is always struggle.
It is the eternal war (155).

War is the reference point for the thoughts of the "I," and war is also the historical reference point. The fact that there is not peace here, but war, radically calls into question the central postulate of the bourgeois public sphere, the ability to organize society according to rational and binding rules and laws. After the nights of bad dreams the "I" leads the everyday life of a writer, where she comes into contact with various forms of the public sphere, whether through interviews that she grants, through social obligations, or through her profession, which takes her to the Frankfurt book fair, among other places.

Very much along the lines of the Frankfurt School thinkers, Bachmann also saw generalized commodification as decisive for social relations.[12] The central metaphor for public life is that of the black market (*Schwarzmarkt*), which she distinguishes in German from that of the *schwarzer Markt* (173). Possibly the difference could be formulated as follows: If the *Schwarzmarkt* in a descriptive sense refers to a specific historical phase, namely the first years after the war—a time period that she also labels an "epidemic," a concept that for her is related to that which she terms "universal prostitution" (290)—then the metaphor of the *schwarzer Markt* can be decoded as the world market in which everyone is entangled. In the tradition of Karl Marx, Bachmann describes the *schwarzer Markt* as a capitalist market that is not interested in the use value of individual products, but merely in their exchange value; one can no longer tell by looking at the products—just as with books—that they were often produced under conditions of contempt for human beings. Borrowing from the critique of a mathematicized world as formulated in *Dialectic of Enlightenment* (26), she continues: "only mathematics allows billions to be beautiful, a billion apples, on the other hand, is unpalatable, a ton of coffee in itself testifies to countless crimes..." (173). In Bachmann's critique of the public sphere, what Höller calls the "historical dimension of patriarchal rule" moves very clearly into consciousness on the linguistic level, and the "intermingling of symbolic and physical relations of violence" cannot be overlooked. Höller has pointed out that "murder scene" (*Mordschauplatz*) is also understood as a designation of the "symbolic murder," that is, the "murder of possibilities of meaning for humans and things in the fraud of mass communication" (265). Thus, in *Malina*, "the building in Vienna where the 'News Service' was housed" seems like a "murder scene" to the female "I" (182). On the semantic level, the murder scene appears at the point where it threatens the taboo areas of sexuality and death (Höller 267). Not least, according to Höller, communication as a "murder scene" is captured in words like "exposed, dissected, and analyzed" or "grind, break on the wheel, torture, and murder" (266). It is not the "worth" (*Würde*) of one's fellow humans that drives the action, but only the economy, big business.

Bachmann again depicts the destructive consequences of this principle of public life in the third part of the *Todesarten* cycle, the fragment entitled *Requiem für Fanny Goldmann* (Requiem for Fanny Goldmann). Here she introduces Marek, only thirty years old, a writer of the younger generation who publishes a book in which he exploits everything that Fanny has told him, her lover, "at night when she was lying next to him, in the afternoon when they were strolling through the woods, when they were bicycling or drinking coffee" (III: 514). It doesn't occur to Marek to apologize to Fanny for this; what is important to him is his contract with the publisher. That Bachmann's critique here is a modern one becomes clear when we recall that the relevant social relations in early bourgeois society were not only relationships of exchange, but also personal interactions influenced by "traditional factors" such as "wit" and "judgment." Kant, the philosopher of the Enlightenment, expressed this by saying that the "market price" had only a relative value, while the "worth" of a human being had an "intrinsic" value. Also, the "internal" limited the "external," i.e., morality was considered to be central not only for social life but also in general, as a social category.[13]

Today, however, public life is characterized by the incompatibility of divergent value systems; this leads the female writer, the "I" in *Malina,* to the following reflections in a letter addressed to her friend Lily:

> You know my prejudices, I have carried over certain assumptions from my education, my background, but also from a certain hierarchy of values. I was easy to deal with since I was accustomed to certain tones, to gestures, to a certain gentle manner, and the brutality with which my world—and yours as well—was injured would have itself sufficed to drive me half out of my mind (91).

Under these social conditions, sensuality and devotion have no place, they can only be formulated as utopian, as in *Malina*: "A day will come when all mankind will have redgolden eyes and starry voices, when their hands will be gifted for love, and the poetry of their lineage shall be recreated" (88).

In the late stories of the *Simultan* collection,[14] in which two of the five female protagonists enter the public sphere, Bachmann rehearses women's various strategies for action.[15] At first glance, one of the most promising seems to be that of her protagonist Elisabeth in the story "Three Paths to the Lake," which was written after *Malina*. Elisabeth, a divorced woman about fifty years old and a successful photojournalist, has learned to discipline her feelings and to use her intellect. The experience of never having met a man "who was exclusively significant for her...not a single one who was really a man and not an eccentric, a weakling, or one of the needy the world was full of," leads her to the conclusion that

> ...the man simply didn't exist, and as long as this New Man did not exist, one could only be friendly and kind to one another, for a while. There was nothing more to make of it, and it would be best if women and men kept their distance and had nothing to do with each other until both had found their way out of the tangle and confusion, the discrepancy inherent in all relationships (175).

This is no solution; on the contrary, it is a deficiency. The women figures of the *Simultan* collection may not be aware of this themselves, but the reader surely is.[16] For all their having adapted to the patriarchal world, for all the professional success that characterizes Nadja, the simultaneous interpreter, and Elisabeth, the photojournalist, feelings still break into the rational patterns of action and we see how thin the protective mechanisms are. For example, Elisabeth's plans for a future together with Manes turn out to be unworkable: "When he suddenly left her she was more shocked by the abruptness—which had not been heralded by any cloud—than by the brutal wound it inflicted and the fact that she was alone once again" (162). What she learns from this is the limit of her ability to love:

> Her increasing success with men was directly related to her increasing indifference to them: what she now, in retrospect, jokingly called sojourns in the desert and dry spells were things of the past, those days when she had cried after each loss and isolated herself in defiance, going on with a sense of pride because there was nothing she could do but keep working (174).

It is precisely this possibility of continuing to work that distinguishes Elisabeth, a figure of the second half of the twentieth century, from the middle-class female figures at the turn of the century. Elisabeth has a profession, and with it she has taken a first step into the public cultural sphere that was formerly male. In this respect it could be said that a reversal of the *Dialectic of Enlightenment* takes place: the women have become subjects, leaving object status behind. At the same time, Bachmann's cultural critique is shown to be a global critique. To be sure, "woman" now has her own voice, but at the price of becoming a co-producer of the patriarchal history of civilization that women have designated as deficient: the separation of sensuality and intellect, the disciplining of their capacity for devotion.

Art, Science, and Practical Action

Bachmann's prose represents the cutting-edge theory of her time. This is reflected, for example, in the change of narrative technique that took place between the *Franza* fragment and the novel *Malina*.[17] She no longer uses conventional narration as in *Franza,* and the *Doppelgänger*-figure proves to be a consciously chosen formal structure that challenges the principle of the self-identical character. Through her narrative technique she thus arrives at the insight that a society in which people are torn from each other and themselves must lead to a type of novel in which the reification of relations between people cannot be overcome by means of "realism." With the novel's content she breaks through the compulsion for identity that leads through the history of civilization, and of which Adorno wrote: "Men had to do fearful things to themselves before the self, the identical, purposive, and virile nature of man, was formed, and something of that recurs in every childhood" (33). Bachmann goes beyond the cultural theory of the Frankfurt School by giving female figures a voice, too. In this, she is depicting something for which the time had not yet come.[18]

Bachmann's art not only gives us information about how we live, but also how we *should* live. However, art cannot overcome the deficiencies that it depicts, cannot rescind the separations of public and private, of intellect and sensuality. That is a question for social practice. Art is the symptom-bearer of the crisis in the bourgeois public sphere. The literary work of Ingeborg Bachmann gives expression to the legal vacuum in the private sphere and the life-threatening penetration of the private sphere by a public sphere that has distanced itself from the need for moral justification (and thus the vulnerability of morality). Thus, her art is also a symptom-bearer of the crisis of Enlightenment postulates. In so far as art also contains the aesthetic possibility of drafting, as a utopia, the beginning of the end of the history of violence, Bachmann reminds us that reality has not yet reached the stage of making happiness possible.[19] What Bachmann achieved in giving expression to this is, not least, that she gave those who were so long oppressed a voice.

And so I would like to conclude with a utopian passage from *Malina* in which the crisis of the private and of the public sphere is imagined to be overcome so that things can get their "aura" back, and the people their "dignity" (*Würde*):

> Even though at one time everyone knew, but since nobody remembers today, I'll disclose one reason why it has to happen secretly, why I close the door, lower the curtain, why I am alone when I present myself to Ivan. I'm not trying to keep us hidden; I want to recreate a taboo, and Malina understood this without my having to explain it, because even when I'm alone and my bedroom door is open, or when he's the only

one in the apartment, he walks to his room as if there never were an open door, as if there never were a closed one, as if there weren't any room at all, so as not to profane anything and so the first bold moves and last tender submissions might have another chance (15-16).

Translated by Jeanette Clausen

Notes

This article is the revised version of a lecture given during my research leave at the University of Massachusetts Amherst in the fall of 1994. My special thanks to Sara Lennox. (Translator's note: Material quoted by the author from German sources is here cited from published English translations, where available. These published translations have been added to the list of works cited. All other translations are my own.)

[1] On the interdisciplinarity of this category and for a literature review that includes discussion of the new reception of Habermas's public sphere theory in America, see Arthur Strum's bibliography.

[2] For example, Regina Dackweiler and Barbara Holland-Cunz allude to Habermas's book in their title, then use his description of the disintegration of the bourgeois public sphere as "an analytical model for the process of disintegration of the feminist public sphere" (106).

[3] In her 1992 article, Karin Hausen asks "what it is that is assigned to the public and to the private sphere, why these assignments were made one way and not another, and what the agreed-upon divisions mean or should mean for women as a group and for men as a group" (81). But, as Elizabeth Mittman asks, "...how does this model apply in a state whose structure challenges the legitimacy of such a public sphere altogether?" (22).

[4] See Carol Pateman: "What can be said is that although the personal is not the political, the two spheres are interrelated, necessary dimensions of a future, democratic feminist social order" (134).

[5] The limitations of this model are well known, since the conditions of participation were property and education. See John Stuart Mill, *Considerations on Representative Government*.

[6] Höller has shown that elements of the crime novel can be traced in the entire *Todesarten* cycle, and that "signifying elements of the crime and horror drama [are] actualized" in the radio play *The Good God of Manhattan* (*Der Gute Gott von Manhattan*) (230).

[7] Peter Brinkemper has called attention to the connection between the content of the statement of dispossession and the narrative technique.

[8] Tanja Schmidt sees specific forms of self-alienation, of "being robbed of one's property" (479), be it the language, the experience, or the history of

women, as "constitutive... for *Todesarten* as well as for the stories in *Simultan*" (480).

[9] The extremely limited ability of the public sphere to perceive what is going on is also noted by Monika Meister (72).

[10] Irene Heidelberger-Leonard finds that for Bachmann "the 'war' between male and female [is] the initial germ for the political monstrosities of National Socialism" (114). However, she sees in "that sort of chronological reversal" a "dangerous terminological blurring of borders" (114).

[11] However, as Constance Hotz has recently shown, *Malina* enjoyed a degree of commercial success. Hotz cites "unexpectedly high sales figures, which necessitated three printings during the first year of publication alone" (150). Thus, a more subtle analysis of the reception history is needed.

[12] Already in 1983 Sandra Frieden emphasized that the explosive social criticism in *Malina* was a critique of "commodity culture," and recognized the irony in the newspaper editor's name, Ganz: "She knows quite well that there can be no wholeness in this society" (67).

[13] Thus, in Kant's *Grounding for the Metaphysics of Morals,* "morality and humanity...alone have dignity," while "[s]kill and diligence in work have a market price," and "wit, lively imagination, and humor have an affective price" (40-41). Within this construction, the relations that have no exchange value and are expressed in terms of affective price can be interpreted as relations in which the subjects do not yet relate to one another as owners of commodities. (Trans. note: The German word *Würde* means both "worth" and "dignity.")

[14] Trans. note: The stories in the German collection *Simultan* are published in English under the title *Three Paths to the Lake,* cited in the text of the article.

[15] Irene Holeschofsky called attention to the significance of irony for the narrative intent of this collection already in 1980. Friederike Eigler builds upon this, attempting, with the help of Bakhtin's dialogic, "a reading of the *Simultan* cycle...that emphasizes its critical potential" (4). However, with her "macroanalysis," she arrives at judgments that are based on a faulty reading. For example, Elisabeth, the cousin of Beatrix in the story "Problems Problems," is not, as Eigler claims, the protagonist of the story "Three Paths to the Lake"; the character in "Problems Problems" is Elisabeth Mihailovics, who is having "an affair with this Marek" (II: 328). More fundamental, it seems to me, is that Eigler does not achieve her intended distance from the feminist readings of the 1980s, which overwhelmingly, as Bärbel Thau has also pointed out, conceptualized the power relations between the sexes as a simple polarity of (male) perpetrator and (female) victim. As early as 1988, however, Sara Lennox stated that "gender relations exist within a context of larger social relations determining their content and the fate of the characters that must operate within their parameters" ("Bachmann Reading" 187). Gender is embedded in a specific social and historical context, as Lennox has shown ("The Feminist Reception"). Sigrid Weigel offers a more differentiated reading than that of the "complicity" paradigm in current scholarship.

[16] As Peter W. Nutting writes: "By articulating Elisabeth's memories, longings and disappointments the narrator helps to shape a truth about Elisabeth's life that she has never been able to tell anyone, even herself" (80).

[17] On the development of the narrative technique in the *Franza* fragment and in *Malina,* cf. especially Monika Albrecht.

[18] Bachmann herself expected this of art. Thus she writes in the first of her Frankfurt Lectures, under the title "Questions and Pseudo-Questions," that a poet could "at best" succeed in two things, "...in representing his time, and in representing something for which the time had not yet come" (IV: 196).

[19] The importance of utopia for Bachmann's understanding of poetics is also emphasized by Michael Benedikt; see especially 104.

Works Cited

Adorno, Theodor W., et al. *The Authoritarian Personality*. Studies in Prejudice. Ed. Max Horkheimer and Samuel H. Flowerman. New York: Harper, 1950.

Albrecht, Monika. *Die andere Seite: Untersuchungen zur Bedeutung von Werk und Person Max Frischs in Ingeborg Bachmanns "Todesarten."* Würzburg: Königshausen and Neumann, 1989.

Althans, Birgit. "'Halte dich fern von den klatschenden Weibern...' Zur Phänomenologie des Klatsches." *Feministische Studien* 2 (1985): 46–53.

Atzler, Elke. "Ingeborg Bachmanns Roman Malina im Spiegel der literarischen Kritik." *Jahrbuch der Grillparzer-Gesellschaft 15*. Wien: Konegen, 1983. 155–71.

Bachmann, Ingeborg. *Malina: A Novel*. Trans. Philip Boehm. New York: Holmes & Meier, 1990.

―――. "Among Murderers and Madmen." *The Thirtieth Year*. Trans. Michael Bullock. New York: Knopf, 1964.

―――. *Three Paths to the Lake*. Trans. Mary Fran Gilbert. New York: Holmes & Meier, 1989.

―――. *Werke*. Vol. 1-4. Ed. Christine Koschel, Inge von Weidenbaum and Clemens Münster. München: Piper, 1978.

―――. *Wir müssen wahre Sätze finden: Gespräche und Interviews*. Ed. Christine Koschel and Inge von Weidenbaum. München: Piper, 1983.

Bartsch, Kurt. "Geschichtliche Erfahrung in der Prosa von Ingeborg Bachmann. Am Beispiel der Erzählungen *Jugend in einer österreichischen Stadt* und *Unter Mördern und Irren.*" *Kein objektives Urteil—nur ein lebendiges: Texte zum Werk von Ingeborg Bachmann*. Ed. Christine Koschel und Inge von Weidenbaum. München: Piper, 1989. 432–48.

Benedikt, Michael. "Wir müssen wahre Sätze finden." *Ingeborg Bachmann: Die Schwarzkunst der Worte*. Ed. John Pattillo-Hess and Wilhelm Petrasch. Wien: Verein Volksbildungshaus Wiener Urania, 1993: 96–108.

Bourdieu, Pierre. *Distinction: A Social Critique of the Judgment of Taste*. Trans. Richard Nice. Cambridge: Harvard UP, 1984.

Brandt, Reinhard. "Freiheit, Gleichheit, Selbständigkeit bei Kant." *Die Ideen von 1789 in der deutschen Rezeption*. Ed. Forum für Philosophie Bad Homburg. Frankfurt a.M.: Suhrkamp, 1989. 90–128.

Brinkemper, Peter. "Ingeborg Bachmanns *Der Fall Franza* als Paradigma weiblicher Erzähltechnik." *Modern Austrian Literature* 18 (1985): 147–82.

Dackweiler, Regina, and Holland-Cunz, Barbara. "Strukturwandel feministischer Öffentlichkeit." *Beiträge zur feministischen Theorie und Praxis* 14.30/31 (1991): 105–27.

Eigler, Friederike. "Bachmann und Bachtin: Zur dialogischen Erzählstruktur von '*Simultan*.'" *Modern Austrian Literature*. 24.3/4 (1991): 1–16.

Frieden, Sandra. "Bachmann's *Malina* and *Todesarten*: Subliminal Crimes." *German Quarterly* 56.1 (January 1983): 1–16.

Habermas, Jürgen. *The Structural Transformation of the Public Sphere: An Inquiry into a Category of Bourgeois Society*. Trans. Thomas Burger with the assistance of Frederick Lawrence. Cambridge: The MIT Press, 1989.

Hausen, Karin. "Öffentlichkeit und Privatheit: Gesellschaftspolitische Konstruktionen und die Geschichte der Geschlechterbeziehungen." *Frauengeschichte—Geschlechtergeschichte*. Ed. Karin Hausen and Heide Wunder. Frankfurt a.M.: Campus, 1992.

Heidelberger-Leonard, Irene. "Ingeborg Bachmanns Todesarten-Zyklus und das Thema Auschwitz." *Kritische Wege der Landnahme: Ingeborg Bachmann im Blickfeld der neunziger Jahre*. Ed. Robert Pichl and Alexander Stillmark. Wien: Hora, 1994. 113–24.

Holeschofsky, Irene. "Bewußtseinsdarstellung und Ironie in Ingeborg Bachmanns Erzählung *Simultan*." *Sprachkunst* 11 (1980): 63–70.

Höller, Hans. *Ingeborg Bachmann, Das Werk: Von den frühesten Gedichten bis zum "Todesarten"-Zyklus*. Frankfurt a.M.: Athenäum, 1987.

Hölscher, Lucian. *Öffentlichkeit und Geheimnis: Eine begriffsgeschichtliche Untersuchung zur Entstehung der Öffentlichkeit in der frühen Neuzeit*. Stuttgart: Klett-Cotta, 1979.

Horkheimer, Max, and Theodor W. Adorno. *Dialectic of Enlightenment*. Trans. John Cumming. New York: Continuum, 1989.

Hotz, Constance. *"Die Bachmann." Das Image der Dichterin: Ingeborg Bachmann im journalistischen Diskurs*. Konstanz: Faude, 1990.

Joeres, Ruth-Ellen B. "'We are adjacent to human society': German Women Writers, The Homosocial Experience, and a Challenge to the Public/Domestic Dichotomy." *Women in German Yearbook 10*. Ed. Jeanette Clausen and Sara Friedrichsmeyer. Lincoln: U of Nebraska P, 1995. 39–57.

Kant, Immanuel. *Grounding for the Metaphysics of Morals*. Trans. James W. Ellington. 3d ed. Indianapolis: Hackett, 1993.

———. *Perpetual Peace*. Ed., intro., trans. Lewis White Beck. Indianapolis: Bobbs-Merrill, 1957.

Lennox, Sara. "Bachmann Reading/Reading Bachmann: Wilkie Collins's *The Woman in White* in the *Todesarten*." *German Quarterly* 61.2 (Spring 1988): 183–92.

———. "The Feminist Reception of Ingeborg Bachmann." *Women in German Yearbook 8*. Ed. Jeanette Clausen and Sara Friedrichsmeyer. Lincoln: U of Nebraska P, 1992. 73–111.

Meister, Monika. "Der Fall Moosbrugger—Der Fall Franza: Machtstrukturen und sanktioniertes Verbrechen bei Musil und Bachmann." *Musil-Studien* 14 (München 1986): 63–80.

Mill, John Stuart. *Considerations on Representative Government*. Ed. Currin V. Shields. Indianapolis: Bobbs-Merrill, 1958.

Mittman, Elizabeth. "Locating a Public Sphere: Some Reflections on Writers and Öffentlichkeit in the GDR." *Women in German Yearbook 10*. Ed. Jeanette Clausen and Sara Friedrichsmeyer. Lincoln: U of Nebraska P, 1995. 19–39.

Nutting, Peter W. "'Ein Stück wenig realisiertes Österreich': The Narrative Topography of Ingeborg Bachmann's *Drei Wege zum See*." *Modern Austrian Literature* 18 (1985): 77–90.

Pateman, Carol. *The Disorder of Women: Democracy, Feminism and Political Theory*. Cambridge, MA: Polity, 1989.

Perrot, Michelle. "Rebellische Weiber: Die Frau in der französischen Stadt." *Listen der Ohnmacht: Zur Sozialgeschichte weiblicher Widerstandsformen*. Ed. Claudia Honegger and Bettina Heintz. Frankfurt a.M.: Europäische Verlagsanstalt, 1984. 71–99.

Ramm, Thilo. "Gleichberechtigung und Hausfrauensache." *Juristenzeitung* 19 January 1968: 41–46.

Saage, Richard. *Eigentum, Staat und Gesellschaft bei Immanuel Kant*. Stuttgart: Kohlhammer, 1973.

Schmidt, Tanja. "Beraubung des Eigenen: Zur Darstellung geschichtlicher Erfahrung im Erzählzyklus *Simultan* von Ingeborg Bachmann." *Kein objektives Urteil—nur ein lebendiges: Texte zum Werk von Ingeborg Bachmann*. Ed. Christine Koschel and Inge von Weidenbaum. München: Piper, 1989. 479–503.

Stefan, Verena. *Shedding; and, Literally Dreaming*. Trans. Johanna S. Moore, Beth E. Weckmueller, et al. New York: Feminist Press at the City University of New York, 1994.

Strum, Arthur. "A Bibliography of the Concept of Öffentlichkeit." *New German Critique* 61 (Winter 1994): 161–202.

Thau, Bärbel. *Gesellschaftsbild und Utopie im Spätwerk Ingeborg Bachmanns: Untersuchungen zum 'Todesarten-Zyklus' und zu 'Simultan.'* Frankfurt a.M.: Lang, 1986.

Tönnies, Ferdinand. *Community and Society (Gemeinschaft und Gesellschaft)*. Ed., trans. Charles P. Loomis. East Lansing: Michigan State UP, 1957.

Venske, Regula and Sigrid Weigel. "'Frauenliteratur'—Literatur von Frauen." *Gegenwartsliteratur seit 1968*. Ed. Klaus Briegleb and Sigrid Weigel. München: Hanser, 1992. 245-79.

Weigel, Sigrid. "Zur Polyphonie des Anderen: Traumatisierung und Begehren in Bachmanns imaginärer Autobiographie." *Ingeborg Bachmann: Die Schwarzkunst der Worte*. Ed. John Pattillo-Hess and Wilhelm Petrasch. Wien: Verein Volksbildungshaus Wiener Urania, 1993. 9-25.

Interview with Elisabeth Alexander: The Mother Courage of German Postwar Literature

Frederick A. Lubich

The interview with the German author Elisabeth Alexander discusses her controversial role among the generation of women authors in post-war German literature. The author talks about her own personal and intellectual development, the cultural differences between Germany and America, her relationship to Germany's fascist past, her strong but ambivalent involvement with Germany's student movement, feminism, and the Catholic church. A substantial part of the interview focuses on her own work, discussing its recurring themes of sexuality, pornography, gender trouble, men as such, and the role of women, especially mothers, in modern society. (FAL)

Elisabeth Alexander was born in the Rhineland in 1922—although until 1992 she persistently claimed she was born ten years later. Raised in a poor family of nine children, she attended a Catholic school for girls and spent one year in a monastery studying home economics (*Hauswirtschaft*). After marrying and relocating permanently to Heidelberg, she was divorced and raised her three children on her own. With various odd jobs she tried to make ends meet and attended acting school and adult education classes.

Alexander dates the actual beginning of her literary career to a spectacular public reading in the Academy Garden of Heidelberg in 1970, an event that attracted attention far beyond the city. The then very popular radical left-wing journal *Pardon* called her a "porno-poetess" and surmised: "After the student revolt, her poems were the hardest thing for the citizens of Heidelberg to swallow."[1] Although Alexander never reached the literary celebrity status of the younger generation of female writers like Elfriede Jelinek or—at one time—Karin Struck, she nevertheless established herself as one of the most controversial woman authors in the Federal Republic of Germany. Verena Auffermann celebrated her in *Die Zeit* almost euphorically as a "plebian poetess" and Gerhard Zwerenz called it a "disgrace for the Federal Republic" that such a "phenomenal word smith" had received hardly any public financial support.

On the other hand, Alexander has always attracted her fair share of ridicule and hostility. After the publication of her first and most successful novel *Die törichte Jungfrau* (The Foolish Virgin, 1978), Christa Rotzoll of the *Frankfurter Allgemeine Zeitung* declared it the "most redundant publication of this year's spring," a "private sex-report," of the "fluffiest intellectual quality." Niels Höpfner of the *Frankfurter Rundschau* called it a "radical confessional novel, almost impeccably constructed, and on a level of reflection of considerable height."

Since then, Alexander has produced a large body of novels, short stories, and poetry as well as numerous articles and book reviews in various newspapers and literary journals. Although focused upon her central themes of sexuality and the role of women and mothers in our society, her productivity covers a much wider array of themes and topics, including nature poetry and children's stories. Her style ranges from the crude, shocking, and sarcastic to the lyrical and elegiac, the surreal and fairytale-like. Whereas some pieces are remarkably crafted, others appear sketchy, more like the raw material of life than elaborate works of art.

Courted by such diverse interest groups as the nascent underground press of the 1970s, the growing feminist movement, as well as a variety of church organizations, Alexander usually managed to please and provoke them at the same time. Her second major novel *Sie hätte ihre Kinder töten sollen* (She Should Have Killed Her Children), equally lauded and lacerated by critics, was almost unanimously praised for its intent to move the "marginal group of the mothers" into the center of public consciousness. Not least because of her penchant for controversy, she became a frequent guest at literary conferences and radio talk shows and on national television programs such as "Literaturmagazin," "Café Größenwahn," "Berliner Salon," and "Literatur Live." Her more recent works are characterized by a tendency toward laconic brevity, describing the vicissitudes of everyday life and contemplating such timely and timeless topics as the ubiquitous cult of youth and the personal experience of aging.

In the 1980s Alexander visited the United States four times as writer in residence or lecturer with the Goethe Institute. She was the first West German author to speak on tape for the archive of world literature at the Library of Congress in Washington, DC. Back home she began to perform with jazz bands, reciting her poetry, and also to teach creative writing seminars at various academies and universities. Up to this day, she participates actively in the cultural life of Germany, giving poetry readings in libraries and city halls of major cities, appearing on regional television, and, most recently, enjoying—through the nomination of the

Baden Württemberg State Ministry for Family, Women, Continuing Education and Art—a two-month stay at the Villa Massimo in Rome.

Notes

Translations are my own.

[1] All quotations in this introduction are from Gräf, Dieter M. "Elisabeth Alexander." *Kritisches Lexikon zur deutschsprachigen Gegenwartsliteratur.* Ed. Heinz Ludwig Arnold. München: Edition Text + Kritik, 1978, 1988. 2-5.

Selected Bibliography of Works by Elisabeth Alexander

Bums: Fünfzig Gedichte. Mit Zeichnungen von Pit Morell. Hamburg: Merlin, 1971.
Nach einer gewissen Lebenszeit. Erzählungen. Illustration von Hans Palm. St. Augustin: Steyler, 1975.
Die Frau, die lachte: Bürgerliche Texte. Leverkusen: Braun, 1975.
Ich bin kein Pferd. Gedichte. Grafik von Martina Etienne. Leverkusen: Braun, 1976.
Fritte Pomme. Kinderroman. Leverkusen: Braun, 1976.
Brotkrumen. Gedichte. Luxemburg: Sisyphus, 1977.
Die törichte Jungfrau. Roman. Köln: Braun, 1978. Taschenbuchausgabe: Frankfurt a.M.: Fischer, 1979.
Ich hänge mich ans schwarze Brett: 43 Gedichte. Hamburg: Merlin, 1979.
Sie hätte ihre Kinder töten sollen. Roman. Düsseldorf: Erb, 1982.
Damengeschichten. Heilbronn: Emig, 1983.
"Meine Kindheit in der Kindheit meiner Kinder." *Das Herz für Kinder klebt an den Autos: Eltern schreiben für Eltern vom Mut sich zu verändern.* Ed. Helga Häsing. Hamburg: Rowohlt, 1983. 16-23.
"Die Dunkelheit ist da." *Jahrbuch schreibender Frauen 2.* Ed. Anne Birk, Regine Kress-Fricke, and Sabine Matthiessen. Karlsruhe: von Loeper, 1985. 17-22.
Zeitflusen. Gedichte. Heidelberg: Heidelberger Verlagsanstalt, 1986.
Im Korridor geht der Mond. Gedichte. Trier: édition trèves, 1988.
Herrengeschichten. Trier: édition trèves, 1990.
Bauchschuß. Roman. Trier: édition trèves, 1992.
Die Uhr läuft rückwärts wenn der Schnee fällt: Ein lyrischer Jahreszyklus. Weilerswist: Landpresse, 1994.
Domizil Heidelberg. Erzählungen. Speyer: Lösch, 1995.

***

Frederick Lubich: Elisabeth Alexander, what would we be missing in present-day German literature if you did not exist?

Elisabeth Alexander: You certainly would miss an absolutely original narrative flow in present-day German literature. I open my thoughts like you open a water faucet, that's how my thoughts flow, unfiltered and pure onto the paper. And when there is an inner stop, I switch the faucet off. It is my principle to correct nothing during this narrative flow, absolutely nothing. On the contrary, I write through to the last period.

That sounds like a stream of consciousness.

That's exactly what it is.

Do you correct your texts, after you let them sit for a while?

Let me give you a concrete example; I wrote a "long poem" with 205 lines: "Die Dunkelheit ist da" (Darkness Has Arrived). After I had left it alone for a while, I started to "correct" some passages, because I thought it wasn't good enough, I'd make it a bit more modern. But when it came to publishing, I changed all passages that I had "corrected" back to the original version. When I correct—edit—I only want the absolutely precise word, it has to be right linguistically and stylistically. The narrative rhythm has to be alive. Today I know that a lot of things that only come from the head lead to emotional amputation. Some of our present-day German writers and intellectuals suffer from this emotional amputation.

Is this something specifically German?

I think so; I have not experienced it in America, where I have lectured four times at universities and Goethe Institutes. In Germany, there is a cultural arrogance. If someone can juggle with foreign words, that makes him an intellectual. The use of foreign words creates an aura of academic education, which in turn excludes others from communication. That creates cultural complexes and instills in many people the feeling that they are stupid.

Is that the flip side of the German tradition of a cultural elite (Bildungsbürgertum)*?*

This is probably so. I myself suffered a lot in the beginning from the fact that I did not know a lot of things. As a twenty year old, I wanted to read all books, and when I realized that this was not possible, I was very upset. Later, I never educated my children in the illusion that I knew everything. It is very overwhelming for children if parents know everything. Then they have no free space to explore the world on their own. I am against the conscious intimidation of people by our academic philistines and the media intelligentsia. At the same time, these so-called intellectuals quite often feel intimidated by me, because I am always unpredictable in my written as in my spoken word...unpredictable also for myself. And that makes me even more prone to take risks, to become more conscious of risks. Because I myself don't know what I will say the next moment.

When I hear you speak about Germany and the Germans, I quite often hear a very critical undertone. What is your actual relationship to Germany, its history, and its culture? In your poem "Vaterland" (Fatherland) you wrote: "Ich liebe dich Land, weil du im Frieden weiter leben mußt, um deine getöteten Menschen wieder in dich aufzunehmen" (I love you, my country, because you have to continue to live in peace, in order to take back into yourself all your murdered people). What does that mean to you today?

What was hurting me for a long time, what almost drove me insane, was the fact that when I was a young girl, I had heard nothing in my hometown of the atrocities of the Third Reich in which I grew up after all. I was not raised in a politically conscious world. Thus, I had nothing to say when later the generation of '68 confronted us about that time. And then I always felt embarassed about it. The most important topic in my childhood was the daily bread on the table. And National Socialism—you can hardly talk about that—had always helped poor people like us with nine children. However, when much later I saw the first mountains of corpses from the concentration camps, I was shocked. I simply could not imagine how these crimes could have happened in a civilized country, committed by supposedly decent, intelligent people. That made me absolutely speechless. I still cannot write about it to this day, because I have to understand and describe it from a human perspective and don't want to explain it politically or theoretically.

And the human aspect in Hitler? His catastrophic career?

Was that not also the scream of a soul tortured in his childhood, in an orphanage? With all that I feel absolutely hopeless. To write poetry about that seems to me to be absolutely perfidious. But you cannot disavow what happened, as Heinrich Böll once told me.

Which one of your books do you consider to be your most important one?

Fritte Pomm, to start with, my first longer work of prose, a kind of children's novel, but then also my first proper novel, *Die törichte Jungfrau.* When I wrote *Fritte Pomm,* my innocence in writing was still completely uncorrupted intellectually. It is pure fantasy, a deeply intimate (*innig*) occidental fairy tale.

Are you a born but lapsed teller of fairy tales?

That could be so, had I not listened so many times to the wrong people.

How did you get started on Die törichte Jungfrau?

My publisher told me that it was time to write a novel. He wanted a "real work," after I had published *Die Frau, die lachte* (The Woman Who Laughed), a collection of stories *Ich bin kein Pferd* (I Am Not a Horse), a collection of poetry, and *Fritte Pomm.* Listening to my publisher, I immediately thought of Dostoevsky, whose novels I like a lot, but he said: "Why don't you simply write about Elisabeth Alexander." The private one or the professional one, I wanted to know—and then I wrote *Die törichte Jungfrau.*

The feuilletons of the German press, from regional newspapers to Die Zeit, *have always characterized you positively as well as negatively as a gadfly and your work as making trouble (cf. "Sand im Literaturbetrieb") in the literary scene. Why?*

What they did not like was the fact that the heroines of my novels, like Josefine Bähr or Magdalena Sand in *Sie hätte ihre Kinder töten sollen,* were "everyday people." Such women—they said—are a dime a dozen. If my heroine had been a psychiatrist like in Erica Jong, or an attractive female student, a successful actress, then these books would have been accepted differently. I also heard such accusations in my lectures. For example, one time a Gymnasium student asked me at a poetry reading in Hockenheim: "Why, Frau Alexander, do you write about a street sweeper? Aren't there better professions?" "Isn't that also a human being?" I asked in return.

The beginning of your literary career coincides approximately with the beginning of the student movement. At that time you quickly became a sort of cult figure in Heidelberg. How did that happen?

Yes, at that time I had organized my first street reading in Heidelberg and I read my poems "Bums," which simply meant something like: Bang, here they are, my poems [*bums* in German also means "to screw"]. I wrote these poems against the rising sex and porno wave, against the objectification of women, rendering them no-bodies, and against the social denigration of the mother. With this volume of poems I became instantly known—some would say notorious—in the German literary underground and it earned me the reputation of a porno princess. My philosophical concerns were of no interest to them. And interestingly enough, what a lot of people disliked the most was the fact that some of the erotically very explicit texts did not arouse them.

Was that a time of social change for you, of sexual liberation from ossified moral conventions?

No, as far as bourgeois morality is concerned, nothing has changed; nowadays there is probably even more of a double standard than at that time. On the contrary, the sex and porno wave of that time turned the whole institution of marriage and family life upside down. On the other hand, I also don't like it when women can't admit that they enjoy intercourse. To come back one more time to the key words "change" and "liberation": During that period I received very important impulses from young Americans. I had rented my apartment with room and board to foreign students. I remember especially well two Americans, one was the son of a well-known film producer, the other was doing his doctorate in English literature. We were constantly debating and discussing, the way everything—as a matter of principle—was endlessly discussed at that time. Those two made me aware for the first time of the macho behavior of my husband and they really supported me in my writing. Those foreign students—from all over the world so to speak—became my major cultural and international experiences. That way I learned a lot about culture in general and gained experiences of the world. These people appreciated me above all as a person. By contrast, the German students at that time were not really interested in discussion but rather confrontation. I remember numerous panel discussions and street demonstrations, where students were only accusing older people of the Hitler regime instead of engaging in a real dialogue.

That probably also explains the radicalization of the German student movement into political terrorism.

Yes, that was a really hysterical time. I caught myself reading the newspaper every day, craving news about the Baader-Meinhof gang. But not until Baader was arrested did I realize to what an appalling degree I had become hooked on the sensational news.

How would you summarize these times?

During the student revolt my intellect was sharpened, my reasoning powers became strengthened. At the same time, I learned to go on the offensive, to develop my instincts and my intuition.

What do you think about contemporary German literature?

In the past I read Böll's works, especially *Und sagte kein einziges Wort* (*And Never Said a Word*) with great fascination; his creative resources were the emotions, the human condition. To him I feel related. However, whereas he in his early phase had a stylistic preference for the adjective, for me the verb has always been more important. There is a danger in adjectives, as their meaning is relative and subjective, whereas verbs are definitive, precise. I was immediately turned off by *Die Blechtrommel* (*The Tin Drum*), its kind of writing, this alienation effect, where the author speaks through a child. And then this Handke. In his novel *Die Stunde der wahren Empfindung* (*A Moment of True Feeling*), the protagonist finds his way back into life because he stumbles upon a shard of a mirror, a braid clip, and a maple leaf in a sand box. That annoyed me. I first would have picked up the glass shard and thrown it away, so that no child could get hurt with it.

And world literature?

In Dostoevsky, I am fascinated with the psychological aspects, the fathoming of the inner world, the plumbing of the abyss of the human soul. And then there is Charles Dickens. I enjoyed reading him. But after all the book reviews I had written for various newspapers, I had to realize that I have to be my own literary model.

How would you define yourself politically?

In the seventies, every German author wanted to be a politically engaged author. The appropriation of this term for the purely political realm always bothered me. I once stood up during a major public reading of young authors and interjected into the long debate: "I can engage myself just as thoroughly with changing diapers."

Literary criticism invented the term "New Subjectivity" for the literature of the seventies.

I could only shake my head about that. These categories of the subjective and autobiographical were self-evident for me. In principle, literature for me means life, to be oneself, to realize oneself, beginning with writing books and selling them. At literary festivals, church conventions, literary conferences, I always had my books with me for sale, and I did advertising for myself. In 1979 at the Frankfurt book fair I went as a sandwich lady, advertising my new book *Ich hänge mich ans schwarze Brett* (I Hang Myself Up on the Blackboard). On the third day, the Suhrkamp publishing house stole my idea and had a sandwich man walking around advertising...

In those days you made headlines...

...and I landed in the limelight. At that time I repeatedly appeared on television.

Frau Alexander, your relationship to feminism?

Feminine actually means soft, tender, fine, doesn't it? And then came this hard-as-a-rock feminism, and that always stunned me. I would have liked to be accepted by this movement, but what bothered me was the women's lack of unity among themselves. Unlike men, women do not have common goals. Alice Schwarzer never had any use for me. Is it because I am not always saying yes to the party line? Don't I have to look at an issue first from all angles? And if you don't want to commit yourself ideologically, if instead you ask questions, then you are an individualist and quickly isolated, and that actually saddened me quite a bit.

Do women write essentially differently than men?

With archaic women, nurturing plays a great role; with that I mean the physical and spiritual nurturing, the sharing with another human being, something that transcends the sexual by far. This virtue was very important in ancient matriarchal cultures. Modern women writers who are after recognition like to imitate male writing, see for example Ingeborg Bachmann. Wohmann, too, has a male way of writing; by that I mean the emphasis on the intellectual in both authors. I always wanted to read a female author with whom I could identify, who has a complex world of emotions and an emotional intelligence and who can express that. I have never found one and I have come to the conclusion that I have to write the way I want, not the way the market wants me to.

With wit and anger...from your guts and not your head.

For me the pleasure (*Lust*) of writing is equivalent to sexual pleasure. For me pleasure is a great gift from God.

Time and again your stories center on the bed...

Yes, I remember how one of these talk show hosts had asked me in front of a huge audience: "Frau Alexander, what do you think when you hear the word 'bed'?" This question in public made me furious and I shouted into the lecture hall: "Take your bed and go home." This man just wanted to make me feel uncomfortable and harass me.

Nevertheless, you participated in a film in which you're already lying in bed in the first scene. The bed seems to mean more to you than just a place to sleep and make love. The bed as the beginning and end of all experiences, the place of the highest pleasure and the deepest space?

Yes, and the bed is also my most intimate place to write. There, my thoughts come from the warmth of all my senses. In *Die törichte Jungfrau* I wrote among other things that Josefine Bähr had been a "mother brothel" for all men. This means to me a sort of homecoming for the man. He was spiritually fed by Josefine, physically nurtured, and then he could go out into the world again. What Josefine wanted to offer men was protection and shelter.

Aren't these quite conventional concepts about women and mothers?

If you like. However, in this sense, I could also say: the sky is conventional, the tree is conventional...feelings are conventional too, no matter in what century they are felt. That has something to do with the human condition. A women is born as a woman and not as a mother, but some have a mother instinct. That's why maternal women (*Mutterfrauen*) have archaic instincts.

You have thematized and problematized woman's mother role like no other female author in post-war German literature.

The mother role is not constant, it has already changed hundreds of times throughout history. I would say the mother role has been subject to changing modes and fashions that are now being redefined on an almost daily basis through the media and their theoretical babble. To be a mother, that has to do with fate, no matter in what times.

That reminds me of Nietzsche's love of fate, but also of your hatred of fate, for example in your novel Sie hätte ihre Kinder töten sollen. *Maybe first to Nietzsche. In* Die törichte Jungfrau *you wrote: "Nietzsche supported her."*

Yes, that was my Zarathustra period; Josefine as well as I could identify with this figure.

In Die törichte Jungfrau *you also depict violent female sexual phantasies. In one passage we read about Josefine and how she bites into a man's penis, that is, she rips off a piece of its skin.*

That is true—and certainly not new. That reminds me now of a certain man. Let me explain it this way: if I can sense with a man that he sees me only as a sexual object and does not accept me wholly as a woman, in other words, if he has this macho thing, then he will be punished, just like Josefine did it. If I can sense this penis arrogance in a man, then his penis will get it. It will not be bitten off—but it will be incapacitated, at least for a couple of days. I speak from experience. At that time I felt as if I were an empress taking revenge on behalf of so many women, do you understand?

I'm afraid I do.

However, above all, Josefine wanted to be a spiritual and maternal mentor and mistress to man.

To come back to your novel Sie hätte ihre Kinder töten sollen. *How in your life and work do you reconcile maternal pleasure and maternal frustration? Your protagonists frequently envision and enact this highly contradictory mixture of feelings in a powerful, if not violent manner. Didn't that sometimes frighten your men as well as your children?*

You have to look at it this way: this great lamento has to be based on vitality, discipline, patience, and the reliability of feelings. These were the virtues my heroines wanted to convey. And in all my exaggerations and my passionate screaming fits, "my men" and my children gladly played their part on my mother stage.

Your last major novel Bauchschuß *(Shot in the Stomach)?*

The way I depicted the hatred of my heroine Henriette Saul was designed to convey to the reader the emotion of hatred as value-free as possible, just like a piece of bread. I wanted to show that nothing is more important in the emotional life of a woman than taking stock of her life, totally and unconditionally—until she feels therapeutically completely cured. As far as men are concerned: I certainly do not say that I hate men. On the contrary, to make a weak penis strong, that is a completely pleasurable feeling. Or as I said it in *Die törichte Jungfrau*: "To create a world in seven rubbings" ("Mit sieben Reibungen Welterschaffen spielen"). But if women nowadays no longer have fun with male bodies, then of course all this falls by the wayside.

In one of your books you speak of sexuality as "God's only power on earth." How did you manage this leap of faith, to overcome the chasm between human sexuality and divine spirituality?

I am a Catholic, let's be clear about that. Since my childhood, God has been my punching ball; but he also has always been my partner. That way I could say to him, "You are a rotten bastard" ("Du bist ein ganz verfluchter Hund"), and five minutes later I would apologize to him. And as a young woman, whenever I went to confession, confessing that I had played around again with a man, I said: "Dear God, I promise that was the last time." Apart from that: Personally, I will not accept a punishing God anyway. I thought many times that God, who knows everything, actually must lead quite a boring life, whereas I had a rather adventurous life. So I always took him with me on my adventure; in other words, I offered him something. If God gave us a human body that can give us pleasure, then it is a divine law that we enjoy this pleasure. I still believe that to this day.

And the Catholic Church's century-old animosity toward sexuality?

Yes, that has a lot to do with envy. That reminds me of Lady Chatterley; she acted all surprised that simple people too wanted to have their sexual pleasure, having thought that this was an exclusive privilege of the upper class. The same way a lot of people think today that only certain people—intellectuals, those with education—have permission to write.

Aren't you on the one hand writing angrily against the porno wave while you at the same time happily ride that same wave?

I have never ridden any wave. The senses, eroticism, sexuality (spirit, soul, instinct) always have been the essentials of my life. This triad provides for the mobility and the elasticity in my literature. In a literature from which eroticism and sexuality have been excluded, something is missing. The salt is missing, the spices, that's why I never really liked GDR literature, because too much was lacking, it was too stiff, not at all alive. A human being who loves freedom also has a different relationship to sexuality. If one lives in fear, one cannot have a healthy, lively sexuality. To come back to the accusation of pornography: What always bothered people was the fact that I express sexual and pornographic themes as matter-of-factly as I describe other everyday activities.

The fact is: Probably no other German female writer before has written with such a sensuous spirituality or spiritual sensuality as you. Do you represent the "sexual correctness" of our postmodern culture?

Correctly or incorrectly, sexuality needs fantasy. The arrival of the pantyhose was the actual demise of male fantasies.

What if you could live your life again. What would you do differently?

I could only live my life differently if I had different feelings and emotions. The main difference would be if I had a more comprehensive education. The preconditions are always pulling the strings. But life is still good to me.

Your relationship to death. You once wrote: "To take death with me, everywhere."

Internally, I have been feeling immortal for a long time. Emotions cannot age. Only logic grows old. Many of my colleagues who write only from their head have not produced anything in years. But when you write from your gut feelings (*aus dem Bauch*), then you still can write on your death bed.

Which brings us back to the bed.

Yes, I have a very special dress—I have not mentioned that to anybody privately or publicly—I have a very special dress that I had custom made in Cologne in the seventies; each strip of this dress has a wonderfully different color, and it cost me a lot of money at that time. It is my poet's dress, and I want to wear this dress in my coffin, because I don't want to lie in my coffin as a woman, mother, or just a mensch, but as a poetess. Whether or not I will have eternal life, that I don't know yet.

Remembering Eastern Europe: Libuše Moníková

Karen Hermine Jankowsky

Libuše Moníková presents in *The Façade* (1987) a range of cultures between Bohemia and Siberia, a Renaissance castle whose symbols are constantly redefined, and a range of gender roles enacted in relation to narratives of the nation-state in Czechoslovakia and the Soviet Union. As the process of German unification casts women's concerns as secondary to the "genderless" goal of building a new German state, Moníková's depiction of intersections of gender and nation grows in importance. References to nation from Homi Bhabha and Benedict Andersen and to gender constructions from Judith Butler and Marjorie Garber inform the investigation theoretically. (KJ)

The boundaries of "inside" and "outside" and the residents of those spaces are simultaneously (apparently) rigidly designated and constantly moving—at least more frequently than exclusionary linguistic, cultural, or national borders might seem to allow.—
Mary Layoun 417

In her 1987 novel *The Façade*,[1] Libuše Moníková, a Czech author living in Germany and writing in German since being pressured after the Prague Spring to emigrate from Czechoslovakia, investigates cultural identities within nations across Eurasia. Moníková declares that she wrote *The Façade* to foster an historically specific memory that relativizes "the comfortable and undefined terms of 'West' and 'East'.... Work on the façade is work against forgetting" (Cramer). Moníková counters notions of "East" and "West" that the Cold War and, before that, racializing assumptions of a "Europeanized" West and an "Asiatic" East had shaped (Nolan; Applegate). She enters into the renegotiation of these ideas during the mid-1980s, a period that was characterized, on the one hand, by Richard von Weizsäcker's remembrance of the Holocaust and an acknowledgment of the twenty million Soviet dead in World War II and, on the other, by Ernst Nolte's assertion of a barbarian Eastern Europe in opposition to a modern Western European German culture. By examining the Czechoslovak past as a national history within Eastern Europe,

Moníková shifts the focus of these German-centered discussions. She calls attention to the long history of German and Slavic influences in Bohemia, to the power differentials between Czechs, Slovaks, and Russians after World War II, and to the more recent tensions over land usage between the Soviet government and indigenous Asian populations in Siberia. In this way she frames the nation not as culturally homogeneous but as shaped by the interaction between different cultures within and across national borders.[2]

Because of the gap in social knowledge between the author's experience with Czechoslovak and Soviet history and the German context of her immediate reading audience, Moníková can call attention to the constructedness of the nation in the sense of cultural identity in its ungendered and gendered forms.[3] In the ungendered narrative, restorers reconstruct the façade of a Renaissance castle outside Prague as a central image for the constant reinterpretation of a memory of the Czechoslovakian nation-state. National narratives are further explored as a group of these workers travels through a series of cultures, enroute via Siberia to an artistic assignment in Kyoto, Japan. The restoration work in "Inner Bohemia," the first half of the novel, demonstrates the construction of a historical memory of the nation-state and of a personalized reconfiguration of that representation. In "Outer Siberia," the second half of the novel, the author constructs imaginations of nation by integrating the travelers' experience of cultural diversity into their work on the castle façade.[4]

Within this overarching narrative, gendered episodes call attention to the role that men's and women's performances of gender differences have on a construction of nation. For example, Moníková portrays gendered behavior as a social performance by both partners in a heterosexual couple and in a woman's memory of her relative's pre-World War II past. In a man's cross-dressing to represent a female Czech patriot, Moníková reflects upon both the tendencies of some men in the nineteenth-century Czech national revival to exclude women from positions of greater influence and of middle-class women to cloister themselves in the private sphere in order to portray their "respectability."[5] Furthermore, through images of a nomadic village that a group of women have established at the eastern margins of Siberia, Moníková differentiates between the ways in which men and women exercise power and suggests the importance for both sexes of the fantasies in which these separatist women resist the Soviet state.

Sites of Memory

The particular way in which notions of nation are contextualized in the book's mosaic of identities and illusions can best be probed by considering Homi Bhabha's distinction between the pedagogic and performative aspects of a national culture. The pedagogic aspect of a culture portrays itself in the allegedly singular voice of its people. The performative aspect of the culture is often excluded in the creation of the pedagogic voice; it is a voice expressed by all individuals and particularly those at the margins when they articulate through words and actions their own particular sense of identity (Bhabha 291-322).

According to Bhabha, both the pedagogic and performative modes of presenting the nation, but especially the pedagogic one, can be communicated with respect to two aspects of time. The modern nation appears in a pedagogic sense as an order based on rationality and fairness in contrast to the irrationality of traditional hierarchies in the medieval cosmology. The image of the nation as orderly and scientifically informed implies the promise of a more humane and advanced society in the future. Within a pedagogic portrayal of the nation, however, symbols of an ancient society evoke a relationship that links a population of "people" with a particular location, often referred to as the "soil" (see Renan). Thus two senses of time—one looking to the future for progress and rationality and one looking to the past for an irrational sense of community—seem paradoxically linked in pedagogic representations of nation. In the construction of a nation's past, archaic symbols appropriated from one group are projected as the identity of the whole nation to produce the image of a historically unified populace (Bhabha 291-322). When Bhabha distinguishes between this pedagogic mode and a performative mode of representing the nation, he describes with this second form the potential for individuals to enact their own notions of cultural and personal identity, which may disrupt the pedagogic narration of the national heritage. As the restorers of Castle Friedland alter the symbols that adorn its outer walls, they are creating in this performative mode new ways of understanding the cultural meaning the castle evokes.

The artistic and rebellious endeavors of the Friedland restorers demonstrate not just the performative abilities of individuals to change the narration of their country's history, but also to reshape key symbols from the pedagogic narration of nation. Pierre Nora offers us a way of thinking about the fluidity of even the pedagogic aspect of signification. Modern nation-states designate historical artifacts like Castle Friedland as "sites of memory" (*lieux de mémoire*) in order to construct the memory of historical origins of the nation (7-25).[6] Using such concrete objects, historical memory sets itself off from personal memory as more substantial. One might expect that such material artifacts have only one hard and fast meaning, which is considered objectively truthful, but this is not the case. Though an object like Castle Friedland appears, through its solidity and age, to have only one shape, the meaning accorded it may take various forms. Thus Friedland's significance lies neither in its artistic value nor in its singular status, but in its image as an historical object whose symbols can be refabricated.[7]

Let us consider more closely the interplay between the pedagogic and performative functions of Castle Friedland. Set in the 1980s, before the reorganization of Eastern European states, *The Façade* portrays the Czechoslovak state's attempt to use Castle Friedland as an artifact for connecting the socialist government with an ancient Czech history. The state tried to redefine Castle Friedland less as a relic of an aristocratic elite, e.g., of the German Thurn and Taxis family who owned the castle for about 150 years, than as an object of cultural heritage for all citizens of a state that was striving to lessen the distinctions of class. The fictional work demonstrates the castle's pedagogic function when workers are rewarded for their contribution to the state with a trip to Friedland, where tour guides interpret the castle in terms of the state's history and identity (20–38). At the same time, the restorers alter Castle Friedland's symbols in the novel and thus express personal interests in recreating its surfaces. In this way, the artists resist both the homogenization of Czech history within this pedagogic presentation and the enduring attempts by former members of the aristocracy to reclaim the structure for their elite circles.

The workers' adaptation of symbols on the façade of the castle shows that an icon of national identity is not the natural outgrowth of a landscape and its people but always an object under construction. A new state can cultivate its history, so argues Benedict Anderson, through museums, as a sign of the length of time its nation has existed as a "people" and as an extension into the future.[8] One of the artists reflects upon this artificial process by making fun of the serious academic interpretation that the sometimes arbitrary, and at other times willful, molding of symbols in the frescoes will take: "A three-eyed Justitia—if anyone on the next tour should happen to notice it, Hanna will have to come up with something. She can use it for the topic of her master's thesis, too: 'Contamination of Classical Motifs by Christian Elements on the Renaissance Façade at Friedland'" (6). The object that represents "home" or the story of a national heritage is an object created by individuals and must be actively preserved by individuals who themselves may choose to express their own concerns and fantasies through it.

The national icon or site of memory, as Nora reminds us, is a floating signifier, and the restorers Maltzahn, Orten, Patera, and Podol explain shifts in meaning for the Friedland façade by talking about their choices of symbols. Maltzahn incorporates traffic sign imagery because he is a motorcyclist; Orten considers evoking the whale from *Moby Dick*; Podol adds a take-off on Munch's "The Scream" (23, 165, 168). Hardly a dead artifact, the centuries-old object takes on new forms through the artistic vision and cultural resonances that the restorers bring to their work. They seem little motivated to inscribe a unified cultural or national identity onto the castle even if the Czechoslovak state may be motivated by this goal in financing the renovations. Instead, an international assortment of high and low culture objects to which they have been exposed lifts their imagination to carve new shapes. After Maltzahn, Orten, and Podol return from being stranded in Siberia for six months, they even incorporate lines resembling Chinese characters into the sgraffiti for future guides and scholars to interpret (373).[9]

In their reformulations, the artists ironize the state's enlistment of the ancient castle to construct a tradition for a government that was in existence only since World War II (Leff 243-73). They mock, for example, pilgrimages to the site. The restorers engage in a farcical battle over the symbols they are restoring when Thurn, a member of an award-winning workers' collective and a representative of the previous owners of the structure, questions the authenticity of the castle coat-of-arms, and when the cadre leader Bullak maligns the artists as bricklayers (27-28). These innuendos cause Podol to sling mortar to fight for the building as belonging to all the Czech people and to defend his creativity.

The restorers struggle with Thurn for their performative reinscription of nation on Friedland's walls in another ironic battle after the Siberian journey. When Thurn attempts to bribe Patera to finish the façade for an upcoming wedding ceremony, Podol and Orten join forces in preventing Thurn from visually symbolizing his family's ownership of the castle before 1855. Podol threatens to denounce Thurn to his cadre leader politically and even Orten appeals to state mechanisms when he claims, "There are in fact several offenses here—sabotage and iconoclasm" (370). Both restorers are making use of institutional structures they otherwise criticize and under which they have suffered. They assert their own values and symbols in shaping the castle's coat-of-arms in a way that is determined neither by the history of the German empire nor by the current politics of the Czechoslovak state.

The restorers' ironic relationship to Castle Friedland allows them to reformulate its symbols performatively to include representations of experiences of Czech resistance and of cultural diversity in the Soviet Union. When the restorers travel through Siberia, they bring their lost history along with them. They insist that the Soviets they meet, like the geologist who is trapped in a cabin with them by a snow storm, learn Jan Palach's name and understand his symbolic protest against the Soviet occupation in Czechoslovakia (290-91).[10] Podol and the other restorers feel that Palach's self-immolation demands that they bear witness to totalitarian incursions against the socialist values they defend (263).

They can articulate criticisms of Soviet power since the state has not yet taken over the Siberian wilderness. Without this control, they can also more directly encounter Soviet ethnic minorities. Here native peoples like the Tungus, Evenks, and other Eskimo groups of Mongolian heritage maintain aspects of their traditional cultures while adapting to the state's attempts to regulate reindeer production (300). Yurts, igloos, and Chinese characters included in the façade represent Asian aspects of Soviet culture whose existence a culturally uninflected goal of a classless society and Russian Eurocentrism had masked (373).

Gendering the Personal and the National

Gender constructions are significant in sections inside the frame story concerning memory and the restoration work on the national icon of Castle Friedland. The third chapter addresses gender codes through a romantic narrative in the relationship between the Friedland archivist, Qvietone, and Marie. Gender roles take on national dimensions in the chapters on the activities of Vilma Janská, Marie's relative, within Czech national liberation struggles (chapter four) and on one restorer's enactment of the role of a nineteenth-century female patriot (chapter six). Finally, in a Siberian shamaness's resistance to the Soviet state, Moníková presents the fantasy of a man's integration into a women's separatist community (chapter fifteen).

Moníková first illustrates the constructedness rather than biological necessity of gender through fantasies of heterosexual love between Qvietone, primarily an entomologist, and Marie, the director of orthopedics in Friedland. In the pursuit of a heterosexual relationship that appears "natural," Qvietone and Marie perform according to a "matrix of intelligibility."[11] Qvietone approaches the "task" through a fascination with biology as displayed by his dissertation on "Mating and Pairing of the Monogamous Desert Sow Bug *Hemilepistus reaumuri* Mercedes" (40). He sees his approach toward Marie also as a performed "mating," but one based on socially rather than instinctively motivated choices. Marie would like to "see herself as the confidante of married men in American films" (72), and since in her real rather than fantasy life, she has for the first time engaged with Qvietone in sex with penetration, she is not sure how to bring those two levels of experience together in the social spaces of her office, apartment, or Friedland castle. During their date in the dangerous shelter of a nearby cave, Qvietone projects himself as a male expert who tries to tantalize Marie with cave lore from the Himalayas, Greece, and Central Europe and with names for the bugs and animals of the dark underground world they explore (46–52). Hardly seduced, she sees him as a "gigantic troglodyte (who) strangles her from behind" (45–48). Uncertain what expression of masculine presence will move her, and cognizant of her Hollywood sense of social communication, Qvietone plummets into a deep cavern searching for a limestone rose that has caught Marie's eye (52–53). Seriously injured by this chivalric performance, he drags himself back to the men at the castle (73-76). Neither Qvietone nor Marie seem comfortable in the performance modes for the projected heterosexual identities that they assume are required in their interaction.[12]

By contrast, Vilma Janská, Marie's distant relative, represents to Marie without irony a heterosexual woman's role and the socio-historical constructedness of gender in Eastern Europe. While Vilma risked her life for her male lover and for her democratic convictions in the period from the founding of the first Czechoslovak state through the Nazi takeover of Bohemia, Marie sought the security of a medical career within what seemed to be, until the late 1980s, a relatively stable Soviet bloc state.[13] Vilma, Marie recalls, had supported Czech troops fighting the Austrians for an independent state in 1917 by working in a military hospital in Kiev. During the communist revolution, she became a refugee in the Ukraine with a deserter from the German Army who wished to join the Czech forces. After this lover, Johannes Herzog, died, Vilma supported herself by dancing in officers' casinos. When the Nazis took over the Czech Republic, she organized escape routes for German socialists until she was killed in a concentration camp. In recalling Vilma, Marie produces an image from the past, of a woman who is heterosexual, socialist, and anti-Nazi in a way that obliterates the extent to which these qualities are constructed within a social process. This effect of naturalness eludes Marie in her attempt to enact a genderless role in the sciences.

Alongside this historical contrast between Vilma's and Marie's roles as women in relationship to the Czechoslovak nation-state, Moníková also contrasts Podol's cross-dressing as a nineteenth-century female patriot with the other restorers' portrayals of men who helped mobilize a Czech consciousness in pursuit of an independent cultural identity. In an improvised national revival for his Friedland co-workers, Podol presents Magdalena Dobromila Rettigová, an author who suggested, in cookbooks such as *Advice to Young Housewives on Achieving Contentment for Their Spouses and Themselves* (1840), that women serve their country in the kitchen (103). When Podol researches and performs Rettigová, he enshrines as women's domain the private sphere of the home. When the other restorers play male figures, such as Smetana and Jan Hus, who are remembered within the history of Czech nationalism for their intellectual and artistic achievements, and when they assert that Rettigová's dumpling recipe will make her famous for nurturing Czech health, they demonstrate the limited framework in which nineteenth-century women could contribute to "history" (102–03).[14]

The narrator presents Podol's double-genderedness by oscillating between the character's twentieth-century male role as restorer and the role of the nineteenth-century female patriot as marked by gender. Podol jokingly presents himself/herself as "auntie" or female confidante to the maids (played by his co-workers) and as a mother figure to the male patriots (104–05, 117). Moníková indicates his split position linguistically by labeling the words that leave Podol's mouth as coming from either Podol (as Podol), or Podol playing Rettigová, or Rettigová herself.

Though Moníková indicates a similar mix of voices for the other characters, Podol is the only actor who presents a gender different from his own. By alternating among different speaking positions, he plays with the representation of masculine and feminine poses. Moníková also directs attention to Podol's masquerade as a woman by having him wear a bonnet while being referred to with masculine personal pronouns (117). Podol goes even further to muddy any absolute dividing line between men and women by playing the roles of both a man and his wife in the restorers' performance of Gogol's *The Inspector General* for scientists at the Siberian think tank *Akademgorodok*. Podol's display of both genders reminds Qvietone of hermaphroditic worms (254–56).[15]

This literary narration of cross-dressing intervenes in both nineteenth- and twentieth-century contextualizations of nation. In the earlier period, the imagination of the Czech nation served the construction of a single cultural identity from which to articulate a separate position within a feudalistic Austro-Hungarian empire and within a European continent fearful of domination by "Asiatic elements" from Russia (Kohn 75–77). This notion of history emphasized the nation-building activities of "great men" and set up an opposition between middle-class male and female roles. In the nineteenth century, while peasant and working-class women toiled and socialized in the public sphere and aristocratic women functioned as symbols of social status, literary and historical texts projected the fantasy that good, middle-class women encapsulated themselves in the inner sphere of the home, where they nurtured the men who ran the state. As a twentieth-century actor, Podol's cross-dressing reflects a disruption of the opposition between masculine and feminine genders through evoking a "third term."[16] Acting in between the two poles of state support and dissidence, Podol positions himself as such a "third term." He paints optimistic nature images that garner him state acclaim, but he has also crafted Jan Palach's death mask (40, 140–41). In the female role of Rettigová, Podol performs this in-betweenness in his relation to the nation.[17]

In another configuration of gender and nation, Siberian women enacting feminine roles represent a resistance to the Soviet state that eludes the male restorers within their own country. Either in a drug-induced chimera or an actual experience, Orten finds himself in an all-women's community that resists both patriarchal and Soviet governmental control and which empowers him to imagine the neutralization of Soviet power that extends to Czechoslovakia. These imaginary or real women are nomads who live in tents, support themselves raising reindeer, and have encounters with men outside their community only when they want to become pregnant. Elueneh, the leader of the women's village, who moves her encampment regularly to protect the young girls from being captured and turned into "slaves" for housework, claims that she turns unwelcome male visitors, including Communist party representatives, into reindeer, but welcomes Orten to have sex with all the adult women in the village in gratitude for their hospitality. These exploits awaken in Orten the fantasy of neutralizing all the members of the Supreme Soviet by transforming them into reindeer (324). For him, the potential for resistance that emanates from Elueneh has to do with her seclusion as a woman within nature and away from political power and the negotiation of notions of nation. In this way, Moníková carries into the present the tangential role for women that Rettigová represented within the nineteenth-century national narrative.

Moníková's *Façade* considers monocultural and misogynistic aspects of images of nation as a means of exploring how individuals encounter, enact, revise, parody, and shift cultural barriers between people of different ethnic groups and genders. With this attention accorded to gender and cultural diversity in individuals' actions within the nation-state, Moníková unsettles efforts to reformulate notions of a national community that ignore the gendered relationships between citizens. In this she goes beyond attempts to apply Johann Gottfried Herder's cultural notions of "a people," or to advocate, as Julia Kristeva has done, Montesquieu's institutionally and culturally oriented concept of *esprit général,* or to develop, in the manner of Jürgen Habermas, a more exclusively conceived "constitutional patriotism" (see Betz on Habermas). While Moníková depicts the individual in a national system of power relationships, she portrays a fluidity between identity positions that visualizes personal and social change. She invites us to recall the construction by which images of social cohesion develop so that we can keep participating in their recreation and alteration and take pleasure in that process.

Collage, parody, ambiguity, and story-telling are Moníková's tools for questioning the logic of familiar norms surrounding personal and cultural identity. Like the artists she invents for Castle Friedland, Moníková restores and reshapes the historical surfaces on which national narratives and cultural differences are imprinted, one paratactically ordered scene after another. Having called attention to the constructedness of imaginations of nation, she can articulate the framing of women's historical memory and present action within those nineteenth- and twentieth-century notions in Eastern Europe. To the extent that a rhetorical evocation of the nation can cast women's concerns in general, and gender analysis in particular, as secondary to the primary, and supposedly genderless, goal of building a new German state, Moníková's analyses and images are necessary reminders of this otherwise unvoiced assumption. Czechoslovakia and Siberia are the sites of this history lesson.

Notes

A summer stipend from the Graduate School at the University of Wisconsin-Madison allowed me to conduct research in the Newspaper Clippings Archive at the City Library of Dortmund concerning the reception of a series of Berlin writers including Moníková. Furthermore, the Nationalism and Community Seminar that Allen Hunter and Mary Layoun conducted for the Haven Center at the UW-Madison provided a forum for cross-cultural scholarship that has been invaluable in the development of this project. As has often been the case, I am indebted to Carla Love's insights in the development of this piece of writing.

[1] Notes will refer to the English translation.

[2] See Renan for a contrasting view.

[3] After the revolutionary changes in France, the United States, and South America, appeals to the rhetoric of nation that spread across Europe during the nineteenth century cast men as genderless human beings who act politically (Uncle Sam) and women as gendered (Lady Liberty and France's Marianne). Women appeared to contribute to the national good through birthing and raising children (see Layoun; Mosse; Andersen; Wallerstein).

[4] The terms "inner" and "outer" set Bohemia and Siberia in a binary opposition to each other.

[5] Mosse analyzes the representation of respectability in heterosexual gender norms for the middle-class in nineteenth-century Germany. Andrew Parker, Mary Russo, Doris Sommer, and Patricia Yaeger continued and consciously expanded upon Mosse's work with a 1989 Harvard University conference, which lead to *Nationalisms and Sexualities,* a collection investigating more national cultures and a range of heterosexual and homosexual identities.

[6] "For if we accept that the most fundamental purpose of the *lieu de mémoire* [site of memory] is to stop time, to block the work of forgetting, to establish a state of things, to immortalize death, to materialize the immaterial—just as if gold were the only memory of the money—all of this in order to capture a maximum of meaning in the fewest of signs, it is also clear that *lieux de mémoire* only exist because of their capacity for metamorphosis, an endless recycling of their meaning and an unpredictable proliferation of their ramifications" (Nora 19).

[7] Misunderstanding the textual function of the Renaissance castle, Wilfried Schoeller suggests that it was not one of the most important of its kind (11).

[8] At a Smetana Centennial celebration, Friedland's director refers to "the nurturing of tradition as exemplified in the renovation of the castle" (Moníková, *Façade* 133).

[9] *Webster's Dictionary* defines sgraffito as "decorations produced by scratching through a surface layer (as of plaster or glazing) to reveal a different colored ground" (2082).

[10] At the Crossing Borders Conference at the University of Wisconsin-Madison, October 1992, Moníková explained that she dedicated her first book, *Eine Schädigung,* to Jan Palach. The rape and subsequent murder of the policeman-rapist in the novel represented the violent occupation that changed her: "Ich hab Panzer gesehen. Ich hab Blut gesehen und wir haben versucht die Panzer anzuhalten. Wir haben mit den Russen gesprochen, die dachten, daß sie in Frankreich waren, und wußten nicht, warum sie da seien—siebzehnjährige Kinder" (Transcription Pam Tesch). This show of military force in Czechoslovakia in August 1968 led to attacks on the democratic renewal: approximately one million people were fired or demoted; new anti-censorship laws were retracted; writes who did not repudiate the Prague Spring were not published (Bugajski 3–7; Wheaton and Kavan 3–22).

[11] "The cultural matrix through which gender identity has become intelligible requires that certain kinds of 'identities' cannot 'exist'—that is, those in which gender does not follow from sex and those in which the practices of desire do not 'follow' from either sex or gender" (Butler 17).

[12] In contrast, Marie relates to Orten by discussing gendered imagery, such as the Japanese male as samurai in Toshiro Mifune films (81–93).

[13] Women in Czechoslovakia, like others in Eastern European states, had not developed an analysis of gendered representations and power differentials within relationships or within the reproduction of the nuclear family. The disintegration of the socialist states was thus particularly threatening to their access to work, child-care, and social benefits. See Funk and Mueller, Drakulić, and *Ohne Frauen.*

[14] The male patriots contribute publicly: Bedřich Smetana, for example, fosters Czech consciousness by musically idealizing the region's landscapes. Alois Jirásek's research on Jan Hus created a sense of Czech history and Jan Evangelista Purkyně helped establish Czech as a language of science by writing his biological studies in it instead of in Latin.

[15] Moníková situates cross-dressing aesthetically in her next work, *Treibeis,* by referring to transvestism in Elizabethan theater.

[16] The cross-dressing male represents the "third sex" or "third term," which is never clearly defined other than as not being the first or second term (Garber 9).

[17] Within the homosexual subplot, roles between men are negotiated, in particular between a gay man from Luxemburg, Nordanc, and Qvietone.

Works Cited

Anderson, Benedict. *Imagined Communities: Reflections on the Origin and Spread of Nationalism.* 1983. New York: Verso, 1991.

Applegate, Cecilia. *A Nation of Provincials: The German Idea of Heimat.* Berkeley: U of California P, 1990.

Betz, Hans-Georg. "*Deutschlandpolitik* on the Margins: On the Evolution of Contemporary New Right Nationalism in the Federal Republic." *New German Critique* 44 (Spring/Summer 1988): 127–57.

Bhabha, Homi K. "DissemiNation: Time, Narrative, and the Margins of the Modern Nation." *Nation and Narration*. Ed. Bhabha. New York: Routledge, 1990. 291-322.

Bugajski, Janusz. *Czechoslovakia: Charter 77's Decade of Dissent*. New York: Praeger, 1987.

Butler, Judith. *Gender Trouble: Feminism and the Subversion of Identity*. New York: Routledge, 1990.

Cramer, Sibylle. "Die Dauer beruht auf dem Fleiße des Schriftstellers." Interview with Libuše Moníková. *Süddeutsche Zeitung* 19–20 September 1987: 164.

Drakulić, Slavenka. *How We Survived Communism and Even Laughed*. New York: Harper, 1993.

Funk, Nanette, and Magda Mueller. *Gender Politics and Post-Communism: Reflections from Eastern Europe and the Former Soviet Union*. New York: Routledge, 1993.

Garber, Marjorie. *Cross-Dressing and Cultural Anxiety*. 1992. New York: Harper Perennial, 1993.

Herder, Johann Gottfried. *Reflections on the Philosophy of the History of Mankind*. Chicago: U of Chicago P, 1968.

Kohn, Hans. *Pan-Slavism: Its History and Ideology*. New York: Vintage Books, 1960.

Kristeva, Julia. *Nations without Nationalism*. Trans. Leon Roudiez. New York: Columbia UP, 1992.

Layoun, Mary. "Telling Spaces: Palestinian Women and the Engendering of National Narratives." *Nationalisms and Sexualities*. Ed. Andrew Parker, Mary Russo, Doris Sommer, and Patricia Yaeger. New York: Routledge, 1992. 407–23.

Leff, Carol Skalnik. *National Conflict in Czechoslovakia: The Making and Remaking of a State, 1918–1987*. Princeton: Princeton UP, 1988.

Moníková, Libuše. Conference comments. Crossing Borders: Contemporary Women Artists in Germany. Madison, Wisconsin, Fall 1992. Transcription Pamela Tesch.

———. *The Façade: M.N.O.P.Q.* Trans. John E. Woods. New York: Knopf, 1991.

———. *Die Fassade: M.N.O.P.Q.* München: Hanser, 1987.

———. *Eine Schädigung*. Berlin: Rotbuch, 1981.

———. *Treibeis*. München: Hanser, 1992.

Mosse, George L. *Nationalism and Sexuality: Middle-Class Morality and Sexual Norms in Modern Europe*. Madison: U of Wisconsin P, 1985.

Nolan, Mary. "The *Historikerstreit* and Social History." *Reworking the Past: Hitler, the Holocaust and the Historians' Debate.* Ed. Peter Baldwin. Boston: Beacon, 1990. 224–48.

Nolte, Ernst. "Vergangenheit, die nicht vergehen will." *"Historikerstreit": Die Dokumentation der Kontroverse um die Einzigartigkeit der national-sozialistischen Judenvernichtung.* München: Piper, 1987. 39–47.

Nora, Pierre. "Between Memory and History: *Les Lieux de Mémoire.*" Trans. Marc Roudebush. *Representations* 26 (Spring 1989): 7–25.

Ohne Frauen ist kein Staat zu machen. Ed. Unabhängiger Frauenverband. Berlin: Argument, 1990.

Renan, Ernest. "What Is a Nation?" Original lecture 1882. Trans. Martin Thom. *Nation and Narration.* Ed. Homi K. Bhabha. London: Routledge, 1990. 8–22.

Schoeller, Wilfried F. "Bröckelnder Putz: Früh gefeiert, zu früh publiziert: Libuše Moníkovás Roman 'Die Fassade.'" *Die Zeit* 9 October 1987: 11.

Wallerstein, Immanuel. "Household Structures and Labour-Force Formation in the Capitalist World-Economy." *Race, Nation, Class: Ambiguous Identities.* Ed. Etienne Balibar and Immanuel Wallerstein. New York: Verso, 1991. 107–12.

Webster's Third New International Dictionary. Ed. Philip Babcock Gove. Springfield, MA: Webster, 1961.

Wheaton, Bernard, and Zdeněk Kavan. *The Velvet Revolution: Czechoslovakia, 1988–1991.* Boulder: Westview, 1992.

Now You See It, Now You Don't: Afro-German Particulars and the Making of a Nation in Eva Demski's *Afra: Roman in fünf Bildern*

Leslie A. Adelson

Promising both a national history (of the Federal Republic) and a particular one (of the "mixed race" protagonist), *Afra* filters both through a textual economy of black-and-white symbolism that alternately foregrounds and backgrounds the "visibility" of different levels of historical experience. By examining competing functions of racialized discourse in the novel, this essay probes the relationship between Afra's story and the national one in which it is made to assume representational status. Not a literary rendition of an Afro-German sociological reality, Demski's text nonetheless invokes a kind of social discourse that does have some bearing on the Afro-German project of self-definition in the 1990s as well as our disciplinary obligation to respond to it. (LAA)

At a time when a newly unified Germany seemed preoccupied with asserting its perceived needs against an alleged flood of undesired would-be immigrants and asylum seekers, the dust jacket for Eva Demski's 1992 novel *Afra: Roman in fünf Bildern* (Afra: Novel in Five Tableaux) promised the book's readers "a panorama of German reality from the end of the forties into our present."[1] This historical overview juxtaposes and blends a national history with a particular one: the story of Afra, the only so-called *Mischlingskind* (mixed race child) in a tiny village in a Bavarian locale (*Gäu*). Both histories are filtered through a textual economy of black-and-white symbolism, at the generative center of which stands this lonely protagonist. The reading of the novel that follows therefore proposes to explore the extent to which Demski's discursive deployment of blackness and whiteness promotes or merely feigns a critical understanding of the Federal Republic's history and its attempts to deal with that history (with history understood to mean either the history of the Federal Republic itself or the historical past prior to its founding in 1949). While this reading is also concerned with the degree and manner in which Afro-German experience can be said (or as is more often the case, cannot be said) to be reflected in Demski's narrative, I do not propose to ascertain the sociological truth content of this novel. This might well be a valid project, but it is not the task that I have undertaken. Rather, it is in the context of socio-discursive tensions between real and imaginary realms that this analysis of *Afra* may prove worthwhile. In this methodological sense it would be silly to fault the author for giving voice to a fictive "black" character without speaking for a real Afro-German community or even to pretend to divine the author's personal intentions. (This is of course different from assessing the function of textual structures, which may well "intend" certain meanings more than others.) What I propose in this instance then is a kind of close textual reading informed by discourse analysis in its broader social, but not necessarily sociological, framework. My conclusion will return to this broader framework.[2]

In order to refine the pivotal question as to the discursive functions of blackness and whiteness in the text, it will be necessary to probe the interwoven functions of visibility and invisibility in the novel. Although one might contend that these are mutually exclusive terms, I shall be using them here in light of a range of gradation, whereby issues and persons may be regarded as "more" or "less" visible or invisible. Complex palimpsests of cultural meaning call for such gradation, as when national and particular histories are superimposed on each other and readers are forced to view one through the other. This type of cognitive filter is already in place when the novel opens and Afra is born. As the village midwife remarks that only girls are being born in the first years following the war, what seems like an unnatural catastrophe to the villagers symbolically renders the vanquished land feminized. The birth of Afra, who "remained of questionable color" (7), signifies something more than simply the loss of the war: an irrevocable invasion by foreign powers. "The villagers recognized that the liberators were Americans because of the Blacks" (12).[3] After the American troops have long since departed, Afra's birth has an unhappy effect on the villagers. "The birth that had just happily taken place made the region visibly American" (13), with the result that the village locale becomes physically occupied from within.[4] Afra's story is discursively cast as inextricably intertwined with national disgrace. The novel's textual economy of black-and-white symbolism is likewise inextricably intertwined with shifting palimpsests of the putative visibility of historical experience. How are we to "see" Afra's story and the national one in which it is embedded and in which it is made to assume representational status?

Demski's repeated allusions to the visibility or invisibility of historical experience must be considered in a larger socio-semiotic context in which certain problems are foregrounded while others are backgrounded. Jeffrey M. Peck (77), Nora Räthzel (45), and Marion Kraft ("Feminismus" 173), for example, have argued that the problem of racial discrimination is rendered invisible by the terminology of debates about the so-called *Ausländerfeindlichkeit*. (Generally translated as "xenophobia," this word more accurately means hositility to those who are not German citizens). Critics of the West German women's movement reproach various factions for their failure to acknowledge the experiences of Black women in Germany by claiming victim status for all women equally and recognizing only men as possible perpetrators of victimization.[5] Leroy T. Hopkins and Carol Aisha Blackshire-Belay alert us to the contributions that studies of Afro-Germans can make to conventional Germanistics and the newer field of German Studies. Others consider the visible presence of Afro-Germans in the German public sphere and its media,[6] while a pathbreaking publication of 1986, *Farbe bekennen: Afro-deutsche Frauen auf den Spuren ihrer Geschichte*, above all created a larger discursive space for Afro-German faces and experiences in contemporary German culture. (An English translation appeared in 1991 as *Showing Our Colors: Afro-German Women Speak Out*. An updated edition of the German original followed in 1992, the same year in which *Afra* was published.) Although this phenomenon may strike many as impossible to overlook, Demski claims never to have heard of *Farbe bekennen* or its authors when she was writing *Afra*.[7]

Pressing topical questions about the status of recently unified Germany as a multicultural society or a land of immigration are no more a focus for Demski's novel than are the possibilities and effects of a real Afro-German public sphere that has been asserting itself since the mid-1980s (see Campt on the latter). If the possibilities for this public sphere to articulate its constituents' interests exist in a field of tension between specifically Afro-German identity and a transnational notion of a "black" diaspora,[8] the isolated dark-skinned protagonist of *Afra* connotes a collective minority of "mixed children" in postwar Germany without having Afro-Germans in mind. (I shall make this argument even though the children of so-called mixed racial heritage who were born in the 1940s and 1950s frequently did grow up in isolation from one another, often not seeing another person of color until they had reached adulthood.) Instead Afra's black corporeality is reduced to a metaphoric function, which alternately emphasizes, mystifies, or disarms the theme of a *national* attempt to come to terms with the past. The allegedly particular life of a single "black" girl is appropriated for a national symbolic, the purpose of which is to render "visible" the repression of the Nazi past in particular. As will be shown (!), Demski's project is not unproblematic.

The notion that it would take the birth of a "black" child to draw the region's attention to the end of World War II or even to the Third Reich is remarkable. The narrator repeatedly insists that the area is "this remote, untouched corner" (13)—untouched as much by war as by Hitler (8, 10-11). The disappearance of Jewish peddlers who were otherwise occasionally visible in the village is, on the other hand, mentioned only fleetingly, and this form of sudden invisibility never becomes the subject of the novel. (I note this, not to suggest that it *should* have been the proper subject of a novel about the past, but rather, to recognize that the text introduces different paradigms of visibility and invisibility and that they in turn carry differing degrees of textual weight.) Before the arrival of the American soldiers, the "green curtain" forms an effective barrier between the isolated region and the rest of the world. Even more important is the apparent separation between the village, untouched by war and the Reich, and the rest of the conquered German nation.

While one may readily believe that the history of a single village does not necessarily run parallel to the history of the nation, this distinction in the novel acquires a particular function by virtue of the fact that Afra's birth pointedly signifies the accession of the region to the (defeated) German nation. The child's "black" skin makes her and the village not only "visibly American" (13), but also visibly guilty. This is at least implied in the novel's symbolic paradigm, which pursues the attribution of guilt vis-à-vis the Holocaust in a highly mediated discursive fashion, via an African-American soldier who impregnates a "white" village beauty and leaves a visibly "black" child behind in Bavaria. The narrator tells the novel's readers something that Afra herself can never know: that her biological father felt forever poisoned by the good cheer of her "white" German mother after he had seen the "corpses of Mauthausen" (22). That which is decisively visible for the father—the corpses of Mauthausen—disappears from the surface of the novel when the criminal responsibility for that which is no longer visible is physically inscribed onto the protagonist's bodily appearance.

In this way Afra's "black" skin stands in for a kind of German national guilt from which she suffers more than anyone else. This figure thus serves both an accusatory and a scapegoating function. This contradictory status arises by means of a complicated nexus of vision, according to which Afra appears as the testimony-bearing legacy of her father and readers are also told, "Not until the other villagers looked at her did the child become black" (77). Afra is driven out of childhood, as we are told, not by being kicked and beaten, but by being looked at ("mit Blicken" 78). As the religious world view of the townspeople allows them to believe that the "black" girl is "no human being" (32), but "something wild" (26) and "from the devil" (27), the American father and that which he has seen recede from view. What remains is a schematic, seemingly ahistorical symbolism of good and evil, from the effects of which Afra is made to suffer, first as a "black" girl and later as a "black" woman. In this sense one might be inclined to believe that Demski does indeed depict the sociological reality of an Afro-German experience of racist prejudice, especially as inflected by discursively mediated social values.[9]

One might consequently conclude that Demski seeks to demonstrate two things: 1) that discrimination against "black" persons in postwar Germany relies on a much older black-white metaphor and 2) that this scapegoating function of blackness serves to cloud or even to block altogether a critical view of a German national history laden with guilt. This interpretation would be supported by the fact that Afra's desperate attempts to be invisible (149) compete with the efforts of those characters, such as the former Nazi sympathizer and current village schoolteacher Wolinski, who seek to make themselves invisible in this remote corner of a Germany undergoing denazification. But these characters are more successful than Afra, especially since no one seems to be searching for those who have been murdered, those who are no longer visible. When the midwife's radio allows the world at large to penetrate the village in the 1950s (120), nothing of the German past comes through. "Of all the stories that led Wolinski to retreat to the godforsaken country behind the green curtains, to that land of the invisible, of all those corpses that no visionary was asked to find even though there were so many of them: nothing. It was as if they were not missed" (137).

This interpretation, which stresses an intended criticism of a postwar Germany whitewashing its own history (in which case "white" is associated with the invisibility of a historical nexus of guilt and responsibility), is called into question by another aspect of the novel's symbolic economy. Whereas Afra's "blackness" (her sole inheritance from her father, 301) stands in textually for the invisibility of a German national past encumbered by the guilt-ridden legacy of the Third Reich, she bequeathes to her milky-white daughter Nivea, whose "white" skin fills Afra with pride and satisfaction, something both invisible and life-threatening. According to Afra, the most beautiful thing about Nivea is that one cannot tell by *looking* at her that she has a "black" mother (316). Yet, the dangerous quality of this legacy does not proceed from any action on the part of the protagonist, but solely from a symbolic paradigm that increasingly distances itself from national history. As an internationally renowned singer, the adult "white" daughter is relatively successful and also doubly identifiable. First, she is recognized as a musical celebrity in a world-wide entertainment industry. Second, she appears ever more clearly as someone who is *visibly* ill with AIDS. These two modes of visibility are closely linked in the novel.

Nivea, readers learn, "wanted to be audible but not too visible" (427, 387). Her musical performances in the United States, however, render her invisible inheritance visible: "Nivea Nightingale's black and white parts will be visible in her band, black and white musicians and technicians, not the beer-tent revelers and orchestras for children's birthdays like back home" (399). The suggestion that there is something essential in Nivea's music that she can consciously choose to reveal or conceal is underscored by the information that her songs are written for Afra ("auf Afra hingeschrieben"), "without the public noticing it much" (426).

In order to understand what is deemed so threatening about this not necessarily visible, now "black" legacy, one must consider more than Nivea's initially imperceptible illness. For Nivea's participation in the international entertainment industry alludes to earlier imagined associations between American jazz and a supposed danger to German national culture after World War I. As Marc A. Weiner cogently demonstrates, conservatives as well as liberals of the Weimar Republic held that jazz posed a challenge to German national identity (although they predictably differed in their valorization of that challenge). The timing of Europe's introduction to jazz coincided roughly with the presence of foreign powers' Black occupation troops between 1919 and 1923. Of this constellation Weiner says,

> By the time jazz was established in the German culture of the twenties, its association with Blacks would have merged in the national consciousness of the recollection of this recent incident, that is, American jazz became the acoustical sign of the transplanted Black and thus it could designate both America as the foreign and victorious New World divorced from European traditions and, at the same time, Africa as the purportedly uncivilized Dark Continent from which the feared Black was seen to challenge Europe's racial and national hegemony (478).

When Weiner analyzes jazz as "the acoustical locus of difference" (483) in Germany of the 1920s and 1930s, this acoustical symbolism remains beholden to some notion of a visibly different corporeality. Nivea's "other" corporeality—her now invisible "black" inheritance—is, on the other hand, optically masked by her "white" skin, which nonetheless does nothing to absolve her of the threat that she seems to pose to German national culture. (After Robert Mapplethorpe has photographed her, Nivea herself loves "the glassy image, in which she appears whiter than all whites" [76]).

The danger embodied by Nivea (one from which she too suffers more directly than anyone else) seems all the more threatening because it is not immediately physically recognizable as such. In order to allow this danger to manifest itself physically, Demski has Afra's daughter become visibly ill with AIDS. In this manner the novel, which simulates the story of an Afro-German, relies on a doubled schematic that has shaped antisemitic discourses since the nineteenth century. According to this antisemitic schematic, Jews are presumed to be physically recognizable as Jews, while the danger ascribed to them derives from their purported talent for self-camouflage (Gilman, *Difference*; *Body*).[10] Because Afra's "black" legacy from her American father thus "disguises" itself in her milky-white daughter, Nivea falls prey to an invisible virus that she herself embodies. That which the American father saw and cannot forget makes him into a historical witness of a guilt-laden, unprocessed German past, while in the third generation this legacy manifests itself as a virulent affliction. Yet, Nivea is not afflicted with German history but with a plague that she has presumably contracted in New York City, a locale where, we are told, one can have as much visibility or invisibility as one desires (475).

The threat presumed to emanate from an international culture industry is thus traced to a particular nation, the United States. Here we find echoes of an older anti-American cultural imaginary as well as a wounded German national stance that resorts to stereotypical discourses of race that doubly target Jews and Blacks. Gilman offers related insights in his comparison of a 1939 novel about Aryans fighting disease in Black Africa and a 1989 novel about Germans combating AIDS in futuristic Europe ("Plague"). Noting the absence of Jewish figures from the earlier novel, Gilman remarks that the text's frequent allusions to syphilis make them an implied presence throughout, since one model of racial ideology under National Socialism posited "the Jews as the carriers of sexually transmitted diseases who transmitted them to the rest of the world" (179–80). One could argue that Afra, who poses a readily visible threat to a homogenous ("white") German identity, bequeathes a deceptively invisible one to her white-skinned daughter. As Gilman explains, the Nazi category of *Mischling*, a term derived from racial science and predicated on biological corruption through "the maternal lineage of the Jew," posits "the exemplary hidden Jew just waiting to corrupt the body politic" (182). The frequent conflation of Jewishness and Blackness in German racial science of the late nineteenth and early twentieth centuries, especially as regards the alleged visibility or invisibility of perceived racial threats to German wholeness, would therefore seem to reverberate in Demski's combined portrayal of Afra and Nivea as well.[11]

Afra's "black" skin stands in symbolically for German guilt rendered invisible, and Nivea's "white" skin emerges as both optical illusion and not entirely successful self-camouflage. This illusion yields no insights into historical connections but, rather, a mere sense of recoiling from a disease that, unlike the German nation, cannot be defeated. Demski's novel thus appropriates the purportedly particular story of a single "black" girl for a national symbolic that seeks to render the repression of the Nazi past visible. In this process discourses of race and guilt are mobilized with the result that a tendentially critical analysis of a German national discourse is undermined, not underscored. The promised "panorama of German reality from the end of the forties into our present" at best mimes familiar mechanisms of repression in topical garb. Persons with AIDS and Afro-Germans serve at best a symbolic, not a sociological function here.

The fact that imaginaries also have political effect is, of course, not new in the context of contemporary literature, especially as concerns the representation of Blacks. Rosemarie K. Lester examines West German serial novels of the 1950s and early 1960s and concludes that the explicit criticism of U.S.-American racism articulated in these texts pursues an implicit agenda designed to distract readers' attention away from the problems of dealing with the then recent German past. Even new images of African-Americans in these novels, such as those associated with the Black Power Movement, served primarily to point out potential dangers of the West German student movement of 1968, which—as is well known—forced a public discussion of the Nazi past ("Beautiful" 191).[12] After the first "black occupation babies" reached school age in 1951, they represented a "very visible indigenous minority" ("Beautiful" 183). "In 1952, public sympathy reached an all time high with *Toxi*" ("Beautiful" 184), a widely seen film by Robert Adolf Stemmle, in which a six-year-old Afro-German, Elfriede Fiegert, plays the leading role (Weber-Nau; Hoffmann and Schokst). The film's sympathy for "black" children of American fathers and German mothers is contingent, however, upon the film's conclusion, which entails the child, who has been abandoned by *both* father and mother, being "brought home" by the African-American father. German audiences could thus be comforted by the knowledge that they had compassion for poor Toxi without having to accept her as one of their own. Blackness belongs, according to the film's symbolism, elsewhere.[13] That this rarely corresponded to the reality of children of African-Americans or Africans in Germany of the early postwar years[14] reminds us of the deceptive economy of exchange that circulates among cultural symbols. The film *Toxi* allows an Afro-German child to be seen without making the history or experiences of real Afro-Germans visible (or even necessarily meaning to do so).

When *Toxi* then appears in Demski's novel, it behooves us as readers to pay close attention. A confused Afra hears of Toxi for the first time when she encounters two city people who have lost their way into the far reaches of the province. Upon seeing the three-dimensional child, they enthusiastically scream, "Toxi, as she lives and breathes!" ("Toxi, wie sie leibt und lebt!" [150]). Afra is thus taken for a figure other than herself and appropriated symbolically when she is made to stand in for that figure. When the film *Toxi* is described by the narrator as "the famous film that deceptively alters life" (160), the narrative stance seems to reflect an awareness of this economy. Many other details similarly point in the direction of recognizing the "black" protagonist as symbolic capital. At the end of the 1960s, for example, when Afra is mistaken everywhere for Angela Davis, her earlier Toxi-function is replaced by her updated Angela Davis-function. Afra's two main occupations as an adult in Munich likewise stress her symbolic disposition to stand in for something that she is not. As a theater actress she feels "comfortable among people who are, to be sure, not interested in her but who had given her a place" (279).[15] This place has less to do with her than with that which her bodily appearance is able to represent (depending in each case on how the director wishes to use her). As an independent prostitute, Afra embodies the exchange value of capital.

Afra's activity as a self-employed prostitute alerts readers, however, to a way in which her character's function in the novel's textual economy extends beyond mere exchange value. Afra wants to determine the terms of exchange herself, something that imbues her with the dual status of exchange capital and an ego, a personal voice, that exceeds it. When three criminals (of whom one is named "Goethe") rape her after she has rejected them as her pimps, her status as an independent self is brutally contested. The rape has decisive significance for Afra, even though neither she nor anyone else in the novel can name that which she has "lost" (362) in the night-time attack. Of narratological significance is the fact that Afra, who is otherwise narrated in the third person, describes and comments on the rape scene in the voice of a narrating I. She even tells the former village midwife, "Since it happened, I know for the first time who I am" (362). This is an astonishing statement for a protagonist to whom an independent ego is nowhere else attributed and who is repeatedly appropriated for a symbolic function that points not to, but beyond her. At the same time, the content of the ultimate identity that Afra allegedly attains by being raped and surviving remains unclarified—*unless* the decisive knowledge of her own essence is supposed to consist of her fundamental reduction to the exchange value of symbolic capital. The assertion of an identity of self in precisely this moment of insight strikes me as ironic.

In her 1989 study of West German serial novels from the 1960s, in which "white" German women give birth to dark-skinned children after having been raped by "black" occupation soldiers in the wake of World War II,[16] Lester asks why these novels go to such lengths to depict "black" American men as rapists of German women and also as victims of U.S.-American discrimination. "To gain the readers' sympathy for the racially mixed children as well as their mothers," she explains, "there had to be an extra-ordinary excuse which at the same time left intact existing racist attitudes" ("Beautiful" 186). Although Afra is portrayed as someone who has been raped and not at all as the child of a rape, we may be dealing with a comparable function. The novel's sympathy belongs to the raped protagonist, which allows Afra to serve as a kind of Toxi for the 1990s. But the symbolic function that she is repeatedly made to fulfill definitively anchors the element of threat to her "blackness." While the Toxi of the 1950s is "brought home" to the United States by her father, the sovreignty of the German nation and German culture is beset by the "blackened" national history that Afra is made to embody in the novel. This history, which novelistically sets Afra's "blackness" into motion, becomes all the more invisible as the AIDS-stricken, "white" daughter of the "black" mother steps more clearly into view.

If that which is "black" and diseased comes from the United States in the novel, the text deviates from familiar paradigms of racist discourse in Germany by foreclosing the notion that this diseased "blackness" can be sent back from whence it came. The visibly "black" becomes all the more threatening because it is no longer foreign but domestic. After Afra's birth we learn of the villagers: "Now they had a new name, a new fear: that which is black. Everything that is black. It was not the foreign that they feared, for strangers had never threatened them and had gone out of their way to avoid the province even a hundred years ago. It was not the foreign. It was the other color" (49). That which lends visibility and a name to what is threatening in the national self—in Germany's own history—is granted no history of its own. In all its corporeal embodiment it becomes virtually invisible—a blind black spot.

Afra's visibility can thus not be said to address racism in the Federal Republic today.[17] The pronounced invisibility of Nivea's "black" roots at best shores up a flawed attempt to deal with the German national past (of either the pre-1945 or post-1945 variety) while it simultaneously evokes older German fears of a plague whose paths of entry are secret and its effects lethal. Even if *Afra* is supposed to show us that history returns to haunt us in diverse disguise, history is barely recognizable as such in this novel. The problematic economy of exchange that propels this symbolism of race and color may well aim a critical finger at a national discourse of repression, but it seems to miss any and all targets. This may be unavoidable when all targets are subjected to so much optical illusion that they eventually disappear from view.

Since blind spots of any shade connote epistemological stumbling blocks to understanding and analysis, one might additionally argue that it is relatively easy for Demski to appropriate an Afro-German figure in this symbolic fashion, given that no major literary publications by Afro-Germans have as yet been widely marketed. Aside from *Farbe bekennen* and May Ayim's 1995 collection of poems, *blues in schwarz weiß,* there have been the scattered publications of the *Initiative Schwarze Deutsche* since its founding in 1986 (see Hopkins for more details on these, which occasionally include poems and short stories). In contrast to, say, Turkish-German or German-Jewish culture, that of the growing community of Afro-Germans is known to an even smaller public sphere and has yet to attract much critical attention in academic circles. (Some of the exceptions to this have been mentioned here.)

To conclude from this that Afro-German culture has not yet produced a sufficient body of literary texts that would warrant serious study would be to miss an epistemological and historical opportunity. A far more appropriate conclusion would be that we German Studies scholars need to expand our understanding of what constitutes cultural activity in the first place. Until we challenge a residual methodological fixation on literary texts that reflect conventional categories of genre, the Afro-German culture that does exist will continue to be a blind spot in the eye of *Germanistik*.[18] While this is a task that the essay at hand does not even pretend to undertake, it does signify the broader context in which this close reading of symbolic and discursive structures in Demski's *Afra* may be seen as meaningful. As collective identities and social values continue to be contested in various macro- and micro-political spheres of German public life, sociological and discursive forms of knowledge and representation encounter and elude one another in unpredictable ways. If we wish to learn what "black" and "white" mean in the Federal Republic of the 1990s, we will need to consider many competing sources and venues for the dynamic negotiation of such meaning. Demski's novel is not a literary account of a sociological reality, though its discursive mapping of a "black" and "white" German national history does invoke and conjure a kind of *social* reality that will also have some bearing on the ongoing Afro-German project of self-definition.

Notes

I would like to thank the anonymous readers of my original manuscript for their helpful comments. Cassandra Bonse, Anita Brown, and John Davidson provided valuable assistance in securing some of the research materials for this project.

[1] At the time of *Afra*'s original publication, Demski, born in Regensburg in 1944, had already authored four novels (*Goldkind* in 1979, *Karneval* in 1981, *Scheintod* in 1984, and *Hotel Hölle, Guten Tag* in 1987) and won several literary prizes (Thomas Kraft). These earlier novels also attempt rather sweeping milieu descriptions of occupied Germany and the Federal Republic in various stages since the end of World War II. *Afra* elicited mixed reviews, including some from well-known personalities. Karin Struck, writing for *Die Welt*, claims to have been able to finish the clichéed novel only "with clenched teeth," for example, while Walter Hinck is favorably reminded of canonical texts by Grimmelshausen, Joyce, and Brecht. The book must have been popular enough to warrant a paperback edition, which followed in 1994.

[2] For an elaboration of my theoretical approach to intersections of the real and the imaginary see Adelson 1993.

[3] Although Demski uses the word *Befreier* (liberators) here, the text otherwise implies that this term is meant ironically, since the village is portrayed as completely untouched, either positively or negatively, by National Socialism.

[4] The notion that America is "foreign, antithetical to Germany and has colonized the German's consciousness" is hardly new to postwar (West) German culture. See Peck (81), as well as Morley and Robins (10).

[5] Sara Lennox addresses this type of criticism in her essay "Divided Feminism." See also Marion Kraft ("Feminismus" 176). A more recent example from the German print media would be Nasrim Bassiri, an Iranian with political refugee status in the FRG, who uses "black" to signify a position of historical, cultural, political, and economic discrimination rather than an allegedly fixed racial identity. In this connection see also Oguntoye; Adelson; and Kraft and Ashraf-Khan.

[6] At the 1993 German Studies Association Convention, where Lennox delivered the paper on which her article is based, Francine Jobatey also discussed the limited visual presence of Afro-Germans outside the bounds of the German entertainment industry today, while Susann Samples addressed the "on again, off again" visibility of Blacks in the Third Reich. Carol Aisha Blackshire-Belay moderated the panel on which Jobatey, Samples, and several others analyzed various aspects of Afro-German identity and experience.

[7] Antonia Holdegel Fore spoke at the 1994 Modern Language Association Annual Convention of her interview with the author during the preceding summer. I should perhaps repeat here that this is not something for which I wish to "fault" the author. This information does indicate, however, that the novel does not directly respond to an actual Afro-German community but draws instead on more widespread traditions of racialized discourse.

[8] This was the thesis presented by Erin L. Crawley at the 1994 Modern Language Association Annual Convention. Crawley's own work engages critically with Paul Gilroy's *Black Atlantic*. My current understanding is that Crawley also has an article, "Re-Thinking Germanness: Two Afro-German Women Journey 'Home,'" soon to appear in *Other Germanies*.

[9] As one Afro-German writer has recently noted, "The color symbolism of the Christian Occident long linked the color black with that which is disreputable and undesirable. The early literature correspondingly offers examples of white human beings who become 'moors' by behaving badly" (Ayim, "Die afro-deutsche Minderheit" 40).

[10] Gilman's conclusion specifically addresses the problematics of Jewish visibility and invisibility ("Plague"). Elsewhere he implies that the Nazis felt compelled to tattoo their concentration camp prisoners precisely because Jews were not in fact as uniformly recognizable as Nazi ideology preached ("Plague" 179).

[11] One might similarly recall that Hitler's *Mein Kampf* charges the Jews with having orchestrated the presence of Blacks in the Rhineland after World War I. See La Capra (63, n. 17).

[12] See Ackermann for a discussion of postwar German literary images of Africa that reveal more about West German politics than those of the African countries depicted.

[13] For a longer historical perspective on this general cultural posture, see Lester ("Blacks in Germany") and Gilman (*On Blackness*).

[14] See Hodges regarding Afro-German women's frustrated relationships to their African fathers (229). Weber-Nau states that U.S. soldiers of the Allied Occupation were not allowed to acknowledge paternity of children they had fathered in occupied territory.

[15] At least two reviewers note striking correspondences between this theater troupe and the group around Rainer Werner Fassbinder (Schmitz-Burckhardt; Endres).

[16] Lester points out that rape by Western Allies "had not been an issue after the Second World War" ("Beautiful" 184), something that might perhaps be viewed differently in light of Helke Sander's controversial film, *BeFreier und Befreite*.

[17] On this subject see various articles in Hügel et al., especially May Ayim's "Das Jahr 1990: Heimat und Einheit aus afro-deutscher Perspektive" (*Verbindungen* 206–22), and the "Focus: Antiracist Feminism" section of *Women in German Yearbook 9* (1994), which contains articles by Ika Hügel, Sara Lennox, and Dagmar Schultz (225–51).

[18] Langston's insightful discussion of constructions of "blackness" in German hip hop culture in the context of transnational media and electronic communities represents an encouraging step in the direction of broadening and even reconceptualizing our disciplinary understanding of cultural production.

Works Cited

Ackermann, Irmgard. "Zum Afrikabild in der deutschen Gegenwartsliteratur." *Stimmen der Zeit* 197.9 (1979): 620–30.

Adelson, Leslie A. *Making Bodies, Making History: Feminism and German Identity*. Lincoln: U of Nebraska P, 1993.

Ayim, May. "Die afro-deutsche Minderheit." *Ethnische Minderheiten in der Bundesrepublik Deutschland: Ein Lexikon*. Ed. Cornelia Schmalz-Jacobsen and Georg Hansen. München: Beck, 1995. 39–52.

_____. *blues in schwarz weiß: gedichte*. Berlin: Orlanda Frauenverlag, 1995.

Bassiri, Nasrin. "Wir brauchen keine großen Schwestern: Die Schwierigkeit, eine 'schwarze' Frau zu sein." *Zitty* 5 (1995): 24–26.

Blackshire-Belay, Carol Aisha, ed. *The Image of Africa in German Society*. Special Issue of *The Journal of Black Studies* 23.2 (1992).

Campt, Tina M. "Afro-German Cultural Identity and the Politics of Positionality." *New German Critique* 58 (1993): 109–26.

Crawley, Erin L. "Journeys Across the Atlantic: Afro-Germans and the Black Atlantic." Paper presented at the Modern Language Association Annual Convention. San Diego, 28 December 1994.

Demski, Eva. *Afra: Roman in fünf Bildern*. Frankfurt a.M.: Frankfurter Verlagsanstalt, 1992.
Endres, Elisabeth. "Schwarzbeerl und die Gesellschaft: Eva Demski erzählt die Geschichte einer deutschen Mulattin." *Süddeutsche Zeitung* (5 August 1992): n.p.
Farbe bekennen: Afro-deutsche Frauen auf den Spuren ihrer Geschichte. Ed. Katharina Oguntoye, May Opitz, and Dagmar Schultz. Berlin: Orlanda Frauenverlag, 1986. Aktualisierte Ausgabe. Frankfurt a.M.: Fischer, 1992. English: *Showing Our Colors: Afro-German Women Speak Out*. Trans. Anne V. Adams. Amherst: U of Massachusetts P, 1991.
Fore, Antonia Holdegel. "'Race' Matters! An Analysis of Women's Relationships in Eva Demski's Novel *Afra* in the Context of Afro-German Discourse." Paper presented at the Modern Language Association Annual Convention. San Diego, 30 December 1994.
Gilman, Sander L. *Difference and Pathology: Stereotypes of Sexuality, Race, and Madness*. Ithaca: Cornell UP, 1986.
———. *The Jew's Body*. New York: Routledge, 1991.
———. *On Blackness without Blacks: Essays on the Image of the Black in Germany*. Boston: Hall, 1982.
———. "Plague in Germany, 1939/1989: Cultural Images of Race, Space, and Disease." *Nationalisms and Sexualities*. Ed. Andrew Parker, Mary Russo, Doris Sommer, and Patricia Yaeger. New York: Routledge, 1992. 175–200.
Hinck, Walter. "Locker: Eva Demskis Roman 'Afra.'" *Frankfurter Allgemeine Zeitung* 5 September 1992: n.p.
Hodges, Carolyn. "The Private/Plural Selves of Afro-German Women and the Search for a Public Voice." *Journal of Black Studies* 23.2 (1992): 219–34.
Hoffmann, Hilmar, and Walter Schokst, eds. *Zwischen Gestern und Morgen: Westdeutsche Nachkriegsfilme 1946–62*. Frankfurt a.M.: Deutsches Filmmuseum, 1989.
Hopkins, Leroy T. "Expanding the Canon: Afro-German Studies." *Unterrichtspraxis* 25.2 (1992): 121–26.
Hügel, Ika, and Chris Lange, May Ayim, Ilona Bubeck, Gülşen Aktaş, and Dagmar Schultz, eds. *Entfernte Verbindungen: Rassismus, Antisemitismus, Klassenunterdrückung*. Berlin: Orlanda Frauenverlag, 1993.
Jobatey, Francine. "Von *Toxi* zu TV." Paper presented at German Studies Association Convention. Washington, DC, 9 October 1993.
Kraft, Marion. "Feminismus und Frauen afrikanischer Herkunft in Europa." *Schwarze Frauen der Welt: Europa und Migration*. Ed. Marion Kraft and Rukhsana Shamim Ashraf-Khan. Berlin: Orlanda Frauenverlag, 1994. 171–83.
Kraft, Marion, and Rukhsana Shamin Ashraf-Khan, eds. *Schwarze Frauen der Welt: Europa und Migration*. Berlin: Orlanda Frauenverlag, 1994.

Kraft, Thomas. "Eva Demski." *Neues Handbuch der deutschsprachigen Gegenwartsliteratur seit 1945.* Ed. Dietz-Rüdiger Moser. München: dtv, 1993. 227–29.

La Capra, Dominick. *Representing the Holocaust: History, Theory, Trauma.* Ithaca: Cornell UP, 1994.

Langston, Richard E. "'Fremd im eigenen Land': Constructions of Blackness and the Quest for Legitimacy in German Hip Hop Culture." Paper presented at the Modern Language Association Annual Convention. Chicago, 28 December 1995.

Lennox, Sara. "Divided Feminism: Women, Racism, and German National Identity." *German Studies Review* 18.3 (1995): 481–502.

Lester, Rosemarie K. "Black Is Not Always Beautiful: The 'Other Americans' in West German Popular Magazine Fiction." *Amerika! New Images in German Literature.* Ed. Heinz D. Osterle. New York: Lang, 1989. 175–97.

———. "Blacks in Germany and German Blacks: A Little-Known Aspect of Black History." *Blacks and German Culture.* Ed. Reinhold Grimm and Jost Hermand. Madison: U of Wisconsin P, 1986. 113–34.

Morley, David and Kevin Robins. "No Place Like *Heimat*: Images of Home(land) in European Culture." *New Formations* 12 (1990): 1–23.

Oguntoye, Katharina. "Die Schwarze deutsche Bewegung und die Frauenbewegung in Deutschland." *Afrekete: Zeitung von afro-deutschen und schwarzen Frauen* 4 (1989): 3–5, 33–37.

Other Germanies: Constructing Identity in Women's Literature and Art. Ed. Karen Jankowsky and Carla Love. Binghamton: State U of New York P, forthcoming.

Peck, Jeffrey M. "Rac(e)ing the Nation: Is There a German 'Home'?" *New Formations* 17 (1992): 75–84.

Räthzel, Nora. "Germany: One Race, One Nation?" *Race and Class* 32.3 (1991): 31–48.

Samples, Susann. "Afro-Germans in the Third Reich." Paper presented at German Studies Association Convention. Washington, DC, 9 October 1993.

Schmitz-Burckhardt, Barbara. "Nivea Nachtigall und die Apo in der Hauptstadt des Scheins: Eva Demskis bayerisches Zeitpanorama über 44 Nachkriegsjahre." *Frankfurter Rundschau* 11 November 1992: n.p.

Struck, Karin. "Lauthals greint die Nachtigall." *Die Welt* 29 Sept. 1992: n.p.

Weber-Nau, Monica. "Inzwischen ist das Besatzungskind Toxi Vierzig." *Stuttgarter Zeitung* 2 August 1986: n.p.

Weiner, Marc A. "*Urwaldmusik* and the Borders of German Identity: Jazz in Literature of the Weimar Republic." *German Quarterly* 64 (1991): 475–87.

Towards an "American Germanics"?: Editorial Postscript

Sara Friedrichsmeyer and Patricia Herminghouse

As most members of our profession are probably aware, concern about declining enrollments and lessened support for programs in German has been addressed over the last few years in a number of conferences, often generously supported by the German Academic Exchange Service (DAAD). At the most recent conference, "Shaping Forces in American Germanics in the Twentieth Century," held at the University of Wisconsin in Madison, we offered our perspectives on the role of feminist scholarship and Women in German (WIG) in shaping the profession. We would like to share some of the views we expressed there; while we will be repeating some history familiar to many WIG members, we will be placing that history in a context that, we recognize, is not uncontroversial.

As our profession has changed over the past few decades, various terms have been advanced to describe the mechanisms at work. We all know that WIG is very much implicated in one of the processes used to describe those developments: the "feminization" of the profession. Recognizing that for many the word and the strategies it denotes are less than positive, we nevertheless gladly claim agency when the term is used to describe the drive to include women writers in the curriculum and in the canon, when it refers to the increased numbers of women engaged in studying and teaching in the discipline, and when it applies to other areas of the profession where women and women's issues have exerted a demonstrable influence.

Here on these pages we would like to explore the part WIG has played in another development, often referred to as the "Americanization" of the profession. Although we doubt that those feminists in the early 1970s who wanted to open the field to new influences framed their goal in terms of an American instead of a German *Germanistik,* many of their achievements, we believe, have led in that direction. The historical and institutional evolution of feminist German scholarship in this country can, as others have remarked, be traced to the women's movement of the 1970s, itself an outgrowth of the civil rights movement of the 1960s. Undoubtedly, it was rooted in the desire for change, in a challenge to an established order. The emerging generation of women Germanists began to indict ingrained practices and habits of mind that had resulted in women's widespread exclusion from the realms of male academic privilege. Some of the few senior women scholars in the profession at that time joined with their younger colleagues and graduate students in calling attention to how few women occupied tenure-line jobs and administrative suites, editorial positions and offices in professional organizations. Together they raised concerns about how this situation affected what literature was researched and taught, indeed which voices were even heard in classes and seminars, and whose works were admitted into the canon.

Thus began the work of literary archeology, leading to discoveries of texts by and about women that had been excluded from the purview of the field. From the belated unearthing of women who had written in the Middle Ages to the exhilarating discovery of the literature being produced even in the present, feminist research in the United States began to flourish as women trained in traditional departments gained access, however limited, to academic citizenship. If it is by now axiomatic that feminism and feminist Germanists in this country have helped shape the discipline, this contribution can be seen as a reflection of the progress achieved in the United States by the feminist movement itself. The changes brought about by this movement have affected not only the content, but also the form of our professional activities. Over the years, for example, WIG has developed certain modes of communication involving a spirit of cooperation and collaboration. These are, in fact, among the most deeply held principles of the organization, yet they have always been more typical of American feminism than of mainstream *Germanistik*. Our inclusion of all ranks of the profession in WIG activities, our WIG newsletter, and the widely read Internet WIG-List all exemplify this spirit.

In many American German departments, the intersection of the feminist movement of the 1970s with the suddenly increased interest in the German Democratic Republic that followed in the wake of *Ostpolitik* served further to establish a distinctive American research agenda. The utopian potential of the GDR as a place where women could be granted legal rights, not only to jobs, but also to training and advancement, and where the government could recognize the needs of children and grant access to abortion, struck a chord with the discontents of feminist Germanists. That women writers were increasingly prominent on the literary scene seemed at the time to underscore the concrete potential of the GDR system. It was, in fact, at the first American conference on GDR literature that the idea for Women in German was born in a moment of inspiration among a group of women faculty and students who once again found themselves excluded from the conversations of "important" men. With the exception of some of the work that had already begun on the biographies and literature of exiles from Nazi Germany, it was the first time that an American professional identity was not a disadvantage: having an American rather than a German passport provided much more ready access to writers and institutions in the GDR.

Other directions pursued by feminist Germanists have also contributed to further differentiating us from *Germanistik*. Following the literary archeological work that began in the 1970s, for example, much attention was devoted to a rethinking of aesthetic and theoretical questions. Gradually feminists began to recognize that the old tools of the trade as practiced by traditional *Germanistik,* the tools with which we had been trained, were inadequate to fundamental changes in the practice of our discipline, at least in the United States. In attempting to transcend the old nineteenth-century tactic of just appending a chapter on the "ladies" to histories of German literature, we established intellectual contacts with other disciplines, especially in Women's Studies programs, where the initial impetus for equality had begun to modulate, sometimes painfully, into an acknowledgment of difference. By the beginning of the 1980s, recognition had begun to dawn that in the attempt to secure equality for the category "women," the dualistic opposition of male patriarchy to female victimization had effectively blinded many of us to our own failure to address assymetrical relations *among* women. Within WIG, lesbian and Jewish colleagues began to call attention to the marginalization of their particular categories within the undifferentiated concept of "women." Drawn into the broader academic context of Feminist Studies beginning to emerge in US institutions, feminist Germanists in this country also encountered a spectrum of ethnic, racial, sexual, and national identifications that further challenged the assumptions underlying the unexamined ethnocentrism of our identification with "things German." Similar developments were not taking place in Germany.

Perhaps because of their experience in Feminist Studies, a field that understands itself as transgressive of disciplinary and national boundaries, feminist Germanists have tended to be among the first to draw attention to the ethnic and androcentric biases in our constructions of the German in German Studies. Being Germanists in the United States has also played a role; perspectives are always different when one is outside the center. The heated discussions of multi-culturalism, racism, colonialism, and essentialism that have shaped feminist and gender studies in recent years have intensified feminist Germanists' uneasiness about some of the assumptions in our field. Until 1989, we were inclined to treat "German" as a rather stable category, one that was not mutable or multi-valenced beyond the East-West dichotomy. Like the masculine-feminine polarity that feminist theory began to abandon after the 1970s, the east-west opposition has been displaced by attempts to register the complexities of culture in Germany: Afro-Germans, ethnic Germans, asylum seekers, lesbians and gays, Roma and Sinti are finally disrupting tidy older representations of a culturally homogenous society. The increased urgency with which questions of "belonging," of nationalism and national identity, are being raised in unified Germany coincides with the issues of identity politics and racism that have been surfacing in Feminist Studies on this side of the Atlantic. These intersections are beginning to be reflected in redefinitions of our disciplinary boundaries, and will surely continue to challenge the nineteenth-century notion of a national literature. The disproportionately high representation of women among the scholars dealing with these topics is certainly not related to any essentially feminine multi-cultural gene—or greater moral endowment—but in most cases to the formative experiences of Feminist Studies, where these issues have been in the forefront of recent research and theory and where the margins and borderlands are proving to be most fruitful locations for cultural insights.

As Feminist Studies has broadened its focus from "women's issues" to more general questions of the construction of gender as it is inflected by issues of race, class, and national identity, it indeed sometimes elides into the general area of Cultural Studies. The emergence of the "cultural studies" approach, with an insistence on closer attention to the question of how its practitioners situate themselves vis-à-vis their object of study, has been influenced by and continues to have major implications for Feminist Studies. This approach has also been significant for German Studies, at least in part because of feminist involvement and influence. As Lawrence Grossberg, one of the major theorists of Cultural Studies, has remarked about the field, "there is no cultural studies which is not 'post-feminist', not in the sense of having moved beyond it, but rather in the sense of having opened itself to the radical critique and implications of feminist theory and politics" (26).

Although many of the initiatives and interests just described have had the effect of distinguishing feminist Germanists—and gradually many branches of the field—from *Germanistik* in Germany, this effect was not necessarily part of a conscious plan. It is only in retrospect that we have become aware of this effect. Some more recent steps, however, have been undertaken with an articulated goal of broadening our relevance for American colleagues in various disciplines. Included here is certainly the 1996 WIG Conference, organized as a response to members' desires to transcend the borders of traditional *Germanistik* by forging links with feminist scholars from cognate disciplines in this country; the conference was a definite step, and one taken knowingly, to push our field in new directions (see the first four contributions in this volume).

And there is yet one more development, this also of recent vintage, that steers us away from *Germanistik* as traditionally practiced in Germany and towards a redefinition of our field that takes into account the increasing need for contact with those of other disciplines. Two years ago at its annual meeting, members of the Editorial Board of the *Women in German Yearbook* resolved to publish all subsequent articles in English. The decision was prompted by a general desire to be part of academic deliberations in this country. The decision was not meant to eliminate contributions from colleagues here or in other countries who preferred to write in German, but simply paved the way for their articles to appear in English translation. It was not a decision casually made, nor was it viewed as irrevocable. There were, however, powerful arguments for an all-English volume. Feminist Germanists have for many years been making their own contacts with feminist colleagues in other fields in this country; yet while we incorporated the results of their work into our own, the reverse was not happening. While our disciplinary journals routinely published reviews of their studies, our yearbook was not being reviewed in journals with mainly English-speaking readers. The policy was adopted, then, largely as part of an attempt to bring scholarship in our field into the American mainstream.

The 1995 volume was the first published after this policy took effect, and thus it is too early to tell whether or not we are achieving what we had hoped. We will be paying close attention to any results associated with this policy, asking ourselves continually if we really are helping to overcome the insularity of our discipline, if we really are helping those in other academic fields to gain access to ongoing developments in our own. We do know that our publisher, the University of Nebraska Press, has adjusted its advertising strategy because of this policy: one recent result was a large ad in *The Women's Review of Books*.

Although we cannot yet measure any external effects, we have noticed some internal effects that bear comment. Having now submitted two all-English volumes—and having worked through numerous translations, some of which we have in the end decided not to publish—we acknowledge that the policy has cost the editors, the translators, the anonymous readers, and even the authors themselves much time and energy. Since we do not want to discourage submissions in German, we have decided to accept or reject each manuscript in its original form. Another review, this time limited to the editors, is required to assess the accuracy of the translation. And between the two reviews is the additional effort of identifying and working with the translator. It is a complicated process, to be sure.

Other considerations have also surfaced, many of them related to the old dilemma of how to reward translators. We have been fortunate to have experienced translators both in our organization and elsewhere who have volunteered their services; we have also begun to develop a network of individuals willing to offer advice on specific problems of translating. But our organization has no money to pay them, and we are reluctant to ask contributors who write in German to hire their own translators. So until now, we have relied on translators who volunteer their time and skills, knowing that they will not receive financial recompense. And knowing that they sometimes will have to do without adequate acknowledgment, as well. In some cases—certainly not all—the translators have actually reworked articles for comprehensibility and general scholarly effect. We have not yet found a fair way to give them credit for their work. A line in a vita claiming a translation seems hardly adequate.

And then there are the problems beyond the actual translation process and evaluation, problems inherent in the very notion of translation. Our recent call on the WIG-List for translators put us in contact with many qualified and willing volunteers. But that call on Internet had another, unexpected, result: a sometimes intense debate on the legitimacy of translating entire scholarly articles or even specific passages quoted to buttress arguments in those articles. Some participants broadened the debate to question the effects of translations on our classrooms and our institutions as well.[1] Clearly it is an issue that evokes strong responses. Some advantages are clear: a chance to reach beyond the small numbers of scholars and students in German departments, an opportunity to help bring developments in our field to a much wider audience, a chance to be part of a larger academic discussion than would otherwise be possible. But there are concomitant disadvantages, and as yet there is no consensus on their magnitude. We have asked ourselves, for example, if this policy could be seen as one more concession to the dominance of the American language, if we are in fact furthering another form of cultural imperialism? Is this policy part of a trend suggesting foreign languages need no longer be learned? Does it thus undermine what we are trying to do as foreign language teachers, i.e., to interest others in learning German? And could it in any way provide fodder to administrations intent on eliminating or "downsizing" foreign language departments? Does it ignore those cultural spaces that refuse expression through translation? And does it, as Dan Wilson suggested at the beginning of the Internet discussion, ignore the language base of culture, the "otherness" of other cultures, by attempting to incorporate everything into the home culture and pretending that we essentially live in a cozy English world.

We grant that the all-English policy has many ramifications, most of which we cannot yet know. Although we acknowledge that this decision might be seen in some corners as a statement diminishing the uniqueness of foreign language expression, we believe the benefits outweigh the disadvantages. At least for the present. For those of us doing work that exceeds the borders of *Germanistik* as traditionally practiced, audiences outside the immediate profession are not merely desirable, but mandatory. From our present vantage point it seems we have the alternative of waiting until they all learn German, or making some compromises.

We want to emphasize that the recent—conscious—moves to a more American kind of Germanics should not be seen as anti-German or anti-German literature and culture; instead our actions and decisions have been based on a desire to make developments in our field more widely accessible and valued. And perhaps it is worth pointing out in closing that, rather than alienating us from German *Germanistik,* the directions we are pursuing have led to some successful attempts to establish more direct links with the few scholars in Germany who are also working in the broad fields of Feminist, Gender, and Cultural Studies, areas defined and still dominated by Anglo-American scholars. The alliances that have been forged over the years culminated, for example, in the 1995 "WIG in Germany" summer conference organized by our colleagues in Potsdam and Berlin. Further, we have increased the number of German scholars on our Editorial Board and, happily, the number of submissions from our colleagues abroad actually seems to increase each year.

It seems clear to us that feminist scholars in our discipline and WIG members in particular have thus helped to provide our discipline with an identity in some ways distinct from German *Germanistik.* But are we contributing to, indeed have we been leading, the process of the "Americanization" of the profession? If by that is meant simply an unthinking embrace of all things American, then the answer is an unqualified no. If, however, the term reflects the desire to be more intimately tied to academic institutions and discussions in this country where most of us live, study, and teach, then—at least for the present—we answer affirmatively and suggest that, as Women in German pursues the goal of opening the borders of our field to the larger debates that are shaping the study of literatures and cultures in the United States today, it remains a force not only for change, but even for survival.

Notes

[1] We thank those of you who expressed your opinions on the WIG-List and invite all our readers to continue this discussion.

Works Cited

Grossberg, Lawrence. "The Formations of Cultural Studies: An American in Birmingham." *Relocating Cultural Studies.* Ed. Valda Blundell, et al. London: Routledge, 1992. 21-66.

Wilson, W. Daniel. WIG-List Discussion. 19 February 1996.

ABOUT THE AUTHORS

Leslie A. Adelson is Professor of German Studies at Cornell University in Ithaca, New York. While still on the humanities faculty of the Ohio State University in Columbus, Ohio, she authored *Crisis of Subjectivity: Botho Strauß's Challenge to West German Prose of the 1970s* (1984) and *Making Bodies, Making History: Feminism and German Identity* (1993) as well as numerous articles on contemporary German literature, feminist cultural theory, minority discourse in the German context, and interdisciplinary German cultural studies. For *Making Bodies, Making History* she was awarded the MLA's first Aldo and Jeanne Scaglione Prize for an Outstanding Scholarly Study in the Field of Germanic Languages and Literatures (1994).

Kathrin Bower is Assistant Professor of German at the University of Richmond. The article printed here is part of an ongoing investigation of the function of writing and the ethics of memory in lyrical representations of the Holocaust in works by German-Jewish poets. She has written and published on Rose Ausländer, Ingeborg Bachmann, and Nelly Sachs as well as on Holocaust poetry and German memory politics. Her research and teaching interests include responses to the Third Reich and the Holocaust in literature and film, gender and performance in twentieth-century German literature and film, and literary constructions of contemporary German-Jewish identity. She is currently working on a study examining abjection and the Holocaust in the presentation of contemporary German-Jewish identity.

Joan Cocks is Associate Professor of Politics and Chair of Politics and Critical Social Thought at Mount Holyoke College, where she teaches modern and contemporary political theory, feminist theory, and cultural theory. She is the author of *The Oppositional Imagination: Feminism, Critique, and Political Theory* (London: Routledge, 1989). She also has published articles on Marxism, feminism, body politics, and nationalism in several edited collections as well as in such journals as *Political Studies, Politics and Society, Differences,* and *Political Theory*.

Myra Marx Ferree is Professor of Sociology and Women's Studies at the University of Connecticut. Her primary area of interest is the social organization of gender, which she studies at the micro level in the household division of labor and at the macro level in the political organization of feminism, focusing particularly on the comparison of German and American feminism. On American feminism, she recently co-authored *Controversy and Coalition: The New Feminist Movement* (2nd ed., 1994), and co-edited *Feminist Organizations: Harvest of the New Women's Movement* (1995). On German feminism she has published numerous articles on the politics of gender equality, the status of women in eastern Germany, and women and post-unification university reform. She is currently working on a large collaborative project that analyzes abortion discourse in the German and American media from 1970 to 1994.

Sara Friedrichsmeyer is Professor of German and Head of the Department of Germanic Languages and Literatures at the University of Cincinnati. Her publications include *The Androgyne in Early German Romanticism* (1983) and the co-edited volume *The Enlightenment and Its Legacy* (1991). She has published articles on German Romanticism, feminist theory, and various nineteenth- and twentieth-century German women, among them Caroline Schlegel-Schelling, Annette von Droste-Hülshoff, Paula Modersohn-Becker, Käthe Kollwitz, and Christa Wolf. She is working on the representation of "Gypsies" in German literature and co-editing a volume titled *The Imperialist Imagination*. She has been co-editor of the *Women in German Yearbook* since 1990.

Atina Grossmann teaches modern European history at Cooper Union in New York City and German, women's, and gender history and feminist theory at Columbia University. She is co-editor of *When Biology Became Destiny: Women in Weimar and Nazi Germany* (1984) and author of *Reforming Sex: The German Movement for Birth Control and Abortion Reform 1920–1950* (1995). She is currently working on "victims, victors, and survivors" in Berlin 1945–48 as well as preparing for publication a collection of old and new essays on "new women," maternity, and modernity in Weimar Germany (University of California Press).

Barbara Hales has just completed her PhD in the Cultural Studies Program at the University of Arizona. She is currently working on a book manuscript dealing with the relationship between Weimar film and Hollywood film noir. Her interests include exile film and literature, representations of the *femme fatale,* and the detective film.

Patricia Herminghouse is Karl F. and Bertha A. Fuchs Professor of German Studies at the University of Rochester. Her research has focused on nineteenth- and twentieth-century literature, particularly on the literature of the GDR and the social contexts of women's writing. Editor of the textbook anthology, *Frauen im Mittelpunkt* (1987), she was also co-editor of *Literatur und Literaturtheorie in der DDR* (1976) and *DDR-Literatur der 70er Jahre* (1983). In addition to on-going work on a book with the tentative title *History, Literature and the Political Agenda in the GDR,* she is currently finishing a volume of short prose works by Ingeborg Bachmann and Christa Wolf for the German Library series and a co-edited volume, *Gender and Germanness: Cultural Productions of Nation.*

Karen Hermine Jankowsky is Assistant Professor of German at Wayne State University. Her book *Unsinn/anderer Sinn/neuer Sinn* (1989) analyzes Christa Wolf's *Kassandra* and its reception in East and West Germany. With Carla Love she has co-edited *Other Germanies—Questioning Identity in Women's Literature and Art* for the Postmodern Culture Series of State University of New York Press. Her current project is a book, *Women Writing over the Wall,* that investigates the applicability of American discussions surrounding the representations of cultural diversity and sexual preference for understanding the literature in German by Libuše Moníková, Herta Müller, and Emine Özdamar, on the one hand, and Christa Wolf, Ingeborg Drewitz, and Waldtraut Lewin on the other.

Todd Kontje is Associate Professor of German and Comparative Literature at the University of California, San Diego. He has published two books on the German *Bildungsroman,* a monograph on Schiller's aesthetics, and articles on eighteenth-, nineteenth-, and twentieth-century German literature. He is currently writing a book on German women, the novel, and the nation ca. 1771–1871.

Irmela Marei Krüger-Fürhoff, a PhD candidate in German Literature at the Humboldt University in Berlin, is presently writing her dissertation on representations of damaged bodies around 1800. In addition, she is working on a DFG-funded research project at the Free University in Berlin, which investigates the interconnections between undergraduates' aesthetic and intellectual choices and their use of the media.

Sara Lennox is Professor of Germanic Languages and Literatures and Director of the Social Thought and Political Economy Program at the University of Massachusetts, Amherst. She is editor of *Auf der Suche nach den Gärtern unserer Mütter: Feministische Kulturkritik aus Amerika* (1982) and co-editor of *Nietzsche heute: Die Rezeption seines Werkes seit 1968* (1988). She has published articles on various twentieth-century German and Austrian authors, on women's writing in the FRG and GDR, on literary theory, and on topics such as feminist pedagogy, feminist theory, the feminist movement in the USA and Germany, antiracist feminism, and antifeminism. She is currently writing a book on Ingeborg Bachmann and co-editing a book entitled *The Imperialist Imagination.*

Frederick A. Lubich, Staatsexamen University of Heidelberg, PhD University of California, Santa Barbara, is currently Associate Professor of German at Rutgers University. Author of books on Thomas Mann and Max Frisch and articles on twentieth-century literature and gender ideology, he is currently finishing a book on the discourse of matriarchy in twentieth-century German literary and cultural history.

Helgard Mahrdt is Associate Professor of German Literature in the Department of Languages and Literatures at the University of Tromsø, Norway. Her research focuses on the Enlightenment and has been influenced by the tradition of the Frankfurt School, especially by Adorno and Habermas. She has published articles on Ingeborg Bachmann, Marieluise Fleisser, and Christa Wolf; an article on Peter Weiss is forthcoming. Co-editor of the *Göttinger Beiträge zur Gesellschaftstheorie,* she is currently revising her dissertation ("Öffentlichkeit, 'Gender' und Moral: Von G.E. Lessing zu Ingeborg Bachmann") for publication and examining the works of Herta Müller.

Charlotte Melin is Director of Language Instruction in the Department of German, Scandinavian and Dutch at the University of Minnesota. She received her PhD from the University of Michigan. Her publications include articles on twentieth-century German poetry (including Enzensberger, Kirsch, Celan, Krechel, and Hahn) and German-American relations.

Helen G. Morris-Keitel received her PhD from the University of Wisconsin-Madison. Since 1991 she has been Assistant Professor of German at Bucknell University. She is the author of *Identity in Transition: The Images of Working-Class Women in Social Prose of the Vormärz (1840-1848).* Her research interests include the intersections of class, gender, and national identities in nineteenth-century women's prose fiction, problem-oriented young adult literature of the 1980s and 1990s, and foreign language pedagogy with a special emphasis on the teaching of reading.

NOTICE TO CONTRIBUTORS

The *Women in German Yearbook* is a refereed journal. Its publication is supported by the Coalition of Women in German.

Contributions to the *Women in German Yearbook* are welcome at any time. The editors are interested in feminist approaches to all aspects of German literary, cultural, and language studies, including pedagogy.

Prepare manuscripts for anonymous review. The editors prefer that manuscripts not exceed 25 pages (typed, double-spaced), including notes. Follow the fourth edition (1995) of the *MLA Handbook* (separate notes from works cited). Send one copy of the manuscript to each coeditor:

Sara Friedrichsmeyer *and* Patricia Herminghouse
Department of Germanic   Department of Modern
  Languages and Literatures   Languages and Cultures
University of Cincinnati   University of Rochester
Cincinnati, OH 45221   Rochester, NY 14627
Phone: 513-556-2751   Phone: 716-275-4251
Fax: 513-556-1991   Fax: 716-273-1097
E-mail: sara.friedrichsmeyer@uc.edu   E-mail: pahe@troi.cc.rochester.edu

For membership/subscription information, contact Jeanette Clausen (Department of Modern Foreign Languages, Indiana University–Purdue University, Fort Wayne, IN 46805).

CONTENTS OF PREVIOUS VOLUMES

Volume 11

Jutta Brückner, On Autobiographical Filmmaking; **Margaret McCarthy,** Consolidating, Consuming, and Annulling Identity in Jutta Brückner's *Hungerjahre*; **Janice Mouton,** Margarethe von Trotta's Sisters: "Brides Under a Different Law"; **Jenifer K. Ward,** Enacting the Different Voice: *Christa Klages* and Feminist History; **Renate Möhrmann,** "Germany, Pale Mother": On the Mother Figures in New German Women's Film; **Barbara Becker-Cantarino,** "Gender Censorship": On Literary Production in German Romanticism; **Dagmar von Hoff,** Aspects of Censorship in the Work of Karoline von Günderrode; **Lewis Call,** Woman as Will and Representation: Nietzsche's Contribution to Postmodern Feminism; **Alyth F. Grant,** From "Halbtier" to "Übermensch": Helene Böhlau's Iconoclastic Reversal of Cultural Images; **Lynda J. King,** Vicki Baum and the "Making" of Popular Success: "Mass" Culture or "Popular" Culture?; **Katharina von Ankum,** Motherhood and the "New Woman": Vicki Baum's *stud. chem. Helene Willfüer* and Irmgard Keun's *Gilgi—eine von uns*; **Friederike Eigler,** Feminist Criticism and Bakhtin's Dialogic Principle: Making the Transition from Theory to Textual Analysis; **Imke Lode,** The Body in the Discourses of Colonial Savage and European Woman during the Enlightenment; **Sara Friedrichsmeyer and Patricia Herminghouse,** The Generational Compact: Graduate Students and Germanics.

Volume 10

Richard W. McCormick, Private Anxieties/Public Projections: "New Objectivity," Male Subjectivity, and Weimar Cinema; **Elizabeth Mittman.** Locating a Public Sphere: Some Reflections on Writers and *Öffentlichkeit* in the GDR; **Ruth-Ellen B. Joeres,** "We are adjacent to human society": German Women Writers, the Homosocial Experience, and a Challenge to the Public/Domestic Dichotomy; **Marjorie Gelus,** Patriarchy's Fragile Boundaries under Siege: Three Stories of Heinrich von Kleist; **Gail K. Hart,** *Anmut*'s Gender: The "Marionettentheater" and Kleist's Revision of "Anmut und Würde"; **Brigid Haines,** Masochism and Femininity in Lou Andreas-Salomé's *Eine Ausschweifung*; **Silke von der Emde,** Irmtraud Morgner's Postmodern Feminism: A Question of Politics; **Susan C. Anderson,** Creativity and Nonconformity in Monika Maron's *Die Überläuferin*; **Ruth Klüger,** Dankrede zum Grimmelshausen-Preis; **Karen Remmler,** Gender Identities and the Remembrance of the Holocaust; **Suzanne Shipley,** From the Prater to Central Park: Finding a Self in Exile; **Sigrid Lange,** Dokument und Fiktion: Marie-Thérèse Kerschbaumers *Der* *weibliche Name des Widerstands*; **Miriam Frank,** Lesbian Life and Literature: A Survey of Recent German-Language Publications; **Luise F. Pusch,** Ein Streit um Worte? Eine Lesbe macht Skandal im Deutschen Bundestag; **Jeanette Clausen and Sara Friedrichsmeyer,** WIG 2000: Feminism and the Future of *Germanistik*.

Volume 9

Ann Taylor Allen, Women's Studies as Cultural Movement and Academic Discipline in the United States and West Germany: The Early Phase, 1966-1982; **Susan Signe Morrison,** Women Writers and Women Rulers: Rhetorical and Political Empowerment in the Fifteenth Century; **Christl Griesshaber-Weninger,** Harsdörffers *Frauenzimmer Gesprächspiele* als geschlechtsspecifische Verhaltensfibel: Ein Vergleich mit heutigen Kommunikationsstrukturen; **Gertrud Bauer Pickar,** The Battering and Meta-Battering of Droste's Margreth: Covert Misogyny in *Die Judenbuche*'s Critical Reception; **Kirsten Belgum,** Domesticating the Reader: Women and *Die Gartenlaube*; **Katrin Sieg,** Equality Decreed: Dramatizing Gender in East Germany; **Katharina von Ankum,** Political Bodies: Women and Re/Production in the GDR; **Friederike Eigler,** At the Margins of East Berlin's "Counter-Culture": Elke Erb's *Winkelzüge* and Gabriele Kachold's *zügel los*; **Karin Eysel**; Christa Wolf's *Kassandra*: Refashioning National Imagination Beyond the Nation; **Petra Waschescio,** Auseinandersetzung mit dem Abendlanddenken: Gisela von Wysockis *Abendlandleben*; **Dagmar C.G. Lorenz,** Memory and Criticism: Ruth Klüger's *weiter leben*; **Sara Lennox,** Antiracist Feminism in Germany: Introduction to Dagmar Schultz and Ika Hügel; **Ika Hügel,** Wir kämpfen seit es uns gibt; **Dagmar Schultz,** Racism in the New Germany and the Reaction of White Women; **Sara Friedrichsmeyer and Jeanette Clausen,** What's Missing in New Historicism or the "Poetics" of Feminist Literary Criticism.

Volume 8

Marjorie Gelus, Birth as Metaphor in Kleist's *Das Erdbeben in Chili*: A Comparison of Critical Methodologies; **Vanessa Van Ornam,** No Time for Mothers: Courasche's Infertility as Grimmelshausen's Criticism of War; **M.R. Sperberg-McQueen,** Whose Body Is It? Chaste Strategies and the Reinforcement of Patriarchy in Three Plays by Hrotswitha von Gandersheim; **Sara Lennox,** The Feminist Reception of Ingeborg Bachmann; **Maria-Regina Kecht,** Auflehnung gegen die Ordnung von Sprache und Vernunft: Die weibliche Wirklichkeitsgestaltung bei Waltraud Anna Mitgutsch; **Maria-Regina Kecht,** Gespräch mit Waltraud Anna Mitgutsch; **Susanne Kord,** "Und drinnen waltet die züchtige Hausfrau"? Carolina Pichler's Fictional Auto/Biographies; **Susan L. Cocalis,** "Around 1800": Reassessing the Role of German Women Writers in Literary Production of the Late Eighteenth and Early Nineteenth Centuries (Review Essay); **Konstanze Streese und Kerry Shea,** Who's Looking? Who's Laughing? Of Multicultural Mothers and Men in Percy Adlon's *Bagdad Cafe*; **Deborah Lefkowitz,** Editing from Life; **Walfriede Schmitt,** Mund-Artiges...

(Gedicht); **Barbara Becker-Cantarino,** Feministische Germanistik in Deutschland: Rückblick und sechs Thesen; **Gisela Brinker-Gabler,** Alterity—Marginality—Difference: On Inventing Places for Women; **Ruth-Ellen B. Joeres,** "Language is Also a Place of Struggle": The Language of Feminism and the Language of American *Germanistik*.

Volume 7

Myra Love, "A Little Susceptible to the Supernatural?": On Christa Wolf; **Monika Shafi,** Die überforderte Generation: Mutterfiguren in Romanen von Ingeborg Drewitz; **Ute Brandes,** Baroque Women Writers and the Public Sphere; **Katherine R. Goodman,** "The Butterfly and the Kiss": A Letter from Bettina von Arnim; **Ricarda Schmidt,** Theoretische Orientierungen in feministischer Literaturwissenschaft und Sozialphilosophie (Review Essay); **Sara Lennox,** Some Proposals for Feminist Literary Criticism; **Helga Königsdorf,** Ein Pferd ohne Beine (Essay); **Angela Krauß,** Wieder in Leipzig (Erzählung); **Waldtraut Lewin,** Lange Fluchten (Erzählung); **Eva Kaufmann,** DDR-Schriftstellerinnen, die Widersprüche und die Utopie; **Irene Dölling,** Alte und neue Dilemmata: Frauen in der ehemaligen DDR; **Dinah Dodds,** "Die Mauer stand bei mir im Garten": Interview mit Helga Schütz; **Gisela E. Bahr,** Dabeigewesen: Tagebuchnotizen vom Winter 1989/90; **Dorothy J. Rosenberg,** Learning to Say "I" instead of "We": Recent Works on Women in the Former GDR (Review Essay); **Sara Friedrichsmeyer and Jeanette Clausen,** What's Feminism Got to Do with It? A Postscript from the Editors.

Volume 6

Dagmar C.G. Lorenz, "Hoffentlich werde ich taugen." Zu Situation und Kontext von Brigitte Schwaiger/Eva Deutsch *Die Galizianerin*; **Sabine Wilke,** "Rückhaltlose Subjektivität." Subjektwerdung, Gesellschafts- und Geschlechtsbewußtsein bei Christa Wolf; **Elaine Martin,** Patriarchy, Memory, and the Third Reich in the Autobiographical Novels of Eva Zeller; **Tineke Ritmeester,** Heterosexism, Misogyny, and Mother-Hatred in Rilke Scholarship: The Case of Sophie Rilke-Entz (1851–1931); **Richard W. McCormick,** Productive Tensions: Teaching Films by German Women and Feminist Film Theory; **Hildegard M. Nickel,** Women in the GDR: Will Renewal Pass Them By?; **Helen Cafferty and Jeanette Clausen,** Feministik *Germanistik* after Unification: A Postscript from the Editors.

Volume 5

Angelika Bammer, Nackte Kaiser und bärtige Frauen: Überlegungen zu Macht, Autorität, und akademischem Diskurs; **Sabine Hake,** Focusing the Gaze: The Critical Project of *Frauen und Film*; **Dorothy Rosenberg,** Rethinking Progress: Women Writers and the Environmental Dialogue in the GDR; **Susanne Kord,** Fading Out: Invisible Women in Marieluise Fleißer's Early Dramas; **Lorely French,** "Meine beiden Ichs": Confrontations with Language and Self in Letters by Early Nineteenth-Century Women; **Sarah Westphal-Wihl,** Pronoun Semantics and the Representation of Power in the Middle High German *Märe* "Die halbe Decke"; **Susanne Zantop and Jeannine Blackwell,** Select Bibliography on German Social History and Women Writers; **Helen Cafferty and Jeanette Clausen,** Who's Afraid of Feminist Theory? A Postscript from the Editors.

Volume 4

Luise F. Pusch, Totale Feminisierung: Überlegungen zum unfassenden Femininum; **Luise F. Pusch,** Die Kätzin, die Rättin, und die Feminismaus; **Luise F. Pusch,** Carl Maria, die Männe; **Luise F. Pusch,** Sind Herren herrlich und Damen dämlich?; **Ricarda Schmidt,** E.T.A. Hoffman's "Der Sandmann": An Early Example of *Écriture Féminine*? A Critique of Trends in Feminist Literary Criticism; **Renate Fischetti,** *Écriture Féminine* in the New German Cinema: Ulrike Ottinger's *Portrait of a Woman Drinker*; **Jan Mouton,** The Absent Mother Makes an Appearance in the Films of West German Women Directors; **Charlotte Armster,** Katharina Blum: Violence and the Exploitation of Sexuality; **Renny Harrigan,** Novellistic Representation of *die Berufstätige* during the Weimar Republic; **Lynda J. King,** From the Crown to the Hammer and Sickle: The Life and Works of Austrian Interwar Writer Hermynia zur Mühlen; **Linda Kraus Worley,** The "Odd" Woman as Heroine in the Fiction of Louise von François; **Helga Madland,** Three Late Eighteenth-Century Women's Journals: Their Role in Shaping Women's Lives; **Sigrid Brauner,** Hexenjagd in Gelehrtenköpfen; **Susan Wendt-Hildebrandt,** Gespräch mit Herrad Schenk; **Dorothy Rosenberg,** GDR Women Writers: The Post-War Generation. An Updated Bibliography of Narrative Prose, June 1987.

Volume 3

Ritta Jo Horsley and Richard A. Horsley, On the Trail of the "Witches": Wise Women, Midwives and the European Witch Hunts; **Barbara Mabee,** Die Kindesmörderin in den Fesseln der bürgerlichen Moral: Wagners Evchen und Goethes Gretchen; **Judith P. Aikin,** Who Learns a Lesson? The Function of Sex Role Reversal in Lessing's *Minna von Barnhelm*; **Sara Friedrichsmeyer,** The Subversive Androgyne; **Shawn C. Jarvis,** Spare the Rod and Spoil the Child? Bettine's *Das Leben der Hochgräfin Gritta von Rattenzuhausbeiuns*; **Edith Waldstein,** Romantic Revolution and Female Collectivity: Bettine and Gisela von Arnim's *Gritta*; **Ruth-Ellen Boetcher Joeres,** "Ein Nebel schließt uns ein." Social Comment in the Novels of German Women Writers, 1850–1870; **Thomas C. Fox,** Louise von François: A Feminist Reintroduction; **Gesine Worm,** Das erste Jahr: Women in German im Goethe Haus New York.

Volume 2

Barbara Frischmuth, Am hellen Tag: Erzählung; **Barbara Frischmuth,** Eine Souveräne Posaune Gottes: Gedanken zu Hildegard von Bingen und ihrem Werk; **Dagmar C.G. Lorenz,** Ein Interview: Barbara Frischmuth; **Dagmar C.G.**

Lorenz, Creativity and Imagination in the Work of Barbara Frischmuth; **Margaret E. Ward,** *Ehe* and *Entsagung*: Fanny Lewald's Early Novels and Goethe's Literary Paternity; **Regula Venske,** "Männlich im Sinne des Butt" or "Am Ende angekommen?": Images of Men in Contemporary German-Language Literature by Women; **Angelika Bammer,** Testing the Limits: Christa Reinig's Radical Vision; **H-B. Moeller,** The Films of Margarethe von Trotta: Domination, Violence, Solidarity, and Social Criticism.

Volume 1

Jeanette Clausen, The Coalition of Women in German: An Interpretive History and Celebration; **Sigrid Weigel,** Das Schreiben des Mangels als Produktion von Utopie; **Jeannine Blackwell,** Anonym, verschollen, trivial: Methodological Hindrances in Researching German Women's Literature; **Martha Wallach,** Ideal and Idealized Victims: The Lost Honor of the Marquise von O., Effi Briest and Katharina Blum in Prose and Film; **Anna Kuhn,** Margarethe von Trotta's *Sisters*: Interiority or Engagement?; **Barbara D. Wright,** The Feminist Transformation of Foreign Language Teaching; **Jeanette Clausen,** Broken but not Silent: Language as Experience in Vera Kamenko's *Unter uns war Krieg*; **Richard L. Johnson,** The New West German Peace Movement: Male Dominance or Feminist Nonviolence.